PRAVDA

PRAVDA

Inside the Soviet News Machine

by

ANGUS ROXBURGH

[Selections from *Pravda* translated
by Neilian and Angus Roxburgh]

George Braziller

NEW YORK

For Ewan

Published in the United States in 1987
by George Braziller, Inc.

Editorial matter © Angus Roxburgh 1987
Translation © Neilian and Angus Roxburgh 1987

George Braziller, Inc.
60 Madison Avenue
New York, New York 10010

Library of Congress Cataloging-in-Publication Data

Roxburgh, Angus.
  Pravda : inside the Soviet news machine.

  Bibliography: p.
  Includes index.
  1. Pravda (Moscow, R.S.F.S.R.) I. Title.
PN5279.M53P77   1987   077'.312   87–11707
ISBN 0–8076–1186–7

Printed in the United States by
the Haddon Craftsmen

Contents

Illustrations

Preface

All Soviet newspapers, as well as television and radio, see themselves as arms of the Communist Party. For them, 'propaganda' is
not a dirty word.

But it would be wrong to infer from this that *Pravda* is devoid of
any criticism of Soviet life. Amid the scholarly ideological tracts and
the overblown claims of economic success, *Pravda* exposes a great
many faults, from inefficiency and bad management to corruption
and hooliganism, from food shortages and poor quality goods to
alcoholism and even the stifling of criticism at Party meetings. Since
Mikhail Gorbachov came to power in March 1985 some taboo
subjects have at last been broached, and new vigour injected into
Soviet news reporting. Indeed, the press is one of the main sources
of all that we know about Soviet politics and life, including most of
what Moscow-based correspondents send to their newspapers
abroad. But there are still huge areas in which criticism is impossible, and others where the truth appears only between the lines.

It is the purpose of this book to guide the reader through *Pravda's*
tangled web of truths, half-truths and omissions. The extracts from
recent issues of the newspaper (Part Two) will speak for themselves,
and provide both an unusual window on Soviet life and some idea of
the image of the world outside which the Soviet people obtain from
their news media. I have tried to give at least a taste of most of
Pravda's styles and typical subjects, but the overall balance of the
extracts is quite different from the newspaper itself: the selection is
more critical (on domestic issues) than *Pravda* as a whole, concentrates more on human interest, and is certainly less stodgy. Specialised economics articles and profiles of model workers are therefore
underrepresented.

Part One looks behind the printed word, at *Pravda's* past and
present. The section on the paper's history examines the various
roles which the Soviet press has been called upon to play over the
years, concentrating on illustrative episodes of particular relevance

to *Pravda*, lest it turn into a mere history of the Soviet Union. There is then a brief survey of today's Soviet news media as a whole – their functions and purpose, and *Pravda's* special role within this system. The next sections look at how *Pravda* is planned and produced, and at the kind of news it contains, and does not contain. How does one set about interpreting *Pravda*? Who reads *Pravda*, and what do they think of it? Finally, how effective is it in its declared aim of assisting the Communist Party in building communism and moulding the 'new Soviet man'? Are the Soviet mass media successful, at home and abroad?

Pravda, as will be shown, is not the most representative of Soviet newspapers, but it is the most important (indeed, probably the most important in the world). The rest of the Soviet press takes its cue from *Pravda*, and the rest of the world studies it – not only as the official voice of the Kremlin, but as a fascinating mirror in which Soviet life is reflected, and at times distorted. If this book sheds some fresh light on the workings of the Soviet media and allows at least a selection to be read in unadulterated form, it will have served its modest purpose.

A word about transliteration: throughout the text itself I have adopted a perhaps idiosyncratic system for rendering Russian names, which aims to indicate the sound of the Russian without being pedantic about letter-for-letter correspondence with the Cyrillic. In the notes, however, a more scholarly approach is used, to make life easier for those who may wish to follow up the references.

I gratefully acknowledge generous financial assistance from the University of Glasgow, where much of the research for this book was carried out. I should like to thank Professor William Wallace and Dr Stephen White of Glasgow University, and George Fodor of the BBC, for reading early chapters and drafts of the Introduction and for their useful advice and comments. Several *Pravda* correspondents kindly discussed aspects of their newspaper with me, and Dr Vladimir Shlapentokh provided invaluable insight. Clive Liddiard and David Reardon helped out with some translating as the deadline approached. All misunderstandings and errors that remain are, of course, mine.

Most of all, I thank Neilian, my wife, who not only translated many of the extracts from *Pravda*, but read every draft and provided ideas and support, in this as in everything else.

September 1986   A.R.

Part One

INTRODUCTION TO *PRAVDA*

1

Seventy-Five Years of Truth:
The History of Pravda

Though its name is unchanged, there are many striking contrasts between today's *Pravda* and the newspaper launched in 1912, five years before the October Revolution that brought the Bolsheviks to power in Russia.

In those days it was hounded by the Tsarist police, and the Bolshevik Party which published it was illegal inside Russia. Today, it is the official organ of the Soviet Communist Party, the only legal political party in the USSR.

In 1912 *Pravda* was produced by revolutionaries in a tiny, cramped office, with someone on guard to warn of police raids. Today, it is edited in a large, comfortable Moscow office block, guarded by a policeman.

Before the 1917 Revolution *Pravda*'s readers learned to understand the coded language it used in order to get its subversive message past the censors. Nowadays foreign Sovietologists scrutinise its censored columns and photographs for hints of Kremlin power struggles and policy changes.

At that time it reported strikes by Russian workers. Now it reports strikes by Western workers.

At that time it sought to overthrow the Establishment. Now it is the staunchest pillar of a new Establishment, and proud of it.

In the days of the last Tsar, when Russian newspapers filled their pages with stock-exchange news and high-society gossip, while remaining silent about the ignominious conditions endured by the workers and peasants, the title – which means 'Truth' – was a direct challenge to the ruling class, and a brilliant name for a workers' newspaper which sought to tear the veil of silence from a rotten society.* Today, workers are more sceptical: as one taxi-

---

*The title was in fact purloined from Trotsky, who had published an illegal newspaper called *Pravda* abroad since October 1908. It was one of the most popular of the workers' papers smuggled into Russia, a fact which no doubt influenced the Bolsheviks in their choice of title in 1912.

driver, asked what he thought of *Pravda*'s coverage of events in Afghanistan, put it, with his tongue in his cheek: 'Well, if it's called "The Truth", I suppose it must be!'

Over the decades, the functions of the Soviet mass media have undergone several redefinitions, in accordance with the demands of the period and of the Soviet leaders. For Lenin, the press was 'propagandist, agitator and organiser'. For Stalin, it was a 'transmission belt' and a 'weapon'. For Khrushchev, it was a 'striking force on the ideological front'. Brezhnev required the mass media to give an 'effective rebuff' to Western propaganda. Under Andropov and Chernenko, the press launched campaigns to tighten up discipline and stamp out corruption at home, and fiercely attacked President Reagan and Western policies in terms hitherto reserved for Hitler's Germany. Gorbachov called for modesty in the leadership and more openness in the press: he banned his own name from *Pravda*'s editorials, and encouraged journalists to investigate social problems such as drug-abuse and even to question some official Party policies.

Pravda's little museum on the top floor of its office block portrays its history as a glorious continuum. But a closer look at the seventy-five years since the paper was founded reveals a good deal more confusion, changes of direction, and manipulation of the truth than the official historians ever concede.

1912–1914: The Pre-Revolutionary *Pravda*

Few Russians are aware that even *Pravda*'s masthead contains a gross distortion of the facts, repeated every day of the year. There, under the paper's three medals, are the words: 'Founded by V. I. Lenin on 5 May 1912.' All Soviet history books – and many Western ones – stress the role played by the Bolshevik leader in 'running' the Party's first legal daily newspaper. Blow aside the mists of legend, however, and the facts suggest something quite different.

It is true that Lenin played an important part at the conference in Prague, in January 1912, at which the Bolsheviks decided to publish a legal daily newspaper inside Russia to spread their ideas among the workers. But during the next months it was Nikolai Poletayev, a Social Democratic Deputy to the Duma (Parliament) in St Petersburg, and publisher of the Bolshevik weekly *Zvezda*, who raised funds and obtained permission for the new daily paper, while Lenin was in exile in Paris.[1]*

Far from 'founding' *Pravda*, Lenin scarcely knew what was happening back in St Petersburg. Thirteen days before its first issue, he was still writing to the editors of *Zvezda*: 'Tell me soon about the daily paper [*Pravda*]. What will its format be? What length of articles may I send?'[2]

Lenin's first article for *Pravda* appeared only in its thirteenth issue, and his second not until the sixty-third issue. Moreover, his letters to the editor show that he was far from pleased with the line it was taking – especially its conciliatory attitude towards the more moderate Menshevik faction of the Russian Social Democratic Labour Party. (The editorial in the first issue, written by Stalin, called for 'peace and cooperation within the movement'.)[3] Even later in the year, when Lenin started contributing more regularly to *Pravda*, he found to his great annoyance that the editors in St Petersburg were toning down his articles, particularly his polemical tirades against the Mensheviks.[4] Forty-seven of his articles were not published at all, and Lenin complained that the editors could at least have the decency to return them to him, rather than tossing them into the wastepaper basket: 'Any contributor, even to bourgeois newspapers, would demand this.'[5]

Lenin's intense interest in *Pravda*, and his impotence in controlling it, were poignantly expressed by his wife, Nadezhda Krupskaya, in her memoirs: 'Ilyich [Lenin] attached enormous importance to *Pravda* and sent articles to it almost daily. He fervently counted up how much money was collected for *Pravda* and where, how many articles were written on each subject, and so on. He was terribly pleased when *Pravda* published successful pieces and took the correct line.'[6]

But Lenin was also furious when *Pravda* took the 'wrong' line, and rejected, altered, censored or delayed his own articles. 'Ilyich grew nervous and wrote angry letters to *Pravda*, but they did not do much good.'[7]

Lenin's initial non-participation in the newspaper he allegedly founded, and his inability to control its political stance or to temper the highhandedness of its editors, were due to a purely practical difficulty, however – that of communicating with St Petersburg from Paris. It was for this reason that Lenin moved to Cracow, close to the Russian frontier, in early July 1912. He moved there with his wife, Krupskaya, and Zinoviev and Kamenev, who, at that time at least, were more prolific contributors to *Pravda* than he was.

Zinoviev wrote that Cracow now became the real base of the Bolsheviks' activities, since it was almost impossible for the illegal Central Committee to exist in Russia. At best a bureau of only two or three people could be maintained in St Petersburg.[8]

From Cracow, only a day's travel from the Russian capital, Lenin and the others kept in close contact with the St Petersburg Bolsheviks, some of whom visited them regularly. The articles which the exiled leaders sent – eventually 'up to six or more a day', according to Zinoviev – now formed the basis of *Pravda*. In the next two years 284 of Lenin's articles were printed.

Krupskaya describes in her memoirs how they got round the problem of censorship of their mail. To avoid arousing the Russian police's suspicion with foreign postmarks, Lenin and his confederates gave their letters to Russian peasant women who crossed the border to the market in Cracow. They were willing, for a small consideration, to hide letters in their bundles and post them inside Russia.[9]

They need hardly have bothered, however, for the authorities were well informed about all of *Pravda*'s activities and intentions: both its publisher, Roman Malinovsky, and its editor from May 1913, Miron Chernomazov, were agents of the Okhranka (secret police). In retrospect, Krupskaya claimed that she did not like Chernomazov from the start, and refused even to give him a bed for the night when he visited them in Cracow, but in fact Lenin was slow to appreciate the danger and ignored warnings from, among others, Nikolai Bukharin.[10] Malinovsky, who was leader of the Bolshevik parliamentary faction, was not exposed until after the Revolution.

So well informed were the police of the Bolsheviks' intentions that the very first issue of *Pravda* was confiscated. The authorities were clearly worried by the paper's aim, which police files rightly described as 'to print reports from the sphere of the working masses'.[11] Both the Bolsheviks and Mensheviks already had émigré publications which they smuggled into Russia, but obviously a legal daily newspaper could reach a far wider readership. (The publication of a legal newspaper even by an illegal party was made possible by the Tsar's October Manifesto of 1905 which guaranteed freedom of conscience and speech, without, however, abolishing post-publication censorship.)[12]

Pravda's purpose at this stage was generally to chronicle the lot of the working classes, and to encourage strikes by publicising them. As well as theoretical articles by Party leaders, the paper printed thousands of reports of strikes and unrest from workers themselves around the country, especially, to begin with, the wave of strikes following the shooting down of protesting workers at the Lena goldmines in Siberia. Speeches by Bolshevik members of the Duma were published, usually in full. 'Press reviews' sought to point up what a Soviet scholar later called the 'grovelling of the bourgeois press before the authorities'.[13] Almost every issue contained a poem on a 'proletarian theme'.

In February 1914 Chernomazov was replaced as editor by Lev Kamenev, who moved to St Petersburg. Even Lenin was impressed by how *Pravda* improved under Kamenev's editorship. 'It's becoming a real beauty!' he wrote. 'A pleasure to look at!'[14]

Aware that about half the population was illiterate, Lenin encouraged the editors to ensure that the paper's language was kept simple and direct. Every issue included a request to literate workers to read out the paper aloud.

In this way, *Pravda* probably reached a fair-sized audience. It appears to have been the most popular of the workers' papers at the time – more popular, at any rate, than the Menshevik *Luch (Ray)*.[15] On its second anniversary *Pravda*'s circulation reached a peak of 130,000, partly as a result of Kamenev's editorial improvements, but the average during its first two years was about 40,000. Half the copies were sold in St Petersburg, the rest all over Russia. The main reason for the periodically much lower circulation was the harassment, censorship and confiscation which it suffered, despite ingenious ruses to avoid them.

Under the press laws of the time, newspapers were not censored prior to publication, but the first three copies printed had to be submitted to a Press Inspector for approval. If the issue was deemed to violate the limits laid down in the newspaper's licence, a fine could be imposed, or the editor jailed, or the issue confiscated, or the newspaper's licence withdrawn.[16] All of these punishments were regularly suffered by *Pravda*.

Eight times it was closed down, only to reappear under a slightly changed name (for example, *Workers' Truth*, *Northern Truth*, *The Way of Truth*, etc.) until 21 July 1914 when its presses were smashed, its entire staff arrested, and the paper disappeared altogether until after the February Revolution of 1917. (See Table 1, p. 275, for a list of the different titles.)

Rather than risk its real editorial staff, *Pravda* employed a total of forty 'surrogate' editors – often illiterate – who were willing to go to prison on their behalf.[17] This was cheaper than paying fines. Of the 645 issues published before the War, 155 were confiscated, and 36 incurred fines totalling 16,550 roubles. (See Table 1, p. 275).

But even confiscation did not necessarily mean that all copies of a particular issue were lost, thanks to the system of post-publication censorship, which the editors exploited to the full. According to an apocryphal-sounding story published in *Pravda* in 1922, the daily task of delivering the first three copies to the censor was entrusted to a seventy-year-old man called Matvei, who was sure to take at least an hour to reach his destination. Meanwhile the presses rolled on. Matvei would stay in the censor's office 'to rest' while the Press Inspector examined the newspaper. If, after reading *Pravda*, the censor turned to another paper, there was no problem, but if he lifted the telephone to instruct a police raid, Matvei would fly out of the room and rush back to the printing-plant by droshky. Waiting watchers who saw him hurrying back sounded the alarm and a clearing-up operation went into action. Newspapers which had not yet been distributed were removed and hidden; the presses were stopped; and by the time the police arrived, all they found were a few copies left for the sake of 'protocol'.[18]

The editors also applied their own pre-publication 'censorship' to prevent incriminating words or phrases from slipping through and risking confiscation. They adopted Aesopian phraseology, referring to the 'underground' rather than the Russian Social Democratic Labour Party, to the 'uncurtailed demands of 1905' rather than the Bolshevik programme of a democratic republic, an eight-hour day and confiscation of the land, and to 'consistent democrats' rather than Bolsheviks.[19] The readers – and the police – soon learned to recognise these terms.

Pravda was not the only left-wing newspaper to suffer from the censorship; indeed, the Menshevik papers were confiscated proportionately more often, and even 'bourgeois' papers were often suppressed. But rather than just close *Pravda* down and be done with it (which the secret police, given their inside knowledge, could easily have done), the authorities preferred to play a game of cat and mouse, so long as they believed it posed no immediate threat to the regime.

Apart from reprisals 'justified' by the censorship regulations, the police mounted surprise raids on the editorial offices – which were in effect the Bolsheviks' headquarters inside Russia. The raids, often conducted without the formality of a warrant, usually took place at night. Writing on the fifteenth anniversary of *Pravda*, one of its original staff, Boris Ivanov, recalled the following incidents.

'It was a warm spring night and the presses were running full speed. The papers, tied into bundles, were tossed to the newsboys and factory workers waiting in the plant courtyard. They heaved the bundles on to their shoulders and went out into the city. Suddenly someone cried "Police!" and almost immediately the courtyard was filled with dark-uniformed figures. The plant was surrounded; the machines were stopped. All the remaining copies of *Pravda* were seized and over one hundred persons were arrested, including many newsboys. . . .

'So many spies and police agents used to loiter around *Pravda*'s premises that they could not even keep track of each other. They were disguised as workers, passers-by, coachmen, and so on. Once, a local police officer in uniform got into a carriage parked in front of the plant and ordered the coachman to start up. The coachman refused, announcing that the carriage was already engaged. The officer was furious and started beating him with his baton. The coachman pulled out a gun and started beating the officer. Police soon arrived to break up the fight. It turned out that the coachman was really a police agent whose sole task was to remain in front of *Pravda*'s printing plant and report on what was taking place.'[20]

Another old *Pravda* worker, A. Gertik, recalled that ordinary policemen considered it their duty to prevent *Pravda* from circulating. They would intimidate newsboys on the street, and confiscate the paper 'often together with its reader'.[21]

Only about half the circulation was sold on the streets, however, the rest being collected from the plant by workers who sold them at their factories. Distribution to the provinces was either done legally, through the post, or clandestinely: for example, sympathetic railwaymen would take bundles on their journeys and toss them to comrades waiting at prearranged points along the route.

Exactly how *Pravda* was financed is not entirely clear, and it is a subject on which Soviet sources are rather reticent. There were undoubtedly workers' donations, and regular collective subscriptions from factories. But these, together with special fund-raising events, appear to have covered only part of the cost of producing the paper and paying its many fines. The balance apparently came from wealthy sympathisers. To help launch the new paper, the writer Maxim Gorky contributed 2,000 roubles, and it is likely that another 3,000 came from the son of a successful Kazan merchant named V. Tikhomirnov.[22]

Eventually, as a secret police report grudgingly acknowledged, *Pravda* achieved financial stability due to its large circulation. And consequently, it became a powerful force in the revolutionary cause, especially as a means of organising protest. The same report noted that *Pravda* and the other legal socialist papers then operating had forged close links with what it called the 'propagandised elements' of the population. The paper's reports, it went on, 'consciously irritate the temper of the population. By falsely explaining the meaning and character of current political and social events, they deliberately discredit the authority and undertakings of the Government.'[23]

One of *Pravda*'s articles on the tragic events at the Lena goldmines, which incurred the censor's disfavour, called on workers to organise against the Government and their employers: 'The shooting of the workers at the Lena made no impression on the ruling classes. Only the unanimous protest of the workers, like a broad wave rolling across Russia, compelled the Government to promise a labour code for miners and promise to designate some sort of Senatorial investigation.'[24]

By the summer of 1914, workers' strikes were reaching a critical level, and *Pravda* both reflected this and attempted to encourage them. But the position of the Bolsheviks themselves was weak, and they were powerless to prevent the closure of their newspaper. Only eleven days later the War with Germany began, and workers' protest melted into an initial upsurge of patriotism.

1917–1921: Revolution and Civil War

In March 1917 the monarchy fell, a Provisional Government was set up, the Petrograd Soviet (Council) of Workers' Deputies was formed, and Russia became what Lenin was to describe a few weeks later in *Pravda* as 'the freest country in the world'.[25]

Among the new freedoms was that of the press, and on 5 March *Pravda* reappeared after almost three years of silence.[26] Now it was not only legal but at liberty to call itself, in its masthead, 'The Central Organ of the Russian Social Democratic Labour Party', and to publish the Bolsheviks' manifesto without recourse to abstruse allegorical language.

But the next few weeks saw such contradictions on the pages of the revamped *Pravda* that the Bolsheviks' supporters were thrown into confusion over the Party's plans.

For the first ten days it was run by several of its pre-war editors, including Vyacheslav Molotov, who advocated policies close to those held by Lenin, now living in exile in Switzerland. *Pravda* totally opposed all cooperation with the Provisional Government and demanded that all power be given to the Soviets (workers' councils); it called for an immediate end to the war and for fraternisation at the front; and it was hostile to the Mensheviks.

A week later, all these points were overturned. Comrades Stalin, Kamenev and Muranov returned to Petrograd from Siberian exile and staged what one leading Bolshevik described as an 'editorial coup d'état'.[27] Now *Pravda* offered the Provisional Government tentative support and advocated continuing a 'revolutionary defensive war'. Stalin condemned the 'defeatist anti-war slogans' and wrote of putting 'pressure' on the Provisional Government to induce the warring states to open negotiations. Kamenev urged that the Bolsheviks and the Left Mensheviks should close ranks.

Pravda's readers were just beginning to digest the new line when Lenin's 'Letter from Afar' was published – cut by 20 per cent to remove what the editors considered were hostile remarks about the moderate leaders of the Petrograd Soviet, but nonetheless breaking once more with Stalin's conciliatory line.[28]

On his arrival in Petrograd on 3 April, Lenin's first words to Kamenev were said to be: 'What's all this stuff being written in your *Pravda*? We saw some issues and thoroughly cursed you!'[29]

Even with Lenin now installed in the editorial offices overlooking the Moika canal in Petrograd, the debate – or argument – did not subside. In his famous 'April Theses', published in *Pravda* on 7 April, Lenin set out what was eventually to become undisputed Bolshevik policy in the months before the October Revolution. The 'imperialist' war should be turned into a civil war; capitalism must be overthrown; there could be no rapprochement with the Mensheviks; and the Soviet, not the Provisional Government, must be supported.

In the next few days *Pravda* was like a lively debating chamber, with Kamenev and Stalin both vigorously opposing Lenin's line. Lenin's general scheme was unacceptable, wrote Kamenev, 'because it starts from the assumption that the bourgeois revolution is ended'[30] (something required, in Marxist theory, before a 'socialist', workers' revolution can take place).

Lenin argued back. And on the 14th, Stalin, who was still an editor of *Pravda*, abandoned his earlier stance in favour of Lenin's.

From now on, *Pravda* reflected the state of the Bolshevik Party, with Lenin in control, but other voices by no means silent.

After an abortive uprising in July 1917 *Pravda*'s presses were wrecked on Government orders, and the newspaper again was forced underground. In the next four months it appeared under five different names: *A Sheet of 'Pravda'*, *Worker and Soldier*, *Proletarian*, *Worker* and *The Workers' Path*. (See Table 2 on p. 276.)

Its circulation fluctuated from an impressive 200,000 in March to about 50,000 in September, and back to 100,000 in October. One edition of *Worker and Soldier* came out in only six copies. A bookshop was started in a working-class suburb of Petrograd, open from five in the morning until late at night, so that workers could collect Bolshevik literature there. Almost half the circulation was sent out of the capital, mainly to soldiers at the fronts and to other large industrial centres.[31]

Even more so than before the war, *Pravda* received substantial voluntary contributions from workers and Bolshevik supporters. Maxim Gorky donated 3,000 roubles, even though he was also running his own newspaper, *Novaya zhizn* (*New Life*). Considerable sums of German money also made their way into the anti-war Bolsheviks' pockets. Finally, according to one historian, 'much of the paper, machinery and other equipment used for publishing Bolshevik materials was stolen or taken by force in the lawless conditions prevailing during the revolutionary months, and so was never paid for at all'.[32]

A whole host of newspapers came out in those revolutionary months of 1917, competing for the hearts and minds of the people. The Bolsheviks themselves had many local papers as well as *Pravda*, including the Moscow daily, *Sotsial-demokrat*, plus special publications for peasants and for soldiers fighting at the front. There were dozens of other papers, covering the whole political spectrum from left to right. Lenin estimated in September that although the left-wing parties commanded 75–80 per cent of the votes in

Petrograd and Moscow, the circulation of their newspapers was 'less than a quarter or even less than one-fifth that of the whole bourgeois press'.[33]

Nor was the debate between them always gentlemanly. John Reed reports in *Ten Days That Shook The World* that the extreme right-wing *Novaya Rus* 'advocated a general Bolshevik massacre' as the only solution to the crisis.

In the event, the crisis was resolved in the Bolshevik Revolution of 7 November 1917, and the first to suffer were the non-Bolshevik newspapers. Banned within three days by Lenin's Press Decree, these now behaved like *Pravda* had before the Revolution, being closed down and re-emerging under different titles. The only difference was that instead of merely closing a printing plant, the Bolsheviks generally commandeered it for their own use.

Most bourgeois papers were closed down even before the Press Decree, the very day after the Revolution. The prominent Menshevik Nikolai Sukhanov wrote of an 'unprecedented *auto-da-fé*', when, on 8 November, all the newly printed copies of *Rech* and *Sovremmenoye slovo* (bourgeois newspapers) were seized from the distribution depots and burned on the streets. 'Even Tsarism', he wrote, 'had never practised such a massive settling of accounts with the press'.[34]

So, having clamoured for months for complete freedom of the press, the Bolsheviks now silenced their opponents on the grounds that if there were total freedom, the wealthy bourgeoisie would use its press to defeat the workers' revolution. The decree provided for its own suspension and the restoration of full liberty to the press 'as soon as the new order is consolidated'.[35] The 'new order', of course, has long since been well established, but has evolved its own new definition of press freedom. (The latest thinking on the role of the communist mass media will be discussed later.)

Meanwhile, a series of moves during the year or so after the Revolution increased the authority of the Bolshevik press in general and *Pravda* in particular. On 1 December 1917 the non-Bolshevik newspapers were deprived of most of their revenue by a decree declaring advertising to be a state monopoly. On 18 February 1918 a Revolutionary Press Tribunal was established with powers to investigate 'crimes and misdemeanours of the press', and as a result of this several Moscow papers were closed down in the spring of that year for opposing the peace treaty with Germany. The Party

Congress of March 1919 criticised certain Bolshevik newspapers
and ordered *Pravda* to 'direct the provincial press'. When the
censor's office, *Glavlit*, was created in June 1922, *Pravda* and the
other central publications were exempt from scrutiny, for the simple
reason that they did not require it, and this appears to have
remained the case until the height of the Stalin period in the 1930s.[36]

During the civil war that followed the Revolution, *Pravda* – vital
though it was to the Bolsheviks' propaganda drive – betrayed all the
scars of a tottering war economy. Its circulation was erratic, averag-
ing 200,000 in 1917, only 58,000 in 1918, and 238,000 in 1920.[37] Its
size fell, at various times, from four pages to two, and its pages
themselves were often reduced to only five columns instead of the
normal eight. Because of the shortage of newsprint, *Pravda* was
sometimes printed on coarse grey or brown paper. Most editions
carried appeals, spread across the top of the pages: 'Comrades!
Save newspapers, do not tear them up, but return them to the
institution where you received them!' and 'There are not enough
newspapers for everybody. Read them aloud or jointly!' The price
soared in line with inflation from 25 kopecks in March 1918
to twelve times that amount – 3 roubles per copy – in January
1921.

On 16 March 1918, three days before the Soviet government
moved from Petrograd to Moscow, *Pravda*, too, transferred its
editorial offices to the new capital. It incorporated the Moscow
Party organ, *Sotsial-demokrat*, and henceforth was published jointly by the Central Committee and the Moscow Committee of the
Party.[38] Its new office was a room in the Hotel Dresden, where
Lenin's younger sister, Maria Ulyanova, appears to have ruled the
roost as the paper's 'responsible secretary' or managing editor,
collecting and sorting material, commissioning articles and preparing them for the presses.[39]

As one would expect of the organ of a party struggling to gain
support, establish a new social and economic system, and win a civil
war, *Pravda* at this time contained a high proportion of purely
practical information: announcements of meetings and other organisational matters. Most of the news space was given over to tele-
graphed reports under such headings as 'Abroad', 'Around Russia',
'News from the Front', 'Petrograd', and 'The Provinces', and there
were also reviews of the press and analytical or theoretical articles
and speeches by Party leaders on the economy, the nature of
socialism, and other affairs of state.

The Twenties: Bukharin as Editor

The decade between the Revolution and Stalin's consolidation of power in his own hands was a period of great debate and conflict within the Bolshevik Party. There was discussion of economic policies and the priorities of industry and agriculture. The New Economic Policy (NEP), introduced in 1921, allowed elements of capitalism to flourish again within the planned economy. And from as early as March 1923, when Lenin suffered his third, debilitating, stroke (and to some extent even before that), there was continual infighting and personal animosity between various factions and individuals, and constant tactical regrouping of alliances within the leadership, both for the sake of policy and for personal advancement.

Where did *Pravda* stand in the power struggles of the period – between Trotsky and the Stalin-Zinoviev-Kamenev 'triumvirate', then between Stalin and Zinoviev, and finally between Stalin and Bukharin? The matter is complicated by the fact that one of the protagonists, Bukharin, was himself editor-in-chief of *Pravda* for the whole of this period, until he himself became the last of Stalin's opponents to suffer defeat.

Nikolai Bukharin was appointed editor on 10 December 1917 by the Central Committee – over the head of Lenin, who wanted him to run a commission on economic affairs instead. The Central Committee overruled him, saying Bukharin was urgently needed at *Pravda*.[40] In February 1918 Bukharin resigned the editorship, and also his Party post, over the question of the peace treaty signed with Germany, but in early July he returned to the job, and stayed in it for ten years.

The first real test of Bukharin's editorial objectivity came in 1923, in the first of the battles for Lenin's mantle. This was closely linked with the economics debate over the so-called 'scissors crisis' (the dangerous imbalance – shown by crossing lines on a graph – between industrial and agricultural prices, which had arisen under the New Economic Policy).[41]

As the economic situation deteriorated throughout 1923, so did relations between Trotsky, who opposed the Party's current line, and the other three Bolshevik leaders, Stalin, Zinoviev and Kamenev, who supported it. On 7 November *Pravda* formally opened its pages to a discussion of economic matters, inviting contributions from all readers. The following month saw the last truly searching discussion in *Pravda*'s history. Trotsky himself did not at first intervene in the debate, but his supporters did, and *Pravda*'s 'Party Life' section contained many articles critical of the Central Committee. Indeed, the Party's Central Control Commission later revealed that 44 per cent of the articles published in the paper at the time put forward opposition views.[42]

But this was not to last. The head of the Party Life section, a twenty-three-year-old called Konstantinov, and his even younger assistant, Vigilyansky, were accused of turning *Pravda* into an opposition paper. Alarmed at the attacks on the leadership, Zinoviev demanded that they publish four articles in support of the leadership. Both men resigned rather than comply, and their going signalled the end of a month of exceptional debate. From now on, *Pravda*'s columns were once again closed to the opposition, and a concerted campaign was launched against Trotsky.[43] His last contribution to the paper, an open letter entitled 'The New Course', published on 11 December 1923, was followed by a full-scale attack on him by Stalin and others.[44]

Having tried at first to edit *Pravda* even-handedly during the debate, Bukharin came under pressure from the triumvirate, and finally he openly joined the anti-Trotsky campaign.[45] His long article, 'Down with Fractionalism', which was serialised in five issues of *Pravda* at the end of the year, was described as the 'reply of the central organ'.[46]

Early in 1924 Trotsky and two supporters protested against *Pravda*'s discriminatory attitude and demanded an inquiry. A committee did indeed look into the matter, but its findings did not help the complainants. The Central Control Commission rebuked Konstantinov and Vigilyansky and explained that 'the organ of the Central Committee is obliged to carry out the perfectly definite line of the Central Committee.'[47] That definition of *Pravda*'s purpose has held true ever since.

In two ways, this period, at the end of 1923 and early 1924, marked a watershed in *Pravda*'s history. First of all, it witnessed the last free discussion in its pages. There is a qualitative difference between the debate of November 1923 and the kind of criticism permitted thereafter (and still permitted today). The November debate was about the form the system was to take (it had not yet really formed) and was directed openly against some of the leaders of the Party and their policies. Such criticism has never occurred again.

If the period saw the 'last fling' before discussion was stifled, it also saw the first great cover-up of a previous Party leader's words. In May 1924, on the eve of the first Party congress after Lenin's death, the late leader's political 'testament', in which he had listed the merits and faults, as he saw them, of his potential successors, was read to Party leaders (including, presumably, Bukharin, the editor of *Pravda*). They decided not even to reveal its contents to the congress at large, far less to the general public. So *Pravda*, naturally, did not publish it. This cover-up was the first example in the Soviet press of the intentional suppression by a new Party leadership of information which was likely to damage their own reputation and prospects. This became standard practice later: Khrushchev denounced Stalin, but the press never mentioned his own role under Stalin; praise of Stalin in speeches made by some of today's Party leaders in their younger years is now routinely excised from their collected works.

In 1925, having defeated Trotsky, the triumvirate itself began to split. The new struggle, between Stalin and Zinoviev, the Leningrad Party chief, was mainly played out in their respective newspapers, *Pravda* and *Leningradskaya pravda*, until the latter was also taken over by Stalin's supporters in January 1926.[48]

Although Bukharin opposed Zinoviev over agricultural and industrial policy, he allowed him to write in *Pravda* too (but censored remarks pointing too directly at himself) Stalin supported Bukharin for tactical purposes. But by 1928 Bukharin himself had moved into opposition, particularly over the harsh grain-collection measures being inflicted on the peasants. Until now Stalin had been able to use *Pravda* to his own ends; now he needed a more obedient editor.[49]

Since early in the year several of Bukharin's associates had been working with him on *Pravda*. They were the first to go. Throughout July, August and September, they were ousted one by one, and replaced by Stalinists. As the Central Committee put it, *Pravda*'s editorial board was thus 'strengthened', and a new bureau of the paper's Party cell was elected, composed of 'the most determined comrades capable of guaranteeing a correct Party line'.[50] Bukharin remained, for the moment, editor-in-chief, but no longer decided the editorial policy or contents. One of his biographers writes that he was reportedly able to influence or compose a *Pravda* editorial as late as 23 September, but the real editors were now the Stalinists

Yaroslavsky, Savelyev and Krumin.[51] Of these, Garald Krumin emerged as *de facto* editor-in-chief, even though Bukharin nominally held the post until the following spring.

Bereft of his supporters on *Pravda*, and now the only representative of the so-called 'Right Opposition' remaining on the editorial board, Bukharin nonetheless succeeded in publishing a few last words of protest before Stalin muzzled the press once and for all.[52] His last public defence of the New Economic Policy and criticism of the headlong industrialisation proposed in Stalin's first Five Year Plan appeared in *Pravda* on 24 January 1929 – the anniversary of Lenin's birth. This article had the significant title, 'Lenin's Political Testament', recalling Lenin's other 'testament', which among other things called for Stalin's removal as General Secretary.

So long as Bukharin was formally editor, his policies were opposed but he was not attacked by name in *Pravda*. But after his removal in April 1929 the way was clear for public personal attack on him. This came on 21 and 24 August, in a *Pravda* which was now totally Stalin's mouthpiece. An unsigned article entitled 'On the mistakes and deviation of Comrade Bukharin' accused him of the heinous crimes of advocating 'giving up the attack on the kulaks [land-owning peasants]', of a 'conciliatory attitude to the Rightists' and of a 'tendency towards slowing the pace of industrialisation'. It played upon his earlier disagreements with Lenin, and vilified him – with an irony which history had still to reveal – for 'addressing the Party like an infallible Pope' and arrogating to himself the role of sole keeper and interpreter of Lenin's behests.[53]

The Stalinist version of Soviet history remains largely unchallenged to this day in the USSR. Consequently, the man who ran *Pravda* for ten of its seventy-five years (and later became editor of *Izvestiya*) is today a 'non-person'. Bukharin's portrait does not hang in the little *Pravda* museum in the editorial offices, and his name does not even merit a mention in any reference book. He was executed in 1938.

Pravda was not merely a forum for the debates on policy in the Twenties; it was also affected by the policies. After the New Economic Policy was introduced in the spring of 1921, newspapers took advantage of the permitted re-emergence of capitalism in the economy to improve their own finances by accepting advertising. Some issues of *Pravda* contained as many as two-and-a-half pages of advertisements, placed both by vendors and buyers. Goods and

Pravda's front page 9 January 1987

1. Leading article on worker participation in management
2. Text of Soviet government statement on Iran-Iraq war
3. Photo of worker at electric lamp factory
4. How dairy farmers in Perm Region are coping with severe winter weather
5. Report on construction of new Polar railway
6. Soviet Prime Minister Ryzhkov visits Finland
7. Foreign news: (a) Portuguese communists support Soviet peace proposals (b) Protests about US TV film *Amerika* which depicts a Soviet invasion of the USA

PRAVDA		5
1	3	
	4	6
		7
2		(a)
		(b)

Lenin reading *Pravda*

Bukharin and Lenin's sister in *Pravda*'s offices, May 1924

services for sale ranged from raw materials and rubbish removal to coke, galoshes, clocks and wine. One advertisement claimed: 'Spots, blackheads and freckles disfigure the face. *Chistotel-Adon* [loosely, 'Cleanbody Adonis'] makes it clean and beautiful.' Most businesses, naturally, used their owners' names, and some state-run stores, with their drab acronyms (or mere numbers) obviously felt at a disadvantage: thus the large department store, 'Mostorg univermag' (an acronym standing for 'Moscow trading organisation's universal store'), felt the need to stress, in large letters, that it was 'in the former building of MUIR & MERRILEES'![54]

1929–1941: Stalin's Weapon

It was in the early Thirties that *Pravda* developed from being merely the country's leading newspaper – with which *Izvestiya* and other papers could still occasionally dare to argue – into Stalin's press gendarme, with a supervisory role over all other newspapers. A former *Pravda* journalist, A. Gayev, describes how this came about.

'The first step in this direction was that the paper was no longer led by one editor-in-chief [Bukharin] but by an editorial board which consisted of representatives of the Press Department of the Party's Central Committee. Later Stalin brought his influence even more strongly to bear. Although the running of *Pravda* remained with the editorial board, to all intents and purposes it was now Stalin's private secretary, who received instructions, guidelines and opinions to be held on individual issues directly from his chief, who set the tone.' It was now totally impossible for any view undesired by Stalin to be expressed. All material, even if it originated from respected journalists, was now subject to pre-publication censorship.[55]

For several years the real head of *Pravda* behind the scenes was Lev Mekhlis, who was Stalin's private secretary until he was appointed chief of the political administration of the Red Army and was succeeded by A. N. Poskryobyshev. In 1933–34, Gayev goes on, 'a personal Press Department was set up in Stalin's private office, which took over not just the actual central running of the Soviet press but also the running of the Central Committee's Press Department. . . . Every word printed in *Pravda* has since had the status of a guideline for the whole Soviet press, including *Izvestiya*, the central organ of the Soviet government.'[56]

By the mid-Thirties *Pravda*'s authority was such that if the editorial board of another newspaper let some mistake slip it was called to order not by the Central Committee's Press Department but by *Pravda*'s editors. If any publication found itself pulled up by *Pravda* it would be obliged to print a public disavowal of its previous 'mistaken' statement.

As Stalin's tool, *Pravda* presented the world to the Russians and Russia to the world through the distorting prism of the dictator's requirements. Thus we read in *Pravda* nothing of the pandemonium in the Russian countryside as collectivisation was enforced or of the starvation as peasants slaughtered their cattle and burned their crops. On the other hand we do read justifications of the 'liquidation of the kulaks as a class'; and it was *Pravda*, above all, that Stalin used to direct from the centre the process of collectivisation in the provinces. The thousands of Party agents dispatched to collectivise the peasants received their instructions via *Pravda*.

The following multiple headline, under the general heading 'Preparation for the spring sowing', was typical of the first days of 1930.

> The collective farms await the leading cadres of socialist agriculture. The resolution of the November plenum of the Central Committee of the All-Union Communist Party (Bolsheviks) to send at least 25,000 workers to the collective farms, which was welcomed with great enthusiasm by the many-millioned masses of proletarians, is being put into practice far too slowly. In a number of districts the trade unions, by relying on spontaneity, have not coped with the recruiting work. Not everywhere is selection sufficiently strict.
>
> Time does not wait. Preparations for the spring agricultural campaign are under way. The collective farms are sounding the alarm. They ask for the fulfilment of the Central Committee's resolutions to be speeded up.[57]

One of the group of articles below this headline quotes some collective farmers who say they lack people to help them in the 'socialist reconstruction of agriculture'. 'We need the help of the towns,' they say.

With the benefit of hindsight and less biased information, it is clear that this is an early example of *Pravda* stating what *should* be as what *is* – a technique widely used to this day.

The disastrous effect of the 'organising campaign' is now notorious and well-documented. It led to a quick retreat, signalled by Stalin's article in *Pravda* on 2 March 1930: 'Dizzy with Success'. Collectivisation, he now claimed, had to be voluntary to be successful. Instead of preparing the peasants carefully for collectivisation, organisers in many areas had merely been 'issuing decrees'. This was undoubtedly true; but though Stalin's article immediately slowed down the pace of collectivisation, the tremendous suffering – both human and economic – caused by the initial 'overenthusiasm' naturally was never described in *Pravda*.

Other slogans from the early 1930s – for example, 'Strike at the kulaks and the right and "left" opportunists,who hamper the spread of collectivisation' – continued without any such rebuff, and the campaign to 'liquidate the kulaks as a class' engulfed far more than just landowning peasants.

It is clear from all this that *Pravda* and the other newspapers played no independent role whatsoever: they simply followed Stalin's personal decisions – in the one case, to curb the enthusiasm of the collectivisers, in the other, to ignore and/or encourage 'over-enthusiasm' in the anti-kulak campaign.

From 1936 to 1938 *Pravda* was turned into Stalin's weapon against those millions who perished in the Great Purge – both those personal enemies, the 'defendants' at show trials, who were subjected to personal abuse and detailed denunciation, and – less obviously – against those nameless millions, classed together as 'enemies of the people', whose individual cases received no mention anywhere in the Soviet press. They were the victims of a mass hysteria whipped up in classrooms and workplaces throughout the country, but directed from the Kremlin through *Pravda* and the central newspapers.

The uncanny ease with which a dictator, in control of all sources of information, can arouse the basest instincts in his subjects, is well illustrated by two occasions in May 1937: one, perhaps the most unusual article in *Pravda*'s history, the other, probably *Pravda*'s most horrifying pages, comparable only with the anti-Semitic outbursts of Hitler's press (occurring at around the same time).

On 8 May *Pravda* readers were astonished to read in their hitherto inordinately prudish newspaper an article which dwelt at length on the details of a case of rape, involving no less than one of the country's best-known physicians. The article, with the eyebrow-raising headline 'A professor is a rapist and a sadist', began by pointing out that the doctor's profession is a dignified one, and that although in pre-revolutionary Russia – and still today in some capitalist countries – doctors turned their surgeries into dens of iniquity, 'this cannot happen in our country'.

Pravda went on to describe the doings of one Professor Pletnyov, a doctor, who 'criminally exploited the trust of his female patient, Citizen B. Having got over typhus, she turned to him with a heart complaint. On 17 June 1934 Pletnyov received her at his home around twelve midnight. Pletnyov's inappropriate compliments struck Citizen B. as strange, and the methods of his medical examination as suspicious. Then the professor committed a repulsive act of violence upon the patient. Quite suddenly, Pletnyov started biting her breast, and bit it until it bled. We shall not go into the details of Pletnyov's sadistic violation of his patient.'

But *Pravda* had already gone into detail of a kind not seen before (or since). And what is more, it did in fact give some more details!

Citizen B. contracted a serious illness in her bitten breast, and Pletnyov tried unsuccessfully to treat it, then bribed her to keep quiet.

The article ended with a call for a 'severe sentence'. (It should be noted that the article appeared three years after the incident, and before a trial had taken place: in the West, *Pravda* would have been guilty of contempt of court.) The next few days saw a flood of letters in *Pravda* damning Pletnyov and reiterating *Pravda*'s call for his sentence to be severe. Then came a note from the public prosecutor to the effect that the affair was to be investigated.

The question is, why did such an unusual article appear at all, and why at that particular time? The answer could be that it was linked with a far more momentous event which eclipsed the Pletnyov affair a few days later – linked not in substance, but in 'mood'. Perhaps the Pletnyov story was discreetly preparing a general mood of indignation in the public, and establishing a precedent for a flood of supposedly spontaneous letters from the public in support of a government initiative.

On 11 May *Pravda* contained an announcement by the public prosecutor that Marshal Tukhachevsky – one of the most successful and highly regarded of Soviet commanders – had been arrested and accused, along with several others, of 'violating their military duty, treason, betrayal of the peoples of the USSR and of the Red Army'.

They had spied for an unspecified foreign power hostile to the Soviet Union and plotted to allow the restoration of capitalism in their motherland. They were to be tried that day.

The following day's edition took the concept of 'popular support' to grotesque extremes. With a speed of coverage which stretched credibility, the newspaper contained five full pages of letters of support and resolutions passed by workers at various factories (in some cases by the night shift, when *Pravda* must already have gone to press). There were even photographs of such meetings – one of them showing a speaker angrily shaking his fist. Such venerable institutions as the Academy of Sciences joined in the public outcry. The original prosecutor's statement which supposedly gave rise to all these indignant protests was very short and lacking in detail – but evidently it was enough for the imagination of the Soviet people to work on.

The poet Demian Bedny – veteran of pre-revolutionary *Pravdas* – even produced a 43-line poem on the subject of Tukhachevsky and his fellow traitors.

The five pages of denunciation included a galaxy of headlines which summed it all up: the following are only a fraction of what appeared.

FOR ESPIONAGE AND HIGH TREASON – EXECUTION!

SPIES, DESPICABLE SERVANTS OF FASCISM, TRAITORS – SHOOT THEM!

TRAITORS OF THE MOTHERLAND WILL BE WIPED FROM THE FACE OF THE EARTH!

SQUASH THE REPTILES!

DAMN THE FILTHY FASCIST RABBLE!

FOR DOGS – A DOG'S DEATH!

IMMEDIATE DEATH FOR THE SPIES!

NO MERCY FOR THE TRAITORS OF THE MOTHERLAND!

THE SPIES WHO AIMED TO DISMEMBER OUR COUNTRY AND RESTORE IN THE USSR THE POWER OF LANDOWNERS AND CAPITALISTS – SHOOT THEM!

THREE-TIMES CONTEMPTIBLE!

THEIR ODIOUS DREAMS WILL NEVER COME TRUE!

'WE ARE ALL VOLUNTEERS OF THE NKVD.'

A WORKERS' THANK YOU TO THE NKVD–MEN AND COMRADE YEZHOV.*

* Yezhov was head of the NKVD (predecessor of the KGB) who masterminded the Purge.

In short, *Pravda* had descended to the gutter and the madhouse. Even had the accusations been true, the language and the obvious stage-management of the 'popular protest' would have been inexcusable. But in 1956 the whole exercise was exposed as a fraud and the accused were rehabilitated. On the ninetieth anniversary of Tukhachevsky's birth, in 1983, *Pravda* about-turned and printed a long article extolling his skills and patriotism, but camouflaging his murder by Stalin in one simple sentence: 'M. N. Tukhachevsky's life was tragically cut short even before the Great Patriotic War.'[58]

The people's will, however, was promptly implemented. On 13 May 1937 *Pravda* announced that the eight fascist spies had been shot. With even more miraculous expedition, the *very same issue* contained dozens of letters and resolutions of approval of this act. No doubt they too would have filled the whole issue, had it not been necessary to devote two pages to the death (of natural causes) of Lenin's sister, Maria Ulyanova. The public anger and applause continued for several days, however, merging with calls for stronger defence for the country. The same method of whipping up public support is used by *Pravda* to this day, if in somewhat less extreme form.

Not all of *Pravda* was as sinister as this, however, even during the Stalinist Thirties. Its overwhelming concerns at the time were collectivisation and industrialisation, and there were a great many pages of output figures for steel, pig-iron and coal production, and stories of Stakhanovites and massive industrial projects. And although the general picture given was of a heroic people selflessly building a glorious future, *Pravda* was not devoid of criticism. Anyone who cared to read the tables of output figures, for example, could learn that on the last day of 1936 the Stalin Motor Works produced only 195 lorries instead of a planned 300. Even the industrial reporting had a good deal more urgency about it than the generally drab and cliché-ridden writing that became the norm in the more complacent Seventies. Criticism was more direct, too. A leader with the headline 'Donetsk coalfield disgracefully lagging behind'[59] would be unlikely today: the same criticism would now appear halfway through an editorial with an anodyne title such as 'Coal for the people'.

The modern technique of wrapping up criticism in 'positive propaganda' and statements of good intent was less developed in the Thirties. An account of an investigation of low teaching standards, for example, was perfectly frank and at times sarcastic. The whole article, of ninety lines, contained not one positive, redeeming word or fact.

In Yuliyevskaya school, Sofiyevsky district, one Savlukova worked as a teacher. She had graduated from an agricultural college. She writes ungrammatically. She could not point to the Caucasus mountains on a map, nor name a single district in the Ukraine. The only literature she had read was 'Gogol's *The Mother*'.* In Shevchenkovskoye secondary school worked a certain Zebelina. She had finished seven years of schooling and only one month on a teacher training course. She does not know metric measures. She could not point out the borders of the USSR on the map.[60]

Amid the politics and the industrial and agricultural news, *Pravda* also contained a number of 'human interest' stories, often with a clear moral. Most of these appeared under a heading which has existed from the very first issue of *Pravda* until the present day: 'Happenings'. The year 1937, for example, began with news of fires in Moscow caused by careless handling of New Year's trees. Highlighting, in typical fashion, just one particular instance, *Pravda* informed its readers that at No. 6, Arbat Street, in the flat of P. I. Manin, a fallen candle set fire to the cotton-wool under the fir-tree. A table, curtains and a bed were all burned, and girls' dresses also caught fire.[61]

The following day there was a report about the 'criminal negligence of doctors', one of whom had bundled a man whose legs had been crushed by a tram off to a sobering-up station, before they had even examined him properly. Crime also surfaced on 3 January 1937, in a report about a drunken 'hooligan' who had burst into a room where census officials were summing up their day's work. He 'threw chairs about and tried to beat up the census workers'. He was arrested, as were four juvenile delinquents who, according to another story in the same edition, attacked a policeman.

As during the period of the New Economic Policy, the back page contained a large number of advertisements, though no longer, of course, for private firms. Now it was mostly subscriptions to journals, new books, and theatre and cinema performances that were advertised, but nonetheless the page retained an attractive layout

---

* *The Mother* is the classic work of socialist realism, by Gorky, not Gogol.

(in contrast to the other pages), with illustrations and individually boxed advertisements, not unlike those in the British press of the same period. 'Buy Cornflakes (*kornfleks*) – nutritious and tasty!' 'We produce tennis-racket strings (*laun-tennisnye struny*).'[62] The foreign words in these advertisements were to disappear in the post-war Stalin regime, but they gave *Pravda* of the Thirties a peculiarly international flavour. Some of the film listings (occasionally, like the film *Chicago*, advertised as 'American hits'), illustrated with drawings of ladies in slinky gowns, and showing at cinemas with names such as 'Chat Noir', seem positively decadent by today's standards.

The foreign pages, meanwhile, portrayed an imperialist world intent on solving their economic crisis by starting a new world war to carve up the world and obliterate the Soviet Union, 'fatherland of the international proletariat'. The working class of the world looked to Moscow for inspiration, and 'progressive writers' such as George Bernard Shaw and Romain Rolland took to the columns of *Pravda*. 'If the future lies with Lenin,' wrote GBS, 'then we can all rejoice.'[63] At the height of the purges, Sidney Webb wrote of the USSR's 'great achievements' and praised the improved position of Soviet women as 'the greatest act of emancipation ever seen by mankind'.[64]

But the 'stormclouds of fascism' had gathered over Europe, and Hitler and Franco became the chief objects of vilification in *Pravda*. Headlines spoke of 'fascist terror', 'anti-Soviet provocations', 'torture of Soviet citizens' and 'the bloody crimes of fascist reaction'. Such was *Pravda*'s world in 1939.

1941–1953: The Conscript Press

On 23 June 1939 the Soviet Union signed a non-aggression pact with Nazi Germany, and *Pravda*'s ritual vilification of Hitler and Fascism, which had characterised the foreign pages in the Thirties, suddenly gave way to tolerant portrayals of life in a 'friendly country'. The very word 'Fascism' disappeared from the press. In some ways it was perhaps a more natural state of affairs. On 26 February 1940 *Pravda* carried a long extract from a Hitler speech on one centre page, and opposite it a detailed article on the communist manifesto.

But less than two years later the Soviet people awoke to discover that this 'friendly country' had invaded Soviet territory. From that day, 21 June 1941, *Pravda* and the other mass media were enlisted for the war effort. The task of the press was now to channel patriotism to the defence of the country rather than to industrialisation or against fictional enemies of the people.

All newspapers were now subordinated to the Press Department of the People's Commissariat [Ministry] of Defence, through which Stalin, now in his capacity as Supreme Commander, exercised absolute control.[65]

Like the press of any country engaged in all-out war, Soviet newspapers understated military defeats and glorified victories and victors. Some of Russia's best writers, such as Ehrenburg, Simonov and Sholokhov, worked as war correspondents, inspiring the troops and those left at home. *Pravda* published the daily reports of the Soviet Information Bureau (*Sovinformbyuro*), journalists' dispatches from the front, and occasionally heart-rending letters sent home by Soviet people taken prisoner and transported to Germany to work as 'slaves' for the Nazis. The heroic work in the rear – on farms and in factories – was not forgotten either. With reports from other fronts filling the foreign page, there was no room for criticism or light relief in *Pravda* during those sombre years.

Important though the press was in mobilising the people to defend the country, paper shortages and economic priorities meant that the number of newspaper titles and also their circulations fell during the war. Between 1940 and 1945 *Pravda*'s circulation dropped from 2 million to 1 million.[66]

When peace came in 1945 and Red Army men returned from the front to their farms and factories, the conscript press did not lay down its arms. There were now new enemies to fight – abroad, the adversaries of the Cold War, and at home yet more 'enemies of the people', suspect intellectuals, and Jews, referred to euphemistically as 'Cosmopolitans'. And of course there was Stalin to glorify. Western radio stations were now powerful enough to shoot holes in the Soviet propaganda and information screen, so in 1949 Soviet jammers went on the air, and the press backed them up in their new role as purveyors of 'counterpropaganda'. The machinery of total press control, built in the Thirties and militarised for the duration of the War, continued to function smoothly in peacetime.

This was the age of stupendous feats of 'socialist competition'. On 29 February 1948 *Pravda* reported that a miner named Shcherbakov had set a new record by doing the work of sixty-four men in a single shift, producing 720 tonnes of coal by himself!

It was also the age of the Personality Cult. Many issues of *Pravda* contained whole pages of pledges by the workers or farmers of such-and-such a region to fulfil some plan. The pledges were always addressed personally to 'The great leader and teacher of the peoples, Comrade I. V. Stalin'. A former *Pravda* journalist says that these collective 'letters' from the working people were composed, almost without exception, in the editorial offices of *Pravda*, following various standard models.[67]

By now, *Pravda*'s leading articles had settled into the style that endures to this day. One 1948 leader, blaming leather producers, shoemakers, and the Ministry of Light Industry for the poor quality of Soviet shoes, could easily have appeared in 1985. 'Shoes are transported from the factories in sacks, in bulk, and become crushed and misshapen,' it wrote. 'Is it really necessary to issue a special directive about despatching finished goods in proper packing?'[68] *Pravda*'s sarcasm was rather misplaced: under Stalin's centralised economy, a special directive was indeed necessary! As today, though, shortcomings tended to be presented wistfully as a failure to match up to illusory world-beating Soviet traditions. We read in the same article: 'Soviet footwear, Soviet fabrics and foodstuffs, deservedly earned universal recognition in the years of Stalin's Five Year Plans. We must revive this glory.'

Perhaps the most damning criticism in the period until Stalin's death in 1953 was reserved for intellectuals – writers, scholars, musicians. As usual, *Pravda*'s role was to prepare the ground for Stalin's pronouncements, and to demonstrate public approval of them. In February 1948 the Central Committee issued a decree on V. Muradeli's opera *A Great Friendship*. The decree accused several Soviet composers, including Shostakovich, Prokofiev and Khachaturian, of 'anti-popular, formalistic perversions' in their work, and of displaying 'antidemocratic tendencies alien to the Soviet people and their artistic tastes'. A few days later *Pravda* published a selection of letters under the headline, 'The Soviet people warmly approve the Central Committee's decree'.[69] A well-known singer said that he had found the part of Fyodor in Muradeli's opera 'not difficult but uninteresting'. A worker, whose claim to authority was that he had initiated the struggle to cut down production losses, said that Soviet music compared unfavourably with Russian classical music. An engineer wrote: 'Our composers should be engineers of the human soul'. The foreman of a tractor factory said that his colleagues were satisfied with the decree, 'which expresses Stalin's concern for our Soviet art, for the ideological upbringing of the working people'. After only two days, the decree was already having a beneficial effect on Soviet music, as this confession by fourth-year music student Molchanov showed: 'For a long time I had disagreed inwardly with the direction taken by Prokofiev, Shostakovich and our other "leading" composers. But as soon as one tried to escape from their influence and satisfy one's own needs in melody and song – one was immediately accused at the Faculty's creative circle of primitivism. When I read the decree I at once heaved a deep sigh. Can you believe it – I now walk about singing to myself, and the thoughts which I used to suppress pour out of me in melodies.' Little has been heard since then of the young composer Molchanov.

Pravda's well-oiled machinery was nonetheless capable of malfunctioning, most notably in 1951, when Stalin objected to an article by one Nikita Khrushchev, then head of the Moscow Party organisation. The next day *Pravda* printed a rare correction note. 'Through an editorial oversight,' it said, 'the article by Comrade N. S. Khrushchev was not accompanied by a note from the editorial board stating that it was published "for discussion". This note corrects that mistake.' A secret circular was then sent out to Party organisations declaring that the article was not just 'for discussion' but misguided and hence to be ignored.[70] This editorial blunder, it must be said, did no harm to the subsequent careers of Khrushchev or of *Pravda*'s editor at the time, Mikhail Suslov, who went on to become one of the leadership's most senior figures for over twenty years.

By now, *Pravda* had settled into the rigid pattern of protocol and nuances that keeps Moscow-watchers guessing to this day. When Stalin died on 5 March 1953, the news was announced in a format retained ever since for the deaths of incumbent Party leaders: black-bordered front page, large portrait, obituary signed by the central authorities, medical report on the cause of death, and the announcement of the setting up of a funeral commission. Next day, an editorial reassured the public that there was no need for alarm. Within a week or so, Stalin's name virtually disappeared from *Pravda*'s pages. Now what became all-important was the order in which the other leaders' names were listed, where they stood in photographs (some of them faked – see Illustrations facing pp. 40–41), and what *Pravda failed* to say, as much as what it did say. 'Kremlinology' came into its own.

1953–1964: Truth Reassessed

In the three years following the dictator's death, while Khrushchev worked to establish his primacy in the collective leadership, *Pravda* was edited by Dmitri Shepilov, who, though a Khrushchev supporter, could not always control *Pravda* in his favour. Even one of Khrushchev's own speeches was 'censored' by the Party's newspaper.[71] In 1956 he was replaced by another Khrushchev man, Pavel Satyukov, who edited the paper until after his patron's fall from power in 1964. In 1959 – two years after Khrushchev had become Prime Minister in addition to First Secretary of the Party – he appointed his son-in-law, Aleksei Adzhubei, editor of the government newspaper, *Izvestiya*. For his last five years in power, therefore, both of the main Soviet newspapers had editors who were well-disposed towards Khrushchev.

It was Adzhubei who, by revamping *Izvestiya*, made the most significant contribution to Soviet journalism at the time. His bolder, eye-catching layout and use of varied typefaces and photographs contrasted starkly with *Pravda*'s still staid and boring appearance, and it clearly appealed to the public: between 1959 and 1964, when Adzhubei was sacked, *Izvestiya*'s circulation jumped from about 2 million to 6 million, while *Pravda*'s hovered around six and a half million. During that period, however, subscriptions to all periodicals were limited, and it was only in 1965, when subscriptions became unrestricted, that *Izvestiya* (now without Adzhubei but still aided by his legacy) overtook *Pravda*, leaping to eight million, one and a quarter million ahead of *Pravda*. It remained ahead for four years.[72]

While these changes in style and presentation were slowly revolutionising the Soviet press, even more significant changes were affecting its content. The glorification of Stalin ended literally within days of his death, and gingerly the process of de-Stalinisation began. In February 1956 Khrushchev delivered a stunning denunciation of Stalin's crimes and personality cult in a secret speech to the 20th Party Congress, but he warned in the same speech that 'we must know the limits, and not give the enemy any ammunition': he

In the first days after Stalin's death, *Pravda* tried to promote Georgy Malenkov as his successor. The picture of him alone with Stalin and Mao Tse-tung (*Pravda*, 10 March 1953) was a doctored version of a group photograph (*below*) published in *Pravda* on 15 February 1950

Politburo member Dinmukhamed Kunayev (*arrowed, 2nd from left*) missed President Andropov's lying-in-state, but *Pravda* inserted him (between KGB chief Chebrikov and future Party leader Chernenko). Being there only in spirit, however, Kunayev could not of course cast a shadow on the ground! (*Pravda*, 12 February 1984)

explicitly forbade the publication of any part of his speech in the press. Nonetheless, its contents were made known to Party members and even non-members at meetings throughout the country, and its spirit quickly became the lodestar of the Soviet press.

Stalin himself was not at first personally condemned in *Pravda*, but the consequences of his rule began to be analysed. It was not a 'free' discussion in the Western sense: the apparatus of press control was still firmly in place, and *Pravda* 'opened up' only to the extent decreed by the top Party leadership. It was only after the 22nd Party Congress in 1961, according to historian Roy Medvedev, that the public could read telling 'assessments of the dark days of a quarter of a century before'.[73] Obituaries of political figures who had perished in the purges were printed. *Pravda* published articles full of praise for Aleksandr Solzhenitsyn's labour-camp novel, *One Day in the Life of Ivan Denisovich*, and even a prepublication extract from one of his stories.[74] Even when the tide was turning against Solzhenitsyn, *Pravda* printed a favourable interview with the editor of the liberal literary monthly *Novy Mir*, in which the publication of *Ivan Denisovich* was held up as 'proof of the Party's broadmindedness on literature and art'.[75]

The story of Nikita Khrushchev's rise and fall, however, is also the story of the flowering and smothering of the Soviet press. The details of how *Pravda* told the Russian people about Khrushchev's overthrow illustrate well the workings of the Soviet press, and deserve to be retold here.

On 13 October 1964, five of *Pravda*'s six pages were given over to the flight of the world's first three-man space-crew, on board a Voskhod capsule. (The previous day's paper had not even indicated that such a flight was in preparation, for fear that something might go wrong during the launch.) The front page contained photographs and biographies of the three spacemen, and a transcript of their conversation from space with Khrushchev.

On 14 October, *Pravda* reported Voskhod's safe return to Earth, and also that Prime Minister Khrushchev had had a meeting in Sochi on the Black Sea with the French Minister for Scientific Research. It also printed telegrams received and sent by Khrushchev. But that day, a meeting of the Central Committee in Moscow was quietly ousting him from power and giving his post of First Secretary to Leonid Brezhnev.

The next day's *Pravda* contained no news of that. But neither did it contain even a single mention of Khrushchev's name – for the first time in a decade. Alert readers might have suspected something was amiss. The President of Cuba, who arrived the day before, was met only by the Soviet head of state, Mikoyan, and the speeches reprinted in *Pravda* did not even contain a reference to the Soviet Party leader and Premier. Roy Medvedev explains that early on the 14th, all the printing presses in the country had been stopped, while thousands of censors went through newspapers, magazines and books eliminating every mention of Khrushchev from manuscripts and page-proofs.

Meanwhile, a meeting of the Presidium of the Supreme Soviet, on the 15th, appointed Aleksei Kosygin in Khrushchev's place as Prime Minister (though the decision had been taken by the Party leaders the previous day).

Only on 16 October did *Pravda* announce Khrushchev's fall from both positions of power. But it gave no hint of the coup which had taken place in Moscow. On the contrary, the official communiqué stated that the two meetings had 'satisfied Khrushchev's request' to be released from his duties 'because of his advanced years and deteriorating state of health'. Portraits of Brezhnev and Kosygin (but no biographies, as would be normal today) appeared on the front page.

Lest readers be worried by the unexpected change of leadership (after all, only days before, Khrushchev had despite his old age and poor health had a jovial, if rather stilted telephone call to Soviet cosmonauts and had been meeting foreign dignitaries) there was a message at the top of page one stating that the Communist Party of the Soviet Union was firmly and consistently putting into practice the 'Leninist general line worked out by the 20th and 22nd Congresses of the CPSU' (which had condemned Stalinism).

Perhaps even *Pravda* was caught on the hop by the coup. Most of that day's issue was devoted to the space-flight and to the 150th anniversary of the poet Lermontov's birth. Only on the next day (17th) did it have an editorial on the political situation, entitled 'The stable Leninist general line of the CPSU'.

Without mentioning Khrushchev by name – or even the fact that the leadership had changed – the editorial gave a clear indication that he had not really resigned but had been ousted, and also of the reasons why: 'The Leninist Party is an enemy of subjectivism and drift in the building of communism. Alien to it are hare-brained schemes, premature conclusions and hasty decisions and actions divorced from reality, bragging and idle talk, love of issuing orders, and unwillingness to take into consideration what has already been worked out by science and practical experience. The building of communism is a living, creative matter; it does not tolerate clerical methods, decisions taken without consultation, or disregard for the practical experience of the masses.' The words 'collective leadership' came up three times.

Khrushchev was already a non-person. His name has been mentioned only twice in *Pravda* since then: once when, at *Pravda*'s bidding, he denounced the 'so-called memoirs of N. S. Khrushchev', published in the West, as forgeries, and again a year later when a terse one-sentence note signed by the Central Committee and Council of Ministers announced 'with sorrow' that he was dead.[76]

Since 1964: The Limits to Free Debate

In November 1964, within a month of Khrushchev's fall from power, the editors of both *Pravda* and *Izvestiya* – both his staunch supporters – were replaced. At *Izvestiya*, his son-in-law Adzhubei was replaced by Vladimir Stepakov, an ally of the new Prime Minister, Aleksei Kosygin; and at *Pravda* the editorship went to Aleksei Rumyantsev. The scene was set for any disputes which might arise between Party and government (as soon they did, over economic reform) to be played out in the two main organs of the press.

The argument, in a nutshell, was about whether *economic* levers should be allowed to regulate the economy (Kosygin's view) or whether *ideology* should take precedence.[77] The latter view was expounded especially vigorously by a 'Brezhnev man', Vasily Stepanov, editor of the Party journal *Kommunist*. On 17 May 1965 Rumyantsev allowed Stepanov to launch a bitter attack in *Pravda* on Kosygin's proposed reform. After days of alleged crisis in the Kremlin, Kosygin's ally on *Izvestiya* (which had totally boycotted Brezhnev's name for three days) responded with a bitterly worded editorial, seen as a thinly disguised attack on the Party leader. 'An engineering diploma is not everything,' it said, alluding to Brezhnev's background. 'To be a leader takes more than having special knowledge of this or that field of technology or economics. The diploma must be supplemented by a talent for organisation, by a correct understanding of the leader's political role and by an ability to motivate people.'[78]

Aleksei Rumyantsev had previously been editor of *Problems of Peace and Socialism*, an official Soviet bloc organ published in Prague. He was, says the émigré dissident Zhores Medvedev, 'a good journalist with fairly independent views whose articles were always carefully read and discussed'.[79] And although part of the reason for his dismissal as *Pravda*'s editor less than a year after taking the job on may have been his inability or unwillingness to argue strongly enough against Kosygin's reforms (which were adopted, albeit diluted, in September 1965), he was in fact a victim of the general political reaction which set in in Soviet politics in the mid-Sixties.

The political debate during these years centred around two related issues: Stalin and whether or not to reverse the process of de-Stalinisation; and literature and the arts, with liberal intellectuals identified with the journal *Novy Mir* coming increasingly under attack. Under Rumyantsev, *Pravda* took up a 'centrist', or even 'progressive' position on both these matters.

Shortly after his appointment, *Pravda* published three leading articles which were critical of the Stalin cult, suggesting that the new leadership would continue a reasonably tolerant policy on this line. In retrospect, it seems likely that the articles reflected Rumyantsev's views more than they did Brezhnev's. Then in February 1965 Rumyantsev wrote – and published in *Pravda* under his own name – one of those rarities of Soviet journalism: an article which literally became the talk of the town, at least in intellectual circles.[80] In this long article, entitled 'The Party and the Intelligentsia', Rumyantsev appeared to reject the calls of conservatives for 'Party-spirited' literature, saying that art could not be 'stimulated to order' or regimented. 'Real creativity . . . is possible only in an atmosphere of search, experimentation, free expression and the clash of opinions.' True, he condemned 'formalism' and 'manifestations of bourgeois ideology', but he went on: 'Everything that promotes the flowering of the human personality, that broadens its outlook, inspires it with high ideals, elevates it morally and intellectually, improves its aesthetic perception of its surroundings, helps it to see more sharply the good and the evil in the world and to react more sharply to them – in a word, all that enhances the truly human in man, is in the mainstream of true art and constitutes its real value.' Rumyantsev also took a swipe at Stalin, who was so sure of his own 'infallibility' and 'considered himself the only intellectual' who could 'decide on behalf of everyone'.

Throughout 1965 the hardliners fought against this apparent liberalism. A new handbook of Party history omitted references to Stalin's mistakes in the conduct of the war and played down the horrors of the purges. First a Writers' Conference in March and then an ideological conference in August signalled an end to tolerance of works that dwelt upon the 'negative aspects' of the Stalin period, and a return to the artistic strictures of 'socialist realism'.[81] In September the writers Sinyavsky and Daniel were arrested, and the manuscript of Solzhenitsyn's *The First Circle* was seized by the KGB.* It was when Rumyantsev tried to oppose the new reactionary line that he was dismissed, together with his assistant, Yuri Karyakin, who had helped him write 'The Party and the Intelligentsia'. The change was announced on 22 September.

Pressure for Rumyantsev's dismissal is said to have come from two of the leaders of the new wave of reaction: Sergei Trapeznikov, the newly-appointed Stalinist head of the Central Committee's Department of Science and Education, and Vladimir Yagodkin, Ideology Secretary on the Moscow Party Committee. One of Trapeznikov's first acts in his new post was to publish in *Pravda* an article in which he described the Stalin era as 'one of the most brilliant in the history of the Soviet state. It is full of the richest experience in the theoretical and practical activity of the Party, in the persistent struggle for the ideological purity of its ranks.'[82] The underground *Political Diary*, edited by Roy Medvedev, specifically linked Trapeznikov's name with the disappearance in the mid-sixties of articles in the Soviet press about the victims of Stalinism. 'Since S. Trapeznikov's sadly well-known article about the "funeral feasters", the number of articles in our press devoted to the memory of the victims of the Stalinist terror has sharply dropped. In most of those articles which do appear there is no indication of the cause of death of such and such a figure. Every editorial board tries to think up as nebulous an ending as possible for such articles.'[83]

---

* Ironically, the *Pravda* offices were the unlikely sanctuary of another copy of the manuscript, which Solzhenitsyn had given to Rumyantsev's assistant, Yuri Karyakin, for safe keeping. Rumyantsev was allegedly thinking of publishing chapters from *The First Circle* in *Pravda*, but Solzhenitsyn is sceptical of this, referring to him as Karyakin's 'oh, so very liberal boss'. See Aleksandr I. Solzhenitsyn, *The Oak and the Calf* (London, 1980), p. 102.

At the end of January 1966 a *Pravda* article entitled 'The lofty responsibility of historians' declared that the phrase 'period of the personality cult', which had become the standard description of the Stalin years, should no longer be used as it was an 'erroneous non-Marxist term'.[84] The phrase has not been officially used since that day.

The paper was now edited by Mikhail Zimyanin, who toed the steadily hardening Party line through the total clamp-down following the Czechoslovak events of 1968 and beyond, until 1976, when he was rewarded with a secretaryship on the Central Committee.

Pravda's position before and after the 'political reaction' of the Sixties is perhaps symbolised by the fate of two of its journalists, Len Karpinsky, a liberal (and son of one of Lenin's close comrades) who became head of the paper's culture section, and Fyodor Burlatsky, who joined as a 'political observer' in May 1964.

It was Burlatsky – one of the Party's leading thinkers – who, under Rumyantsev's editorship, initiated a discussion in the pages of *Pravda* about the need for a separate academic discipline of 'political science' to be established in the Soviet Union – a discussion which led ultimately to the revival of Soviet political and social science research, which had been stifled under Stalin. Karpinsky became the centre of a group of young *Pravda* journalists and intellectuals who favoured liberal reforms in the Soviet system.[85]

In 1967, after Solzhenitsyn had written a letter to the Union of Writers attacking censorship, Burlatsky and Karpinsky together penned an article criticising censorship in the theatre. The article caused a heated argument in the editorial board, of which both men were members. The editor, Zimyanin, saw that the political climate was no longer such that he could print the article. The two journalists therefore took it to *Komsomolskaya pravda*, whose literary editor mistakenly assumed that it must signify the beginning of a new trend, to be initiated at a lower level than *Pravda* itself. He printed it, and was promptly sacked.[86]

Karpinsky and Burlatsky also lost their jobs on *Pravda*, apparently on Brezhnev's orders, and received Party reprimands. Karpinsky was sent to *Izvestiya*, Burlatsky to the Institute of International Relations. Karpinsky was soon sacked from his post as special correspondent at *Izvestiya* after making a strong anti-Stalinist speech at an editorial meeting in 1969. He found refuge in the newly founded Institute of Sociology, whose director was his former boss at *Pravda*, Aleksei Rumyantsev. In 1972, again under the influence of the reactionary Trapeznikov, Rumyantsev was removed from the directorship of the Institute, and Karpinsky left to head a department of Progress Publishers. Karpinsky's downward career ended with his becoming a dissident and starting up a *samizdat* (underground) journal. He was sacked once again, and thrown out of the Party. He now works as a bibliographer.[87] Fyodor Burlatsky, on the other hand, is now head of the Philosophy Department of the Institute of Social Science attached to the Central Committee, deputy chairman of the Association of Political Science, and one of the most interesting Soviet commentators on foreign and internal affairs, writing chiefly in *Literaturnaya gazeta*.

The year of Rumyantsev's editorship of *Pravda* stands out both because of the unusually clear (if subtly expressed) confrontation over economic issues which developed between *Pravda* and *Izvestiya*, and because it shows that the Party's own newspaper is not always a perfect mouthpiece of the leadership, particularly when it is edited by a man of such pronounced abilities and views as Rumyantsev evidently had.

Internal debates over the economy and ideology waned as Brezhnev established his supremacy in the 'collective leadership'. Under Mikhail Zimyanin, *Pravda* became once more the spokesman for the mainstream of Party thought (and 'permitted' debate), and it has continued in this role since Viktor Afanasyev took over the editor's chair in 1976.

There were numerous outward signs of internal dissatisfaction with the work of the mass media at this time, however. In 1966 the Central Committee's Department of Agitation and Propaganda ('Agitprop') was renamed the Propaganda Department, and presumably had its functions trimmed accordingly, with 'agitation' – the explanation of particular current issues – being hived off to lower bodies, leaving it to concentrate on the wider ideological concerns of 'propaganda'. In 1967 the journalists' 'trade journal', *Sovetskaya pechat*, was criticised and closed down. Its successor, *Zhurnalist*, was put under *Pravda*'s guidance. Finally, there was a growing perception of the diverse uses to which the various news media could be put. Audience surveys were commissioned – for the first time since the demise of Soviet sociology under Stalin – to discover who read what and why. The aim was not – as it might be in the West – simply to find out the audience's preferences and to tailor newspapers and broadcasts to suit them (and thereby to win bigger audiences), but to find out which aspects of propaganda were 'ineffective' and to make better use of the specific potentials of the press, radio and television by discovering why people used each of them.[88] That may have been the intention, but to this day, despite undeniable improvements in all three media, Soviet television still has newscasters reading the complete texts of long statements, without so much as a still photograph to accompany them, the night before the same text is printed in *every* Soviet newspaper!

It was during the Brezhnev years that *Pravda*'s present layout and 'face' took shape, with an obvious effort being made to introduce more eye-catching typefaces and formats. There was a distinct shift in the content, too, following a stream of complaints by Brezhnev and various Central Committee decisions and resolutions on the mass media and ideology.[89] This was the period of détente, culminating in the Helsinki accords of 1975, which included calls for freer exchanges of information between East and West. Jamming of most foreign radio broadcasts ceased, and there was more personal contact between Russians and visiting Westerners. Because of the increasing effect of such 'anti-Soviet' influences (including the rebroadcasting into the Soviet Union of the *samizdat* writings which had proliferated as a result of the internal political reaction), the leadership perceived a need for 'counterpropaganda'. This soon left its mark on *Pravda*'s foreign pages, which became more vociferous in denying Western allegations of human rights violations in the USSR and also started throwing back 'counter-claims' – that there was no freedom of speech, and so on, in the West. The West's 'free society' became known as the 'society of violated rights'.

On the home front, however, fossilisation set in. To add to the tedium of rigid ideology and endless boasting about production successes, came a new element – Brezhnev's own personality cult. His name, with all his titles, littered the pages of *Pravda*. Scarcely an article could be written without a quotation from one of his speeches being inserted to 'justify' its appearance. His memoirs were serialised and read on the radio, turned into films, and awarded the Lenin Prize for literature.

It took Brezhnev's death in 1982, and the energy of Andropov, while it lasted, to shake the press out of its torpor. There was no question of radical changes in approach, however. Rather, it was the same rusty and ineffective machinery merely being turned to new tasks, the priorities of a new General Secretary – corruption and indiscipline. Of all the central newspapers, only *Izvestiya*'s editor was changed. Under Chernenko's brief rule, the pace slackened slightly but the priorities remained basically the same.[90]

Coming to power in March 1985, Mikhail Gorbachov seemed to understand that the old machinery and approaches were not going to help him achieve his more ambitious goals. In the press, as in other parts of the state apparatus, he made several personnel changes. He called media chiefs together for 'pep talks', and tried to stimulate initiative by encouraging bolder criticism and giving editors the freedom to explore previously forbidden subjects. *Glasnost* (openness or publicity) became the new watchword.[91] There was more coverage of domestic bad news – especially after the accident at the Chernobyl nuclear power station in the Ukraine. Under Gorbachov the media intensified Andropov's campaign against corruption and mismanagement, took up the fight against alcoholism, and widened the economics debate. Gorbachov's own speeches and walk-abouts were given saturation coverage.

Pravda itself came in for criticism at the Communist Party Congress in February 1986. Yegor Ligachov, 'number two' in the Politburo, indicated that it had gone too far in the debate of current issues which was encouraged during the months before the Congress.[92] Apparently he had been particularly displeased by an article which raised – for the only time ever in the Soviet press – the question of privileges enjoyed by the Party élite, and the resentment they cause in the general population.[93] The criticism gave rise to speculation that the paper's editor, Afanasyev, had fallen into disfavour. But there was no indication that he did not enjoy Gorbachov's support, and at the time of writing he was still in charge.

Despite Gorbachov's calls for greater honesty and openness, the bright red birthmark on his forehead, which was there for all to see on television, miraculously disappeared from *Pravda*'s retouched photographs. Was it really being any more honest about the blemishes in Soviet society? Before attempting to answer that question, it is time to take a broader look at the Soviet news media as a whole.

2

Pravda and the Soviet Mass Media

As *Pravda* evolved through the decades, changing to suit the economic and political conditions in the country, some developments proved to be temporary; others stayed, and go to make up the character of the paper that exists today. The free debate of the early Twenties, the advertising of the NEP period, the hideous ravings of the Stalin period – these things have gone. But the system of news control, and the organisation of *Pravda* and the mass media today, contain elements that date back to Stalin or even further. Soviet theories of the role of the press have moved on, although Lenin's dictum that a newspaper is 'not only a collective propagandist and collective agitator but also a collective organiser' is still trotted out.

From the start, the newspaper's relationship to the Party has indicated a role very different from that of the Western news media. Indeed, 'news' would seem to be the least of *Pravda*'s worries: in a leading article on 'Press Day' (5 May) 1985, it defined the Soviet press as the 'faithful assistant of the Leninist Party, a tireless propagandist of the ideas of Marxism-Leninism'. So what exactly are the functions of the Soviet mass media, and of *Pravda* in particular?

The starting-point of all Soviet discussion of the subject is the question of ownership. In contrast to the privately-owned 'bourgeois' newspapers of the West, which must necessarily express their proprietors' – or at least the Establishment's – views, the argument goes, the Soviet press is publicly owned and therefore reflects the views of the people. Since 'the Party and the people are one', there can be no question of the Party press acting against the people's best interests. It is the same argument, in other words, as that used to justify the one-party state and lack of political opposition.

Similarly, it is argued that Western newspapers, and hence their content, are essentially 'commodities' which must be commercially viable. Because they depend on advertising, they must also reflect their advertisers' views, and because they must sell well in order to attract advertisers, they resort to sensationalism. In the communist press, one Soviet academic writes, 'it is impermissible to employ invented, unverified, socially contentless facts, exaggerated sensations, or the cult of violence, or to interfere in interpersonal relationships'.[1]

Western definitions of the political functions of an independent press tend to centre around three main points. First, the media should provide people with sufficient objective information for them to be able to follow public events with critical awareness. Secondly, they should play a part in forming public opinion, by suggesting political alternatives in commentaries and editorials, by running campaigns for or against various projects or policies, and by publishing interviews with public figures. Thirdly, the press should support democracy by criticising those with power and thereby helping to control their activities. Most serious Western newspapers would at least subscribe to these ideals, even if not all of them consistently implement them. In the case of the 'popular press' a fourth function – entertainment – becomes so important as to swamp the other three, often leading to trivialisation of important issues.

It is only recently that Soviet scholars have begun to ascribe any of the above functions to the Party-controlled press. In the standard description, its role is not to reflect but to organise, not, in *Pravda*'s words, to 'strike the reader's imagination' but to 'urge him to action, to competition, to the achievement of high productivity of labour'.[2] Journalists are not reporters, but are purposefully engaged in the administration of society and the economy, publicising and explaining the Party's decisions. Far from providing political alternatives, the task is to channel public opinion in the direction of the Party line. And although Soviet theorists extol the virtues of 'self-criticism' it is clear that this can be only partly compatible with the goal of being the Party's 'faithful assistant'. As for world affairs, says *Pravda*, the Soviet press is 'a fiery champion of the Leninist foreign-policy course. It affirms the ideals of peace, security and friendship between peoples, and exposes the disinformation and slander of bourgeois propaganda.'[3]

Students at Soviet journalism faculties learn to trot out the accepted wisdom that the 'four principles of Soviet journalism' are *partiynost'* (Party-spiritedness), *ideynost'* (ideological correctness), *narodnost'* (being for, by and close to the people) and *pravdivost'* (truthfulness).[4]

More diverse definitions of the Soviet media have appeared in recent years. One writer pointed to six functions which would seem to be a more realistic assessment of what *Pravda* and the other papers see as their aims.[5]

- Ideological education: that is, propaganda of Marxism-Leninism and 'correct' formation of public opinion.
- Organisation: mobilising the population to perform vital tasks, publicising the experience of the best work-teams, and criticism of shortcomings.
- Chronicling: provision of day-to-day information, allowing people to orient themselves quickly in the flow of events at home and abroad.
- Education: spreading knowledge in the fields of science, culture, art, etc.
- Entertainment.
- Advertising: (*Pravda* only advertises television, radio and theatre programmes, but local papers also advertise goods and educational courses.)

All these functions are means to an end, though. Writing on *Pravda*'s seventieth anniversary, its editor-in-chief, Viktor Afanasyev, summed it up as follows:

We inform the masses of the decisions of the Party and government, propagandise these decisions, mobilise and organise the Soviet people to carry them out, accumulate and mould public opinion, and concentrate people's efforts on solving precisely those tasks which are most important and most necessary for the country and for the Party. We study and spread advanced experience, and together with the Party and people seek internal reserves for our movement forward. We help the Party to bring up the new man, strive to show . . . the greatness of his affairs, his successes, needs and interests, the difficulties he encounters, the problems he solves; we criticise shortcomings, mistakes and omissions, and we try to find ways of overcoming them. We raise the Soviet people in a spirit of peace and cooperation between peoples, striving to make real patriots and internationalists of them, ready to defend their country and the gains of world socialism.[6]

That, at least, is the theory. We shall see later how successfully it is translated into practice.

There are no privately-owned or 'independent' newspapers in the Soviet Union. The entire system of public communications serves the interests of the Communist Party and the state, and, backed up with jamming of hostile foreign radio broadcasts and strict control of imported literature, attempts the total indoctrination of society. But for the vagaries of short-wave reception and less than total efficiency of customs officials, it might well achieve it.

Newspapers, from *Pravda* down to factory broadsheets, come under the control of the Party organisation at the appropriate level of the hierarchy – the Central Committee in *Pravda*'s case, the factory cell for an enterprise's 'wall newspaper'.

All the central newspapers published in Moscow, as well as the news agencies TASS and APN, and radio and television, are answerable to the Propaganda Department of the Central Committee, headed by Yuri Sklyarov, a Gorbachov appointee, and a most important behind-the-scenes figure in the Party apparatus.[7] This department has sectors for the press, the radio, television, book-publishing, and so on, through which it issues instructions downwards and also checks the published or broadcast output of the media. It is known that in the Sixties the press sector held a fortnightly 'instructional conference' for the editors of the main newspapers, at which past performance was criticised and guidelines were laid down on priorities in the coming two-week period.[8] It would appear that this practice may have been abandoned – or, more likely, restricted to lower-level newspapers, in view of the close contact which is in any case maintained between the Party leadership and the editors of the chief newspapers (see below). But *ad hoc* conferences on major campaigns and policy changes, attended by all the top editors, are still held.

Sklyarov – a former First Deputy Editor-in-Chief of *Pravda* – was in fact the second person appointed by Gorbachov to head the Propaganda Department. The first was Aleksandr Yakovlev, appointed to the post in July 1985. The swiftness with which Gorbachov moved his own man into this position – only four months after he came to power – demonstrated the importance he attached to the work of the mass media. But it was also a rather curious appointment, since Yakovlev's predecessor, Boris Stukalin, had been in the job for only two-and-a-half years, had a journalistic background, and was appointed by Andropov, Gorbachov's own 'mentor'. Most other Andropov placemen continued to enjoy Gorbachov's confidence, but not, apparently, Stukalin, who was made ambassador to Hungary in the reshuffle – a clear demotion. Gorbachov had already underlined his dissatisfaction with the work of the mass media by holding a meeting in June in the Central Committee with top editors and broadcasters, at which he called for 'open, concrete and constructive' criticism of shortcomings, and stressed the role of the media in 'restructuring the public conscious-ness in the spirit of the new demands of life'.[9]

But the real clue to Stukalin's fall from favour may lie in a short announcement printed prominently on the front pages of the main newspapers just one day before the major Central Committee meeting held in July, at which Gorbachov decisively consolidated his own power by ousting his rival Grigory Romanov from the Politburo and Secretariat, kicking veteran foreign minister Andrei Gromyko 'upstairs' to the Presidency, and promoting his comrade Eduard Shevardnadze. The announcement itself was innocuous: a decree that the Baikal-Amur Railway was to be named after the Komsomol. But it was signed by 'Secretary of the CPSU Central Committee, M. Gorbachov.'[10] Not *General* Secretary, just 'Sec-retary' – one of a dozen men who held that title. Somebody at a very senior level had dared to remind Gorbachov, on the front page of every newspaper, that he should not get above himself, and whether or not that somebody was Stukalin himself, it seems that he, as propaganda chief, had to carry the can. He was dismissed – possibly within days – and dispatched to Hungary three weeks later.[11] (It is not impossible that it was Stukalin, too, who insisted that Gorbachov's speech to that Central Committee meeting should not be published – contrary both to precedent and to Gorbachov's own insistence on 'openness' in the press.)

Stukalin's successor, Yakovlev, had worked as first deputy head of the Propaganda Department from 1965 until 1973, when he is thought to have fallen into disgrace for attacking Russian national-ism. He was 'gracefully demoted' to the post of ambassador to Canada, but brought back to Moscow in 1983 to head a key foreign policy 'think tank', the Institute of World Economy and Inter-national Relations.[12] He is believed to be close to Gorbachov, and was promoted to become a Secretary of the Central Committee in February 1986, handing over the day-to-day running of the Propaganda Department to Sklyarov, but continuing to supervise its work in his capacity as 'propaganda secretary' (the title itself does not exist). Yakovlev is answerable only to the General Secretary himself and to Gorbachov's second-in-command, Yegor Ligachov, who is both a full Politburo member and Secretary in charge of ideology.

Russians have a huge number of sources of information at their disposal. In 1984 a total of 8,327 daily and weekly newspapers were being published in the Soviet Union, with a total circulation of 185,275,000. Of these, the vast majority are local or republican papers, while 31 are 'central' or 'all-Union' newspapers, published in Moscow but printed in several centres and sold throughout the country. There are about 1,500 magazines and journals, with a total printing of 182,275,000.[13] (See diagram on p. 281.)

Pravda (daily circulation 11.3 million) is the most important of the central newspapers because it is the organ of the Communist Party's Central Committee. Given the primacy in the Soviet system of the Communist Party over the Government, it is slightly more authoritative than *Izvestiya* (*News*) (circulation 6·4 million), published by the Presidium of the USSR Supreme Soviet. *Izvestiya* has an evening edition for Moscow and a morning edition for elsewhere. The content of these two main organs reflects the bodies which publish them – in coverage, at least, although their editorial stances, as has been seen, have rarely diverged throughout their history.

Trud (*Labour*), published by the Central Trade Union Council, is now the USSR's best-selling newspaper, with a daily circulation of over 18 million – probably not because it concentrates on trade union matters but because it is certainly the liveliest of all the central papers, less formal, and with a good deal more non-political information and human interest than the others.[14]

Selskaya zhizn (*Rural Life*) is, like *Pravda*, published by the Central Committee, but it is directed towards a rural readership, concentrating more on farming and the problems of village life. It has a circulation of 9.5 million.

Komsomolskaya pravda (*Young Communists' Truth*) (circulation 13.6 million) is published by the Communist youth organisation, the Komsomol. It is aimed at young people and accordingly treats its 'propagandist' role seriously, including among other things many unflattering stories of capitalist life to disabuse young people of any notion that the West might have more to offer than just abundant consumer goods – or even that the consumer paradise is open to more than just the privileged élite.

For children, *Pionerskaya pravda*, put out by the Young Pioneers organisation with a daily print-run of 9.7 million, is carefully designed to inculcate the 'correct' values – especially 'love of the motherland' – at an early age.

Sovetskaya Rossiya (*Soviet Russia*) is not strictly speaking an 'all-Union' publication as it is only distributed within the Russian Federation, but it reaches a large readership in this most populous of the fifteen Soviet republics. Each of the other republics publishes two main daily newspapers, one in Russian and the other in the republic's chief national language. *Sovetskaya Rossiya* has been one of the boldest papers, together with the thrice-weekly *Sovetskaya kultura* (*Soviet Culture*) and *Komsomolskaya pravda*, in taking up Gorbachov's challenge for franker reporting of domestic affairs.

Other important central newspapers are the daily *Krasnaya zvezda* (*Red Star*), published by the Ministry of Defence, and *Literaturnaya gazeta* (*Literary Gazette*) (circulation 3.1 million), a sixteen-page weekly read mainly by the 'educated classes', which covers not only literary life but also international affairs, and is particularly popular for its 'sociological journalism' – detailed and often remarkably frank features on problems of Soviet society. For sports fans there is a daily entitled *Sovetsky sport* (4.6 million).

The most popular Soviet magazines are *Zdorovye* (*Health*) (16.5 million); *Rabotnitsa* (*Working Woman*) (14.9 million) and its rural counterpart *Krestyanka* (*Peasant Woman*) (10.7 million); the children's magazines *Vesyolye kartinki* (*Jolly Pictures*) (9 million) and *Murzilka* (5.7 million); a small-format layman's guide to laws, regulations and citizens' rights entitled *Chelovek i zakon* (*Man and Law*) (8.6 million); and finally, the thrice-monthly satirical magazine *Krokodil* (*Crocodile*) (5.3 million). Mention should also be made of the Party's two theoretical journals, *Kommunist* and *Partiynaya zhizn* (*Party Life*), and of the literary monthlies known as the 'thick journals' – *Novy mir* (*New World*), *Oktyabr* (*October*), *Druzhba narodov* (*Friendship of Peoples*) and others – which publish new poetry and prose, literary criticism, and serialise novels before they appear as books.

Also competing for the citizen's attention – though in the Soviet context 'competing' is perhaps not quite the word – are radio and television. They are particularly valued, according to an opinion poll, for relaxation and entertainment, and television also for its programmes on literature, art and sport. The local press is seen as a prime source of 'useful information and advice', recipes, weather reports and advertising. The central newspapers, on the other hand, despite the recent rapid growth in the availability of television, are apparently valued by the public for their 'quick reporting of events' and are regarded as a better source of 'objective, reliable news' than either television or radio.[15] These attitudes may be changing, however. The daily evening news broadcast on Soviet television, known as *Vremya* (*Time*), is said to have an audience of 150,000,000, making it the most popular regular programme on television, and also the most widely used single news source in the country. For 30 per cent of viewers it is the main or only source of information for the whole day. Also popular are the 45-minute *International Panorama* broadcast each Sunday, which includes extended reports from correspondents around the world (usually colourful and sometimes non-political), and a fifteen-minute summary of international events called *In the World Today*, two editions of which are screened each evening.[16] Research carried out in Leningrad established that television was easily the most popular source of foreign news (used by 86 per cent of those questioned), followed by newspapers (79 per cent), with radio some way behind (64 per cent).[17]

Thanks to a system of six communications satellites and hundreds of ground relay stations, at least one television channel can be picked up by 92 per cent of the population, and 76 per cent can receive two programmes.[18] In Moscow and other major cities, four channels are available. There are 85,000,000 television sets in the country, 15,000,000 of them for colour reproduction (1983). Radio is available not only via wireless sets, but also through a network of 75,000,000 wired loudspeakers in almost every home and place of work throughout the country (which can, of course, be turned down or unplugged, at least at home, but cannot receive foreign broadcasts).[19]

Lastly, mention must be made of the two news agencies, TASS and APN, which supply a large proportion of the information carried by the media. TASS (Telegraph Agency of the Soviet Union) has a huge network of correspondents at home and in about 110 countries abroad. It provides 'hard news' and authoritative commentaries, and also handles official government materials – the texts of leaders' speeches, reports on official visits and meetings, government appointments, and so on. In addition to the regular services, wired to Soviet newspapers and foreign subscribers, TASS produces two voluminous 'secret' versions of domestic and foreign news, graded according to the confidentiality of the information they contain and the rank of their recipients. One service, which includes translations of foreign press commentaries, is intended mainly for Soviet commentators, while the other is fit only for the eyes of the country's rulers – although it allegedly contains little that would not appear in ordinary Western newspapers.[20]

Sometimes described as 'semi-official', APN (Novosti Press Agency) is nonetheless equally devoted to the Party line: it was set up in 1961 as a 'public information organisation' and specialises in 'soft propaganda' – features, cultural matters, 'international friendship', and the like. It also publishes many booklets about Soviet policies and life intended for readers abroad, especially in the developing countries. Western security services regard its foreign correspondents with great suspicion.[21]

The Soviet mass media have been described – by both a supporter and a detractor – as an 'orchestra' and a 'symphony', with each instrument playing its own part, every player note-perfect, and the whole harmonious piece conducted from the centre.[22] If that is the case, then *Pravda* is undoubtedly the first violin. It is not strictly speaking representative of the press as a whole, since most papers are either specialised or local. But it is the leading Soviet newspaper in several senses. It is rightly regarded abroad as the most authoritative voice of the Soviet state, and at home as the main channel by which the Party's instructions and opinions are filtered down to lower-level bodies and to the population. Its journalists have a special status: a *Pravda* correspondent, for example, has the right to demand – as the full representative of the Party's central organ – an interview with any local Party first secretary. Its internal structure and editorial processes are literally copied by the rest of the Soviet press. Until 1969 television and radio were not allowed to report any news or government decisions until *Pravda* had printed them; nowadays they take such items directly from the TASS news agency, but it is still *Pravda*'s comment that sets the political and ideological tone for all the other media. Finally, only *Pravda* criticises the rest of the press; *Pravda* itself, as the model newspaper, is never criticised.

How Pravda is Made

Pravda Street is one of the quieter corners of Moscow. Not much traffic goes along it; there are few passers-by, and no large shops – only modern office blocks, a small cinema, a poorly-stocked food shop, and, opposite it, the two *Pravda* buildings. The older one, built in the Thirties, now houses the offices of other newspapers – *Selskaya zhizn*, *Komsomolskaya pravda*, and others. *Pravda* itself is produced in a new ten-storey building, emblazoned with the word 'PRAVDA' in the instantly recognisable lettering of the paper's masthead.

The calmness of the street continues inside the editorial offices. On the ground floor there is a large, high-ceilinged waiting-room with rows of leatherette chairs. Beside the lifts there is a cloakroom, and a policeman, with a telephone and a list of internal numbers, who checks passes. The only sound is the piped radio quietly rasping from a loudspeaker.

Upstairs there are long corridors with carpet runners, and doors opening into small offices like studies or seminar-rooms, where the journalists work. There is no Western-style open-plan newsroom with clattering typewriters, telephones ringing, and reporters bustling round in shirt-sleeves. The atmosphere is scholarly and calm. Any visitor to these offices instinctively understands why *Pravda* has so few misprints, why it takes so long to react to events, and why it is so predictable.

The academic atmosphere extends to its staff. Its present editor, Viktor Afanasyev, has been described as resembling 'a slightly bohemian college lecturer', with his thick grey hair over his collar and his casual style of dress. And indeed, he is a doctor of philosophy and corresponding member of the Soviet Academy of Sciences. Before he was appointed editor in 1976 he had published books on scientific communism, management problems, and philosophical problems of biology.[1]

The post of editor of *Pravda* is the most senior in Soviet journalism and normally brings with it a series of other promotions. Afanasyev's predecessor, Mikhail Zimyanin, for example, within a year of becoming editor of *Pravda*, was elected Chairman of the Union of Journalists, although according to the Union rules he was not even eligible to become an ordinary member, far less Chairman, since he did not have the minimum three years' journalistic experience required for admission.[2] Zimyanin left *Pravda* to become a Secretary of the Central Committee of the Communist Party.

Afanasyev himself, since his appointment as editor, has become a member of the Central Committee, Chairman of the Union of Journalists, a deputy of the Supreme Soviet (or Parliament), and was awarded the Order of Lenin on his sixtieth birthday in 1982. He is the vital link between the paper and the Party leadership, who trust him implicitly to represent their policies correctly.

According to a source on *Pravda's* staff, the editor-in-chief attends the weekly meetings of the Party's Secretariat and sometimes even of the Politburo. It was President Brezhnev's custom to hold regular extra meetings with the editors of *Pravda* and *Izvestiya*, and the directors of the two news agencies, TASS and APN. Andropov, presumably because of ill health, only did this twice during his brief rule. At one of these meetings he is said to have complained about the lack of good literary criticism in *Pravda*.

Differences between the Party leadership and *Pravda*'s editor rarely come into the open. Commenting on what Western observers saw as a muddled Soviet reaction to the shooting down of a Korean airliner in September 1983, Afanasyev was careful to direct his criticism at the military, not the political leadership.[3] But the fact that he criticised the handling of the affair at all, while on a visit to Britain, was an indication of his high standing in the Party.

He appears to be a staunch supporter of Gorbachov, and during Chernenko's brief interregnum he felt confident enough to make unusually unorthodox statements while abroad which tended to undermine Chernenko's authority and boost Gorbachov's. In 1984 he referred to Gorbachov as 'our second secretary' (in other words, Chernenko's deputy), even though there is officially no such position in the Kremlin hierarchy. Later he broke Moscow's usual vow of silence about the leader's state of health by admitting in an Italian television interview that Chernenko was ill.[4]

Afanasyev is thus one of a handful of Soviet journalists and academics on the fringes of real power who are permitted to travel abroad and be interviewed by Western journalists, often expressing personal views which may be at variance with official policies. Others in this privileged position include broadcaster Vladimir

Pozner, who once said he believed Soviet jamming of Western radio broadcasts was counterproductive, and the foreign affairs expert Georgy Arbatov, always prepared to be interviewed – live, and in English – on Western radio and television. This group of Soviet 'pundits' has come into its own with Gorbachov's efforts to project a softer Soviet image abroad. Together with the public relations men who front press conferences in Moscow, they represent the new, reasonable face of Gorbachov's Kremlin. Ironically, they are responding to Western news values (human interest, off-the-cuff comments, and so on) which have yet to be accepted at home, even in Afanasyev's *Pravda*.

Of Afanasyev's personal life it is known that he has two children, a son and a daughter, and is a skilled water-skier. He is articulate, but soft-spoken, almost shy. The son of a peasant, he spent thirteen years in the military and was wounded during the last war. He reportedly told American newsmen with pride that IBM once offered him a million dollars to work for them and 'think up a couple of ideas'.[5]

The editor is in charge of an editorial board, consisting of his deputies, the heads of some of *Pravda*'s 22 editorial departments, the chief 'political observers', and the so-called 'Responsible Secretary' (or managing editor), one of the most important figures on the staff. The editorial board – over twenty people – has overall responsibility for the content of *Pravda*, while the secretariat (seventeen members), headed by the Responsible Secretary, is the paper's 'planning centre' which coordinates all the long-term and daily activities involved in the making of a newspaper.[6] (See diagram on p. 62.)

The editorial departments, where the actual writing and editing is done, deal with the following areas:

- Party life
- Propaganda of Marxism-Leninism
- Industry and the economy
- Agriculture
- 'Socialist competition'
- Literature and the arts
- Letters
- Culture and problems of everyday life
- Science
- Education

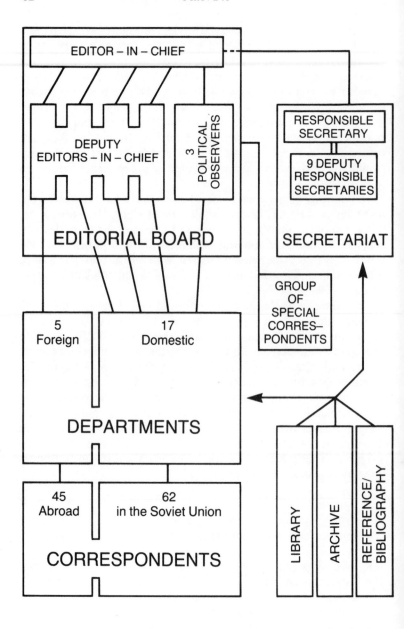

Editorial structure of *Pravda*

- Current news
- Military affairs
- The press, criticism, etc
- 'Feuilletons' (satire)
- Illustrations
- Local correspondents
- Socialist countries
- Capitalist countries
- International problems
- Developing countries
- International news
- External relations

Altogether they employ about 180 journalists, 70 of them in the letters department.[7]

In addition, *Pravda* has 62 correspondents around the Soviet Union and 45 abroad.[8] Most of the foreign correspondents are in Europe, while Africa and Latin America have far fewer. As a result, *Pravda* relies heavily on reports from the TASS news agency for its coverage of these areas.

Other important figures on *Pravda*'s staff are its 'political observers' – experienced journalists such as Yuri Zhukov, who in his other role as Chairman of the Soviet Peace Committee has become known in the West for his criticism of Western peace movements (especially of their support for 'independent' peace campaigners in the USSR). Zhukov is also a candidate member of the Party's Central Committee and therefore in close contact with the Party leadership. He is a notorious hardliner, however, seen as something of a bore even by many of his fellow journalists.

Pravda's staff reporters receive royalties for published articles, according to their length, in addition to their fixed salary, which varies from 150 roubles a month for a junior member of the Moscow staff, to 450 roubles for a member of the editorial board. The average Soviet wage is 190 roubles a month. Correspondents in the Soviet Union receive 250–280 roubles, while those abroad are paid 300 roubles in hard currency. The salary of the editor-in-chief is a secret.[9]

Like all Soviet journalists, *Pravda*'s staff are entitled to flats with an additional 10 square metres of 'living space' or an extra room. Top journalists undoubtedly also enjoy 'perks' in the way of access to special shops. *Pravda* has a special rest home in Pitsunda on the

Black Sea, and another outside Moscow. For a shorter break, *Pravda*'s journalists can use a 'three-day house' – a private dacha in a wooded area of Moscow – paying only about £3 for a weekend.[10]

The planning process of a typical working day in *Pravda*'s offices is much more extensive than that of any Western newspaper, and is one of the most significant features of Soviet newspaper production.

Soviet textbooks on journalism stress that the planned nature of the Soviet economy and Soviet society as a whole is equally applicable to the ideological sphere and the production of newspapers.[11] This is not mere phrase-mongering. Since it is the press's primary task to illuminate and justify the policies of the Communist Party, it is logical that this task can be, and must be, planned in step with those policies.

Like the economy, therefore, newspapers have long-term guidelines based on the current Five Year Plan, and a series of progressively more detailed plans, ending in the concrete design of each day's edition. *Pravda*, for instance, has an annual plan, a quarterly plan, and a weekly plan.[12]

The Quarterly Plan, six to eight pages long, outlines the overall priorities and campaigns to be mounted in the three months ahead, including assignments for all the departments and correspondents.

While the editorials or leading articles of Western papers are reactions to the latest news, *Pravda*'s editorials are planned well in advance. By the 14th and 29th of each month the Secretariat submits a timetable of planned leaders to the Editorial Board for approval. This allows plenty of time for writing and rewriting, and means that there is always a batch of editorials 'in stock'.

The Weekly Plan, drawn up each Friday by the Secretariat, gives precise details of every feature article to be published the following week: its 'genre', the department responsible for its preparation, its author, its approximate length (in lines of print), the deadline for submission to the Secretariat, and even the page on which it will appear. What goes into *Pravda* is based on suggestions from the departments and correspondents, but will also take account of any special events to be commemorated: for example, May Day, or Constitution Day, or Press Day (celebrated on 5 May, *Pravda*'s anniversary). The Secretariat also tries to ensure that a correct balance is kept over the weeks between different themes, geographical areas, positive and critical articles, and so on.[13]

As a result, the basic shape of each day's *Pravda* is decided well in advance. It is little wonder that the finished product is such a polished article.

Let us look inside the *Pravda* offices on a typical day – a Monday, for instance. Throughout the day, two separate editions are being worked on. The Secretariat's duty service produces a mock-up of Wednesday's edition, pasting proofs of feature articles on to the relevant pages to give a clear picture of how they will look and how much space will be left for news reports.

Meanwhile, members of the Editorial Board, arriving at their desks around ten a.m., receive page-proofs containing the major articles for Tuesday's edition (produced by Sunday's 'duty service'), with which they familiarise themselves before the editorial meeting at eleven a.m. In the foreign department, a duty officer reports on the latest world developments reaching the teletype room, and a decision is made about the subject for the next day's 'Commentator's Column', a daily signed 'mini-editorial' on foreign affairs.

At eleven o'clock the Editorial Board meets on the eighth floor of the *Pravda* office block. It is usually a brief conference – rarely more than about ten minutes. The Secretariat reports on the production of Sunday's edition (whether it was late, and if so, why), and a representative of the publishing house reports on its distribution. Then the board turns its attention to Tuesday's edition, and any criticisms made of the articles in the mock-up are noted by the departments concerned. Some may have to be rewritten or at least stylistically edited, and one may even be postponed for a day.

After the meeting, the departments set about revising articles, sending them to the composing room as soon as they are ready, while the Secretariat's duty group selects the most important news items arriving from the news agencies and *Pravda*'s own correspondents at home and abroad.

The deadline for feature articles (i.e. everything not classified as 'news') is two p.m., but most of this material is ready long before then. The deadline for news items (for the first, provincial edition) is four p.m. Most of the last-minute work, naturally, goes on in the department of International News, which sifts reports from agencies and correspondents for inclusion in the foreign news page (page five), and in the reference departments, where names, dates and spellings are meticulously checked.

Between five and six p.m. a series of lights comes on in the offices of the editor-in-chief, his deputies, the responsible secretary and the duty editor, indicating that each page is now ready for printing.

When all six lights are on, the duty editor signs the front page, and the text of the first edition is transmitted by phototelegraphy to thirty-nine provincial cities for printing. Matrices are flown out to a further four cities.

From six to eight p.m. the editorial staff rest. At eight they return to their offices to finalise the second edition. Although the main articles will normally be untouched, an effort is made to keep the news columns as fresh as possible. On average, some 10–12 per cent of the news reports in the second edition are new (and repeated in the next day's first edition). Even main features from the first edition are sometimes rejigged – or thrown out altogether – to make way for, say, an important obituary or late speech.

At eleven o'clock the second edition goes to press – in Moscow, and by facsimile transmission in Leningrad, Kiev and Minsk.[14]

No description of the daily editorial process is quite complete, however, without one stage which is never mentioned by its proper name in Soviet sources – censorship.

Like all printed matter in the Soviet Union, *Pravda* is censored by a representative of *Glavlit* (the Chief Administration for the Protection of State Secrets in the Press) – twice, according to one of its former journalists: once before printing, and once before distribution.[15] The censor has a list of items which must be kept secret. These have been defined variously at different times, but have generally included certain military information, crime figures, other statistics, personal information about leading politicians, and so on. In *Pravda*'s case the censor is presumably less concerned with ideological 'errors', which in any case will have been eradicated at an early stage, than with ensuring that there are no unfortunate juxtapositions of headlines or articles in the finished pages. (Wily journalists on another newspaper, *Literaturnaya gazeta*, managed to place an article with the headline 'A magician of poetry' next to the tiny announcement of Boris Pasternak's death in 1960, after the poet had been discredited officially because of his novel *Doctor Zhivago*.)[16]

However easy the task of censoring a newspaper like *Pravda* may be, it is certainly done (though some of the staff seem to be genuinely unaware of it). The responsible secretary, in a description of a day's work on *Pravda*, writes that the paper is 'ready' at six p.m. (when all the lights come on), and that 'half an hour later the "duty editor" writes on the front page "Ready for printing".'[17] Why the delay of half an hour, if not for censorship?

A censorship number appears at the foot of the back page of every edition, in the form of the letter B plus a five-digit number, which changes every day. A study of these numbers shows that *Pravda* has in fact three censors, who work on a three-week rota, with one month's holiday a year![18]

Only one-quarter of Pravda's copies are printed in Moscow. The remainder are run off in forty-six cities throughout the country, forty-two of which receive it by facsimile transmission – either by landline or via the 'Orbita' satellite system. It takes only three or four minutes for a photograph of each page to be transmitted. Before the first regular facsimile transmissions began – in January 1965 to Leningrad – matrices had to be flown out to all the printing centres. This was highly unreliable: twenty-five to thirty out of every hundred would arrive late, and even more when the weather was bad. The use of satellites has meant that *Pravda* is now available in all but the most remote areas on the day of issue.[19] (It also means, incidentally, that Western intelligence organisations can intercept the signals and print out copies of *Pravda* and other central newspapers long before they reach the newsstands in the Soviet Union.)[20]

Pravda is produced on letterpress printing presses, although some other Soviet newspapers, such as *Selskaya zhizn*, have moved on to the offset system.[21] Up-to-date photosetting equipment using lasers is being produced in Leningrad and will gradually be introduced at *Pravda*'s printing plants.[22]

Distribution is handled by the Central Subscription Agency and the Central Retail Agency (both parts of the *Soyuzpechat* organisation. Of the 11.3 million copies printed each day, 10 million are delivered to subscribers by the Post Office, with the rest sold at kiosks or sent abroad.[23]

The price went up by one kopeck in January 1982, but *Pravda* still costs only 4 kopecks for the normal six-page edition, and 5 kopecks (about 5p) for Monday's eight-page version. This provides an annual sales revenue of some 160 million roubles (about £160 million), and even though the newspaper carries no advertising it actually appears to make a profit.[24]

4

All the Views Fit to Print:
Content and Policy

Mikhail Gorbachov came to power proclaiming the right of Soviet citizens to know. In his first speech he said: 'The better informed people are, the greater the awareness with which they act and the more active their support for the Party and its plans and goals.'[1]

A year later, at the Party Congress in early 1986, he stoutly defended his policy of *glasnost* (openness, or publicity) against its detractors. 'Sometimes when speaking about *glasnost*,' he said, 'one hears appeals that we should speak more circumspectly about our shortcomings and omissions, and about the difficulties that are inevitable in any living work. There can only be one response here – the Leninist one: communists always and under all circumstances need the truth.' Openness, moreover, could not be selective: it had to be turned into what Gorbachov called a 'failsafe system'.[2]

Those words were spoken in February. The accident at the Chernobyl nuclear power station in the Ukraine at the end of April was to be a test case for the new policy. And judged by Western standards, coverage of the disaster was abominable. For several days, the Soviet mass media tried to pretend that nothing at all had happened. Only when the countries of Europe began protesting at the radiation cloud spreading from Chernobyl did the media start reporting the accident, and even then the details – about its causes, its effects, casualty figures, precautions to be taken by the population, and so on – came late and in small doses. Really vital pieces of information appeared as if by chance in various publications, half-hidden in stories about the heroic efforts to cope with the damaged reactor and evacuated population. Western news media slotted together all the pieces of the puzzle, but no newspaper in the USSR ever did the Soviet people that favour. If you bought the wrong paper one day you would not learn the latest death toll, and on most days no paper gave any casualty figures at all.

But judged by Soviet standards – even under Gorbachov's policy of openness – the coverage was not surprising. *Glasnost* was never intended to mean freedom of information for information's sake. It applied only to the new leadership's stated concerns – indiscipline, drunkenness, corruption, inefficiency, inertia, and all those short-comings that stood in the way of the two major goals of the day: 'reconstruction' and 'acceleration'. An unexpected nuclear acci-dent never came into this scheme of things at all, and the media's first instinct was to maintain their traditional secretiveness on such matters. Even when the propaganda machine recovered from the initial shock (and it is said that Gorbachov's wish to come clean immediately was opposed by a majority on the Politburo),[3] in-formation was still only prized out of the authorities by a succession of unavoidable needs:

- the need to admit to neighbouring countries that there had indeed been a nuclear accident (had the radiation not spread, there would have been no need);
- the need to inform the local population about necessary health precautions (to be balanced against the need to avoid panic, which Soviet leaders still believe can be caused by too much information);
- the need to put a stop to the rumours which spread throughout the country precisely because of the lack of reliable infor-mation (that a mixture of vodka and red wine was an antidote to radiation, for instance).

Much of the information divulged at press conferences seemed to be intended to impress the West rather than to help the Soviet people understand the situation.

Nonetheless, Chernobyl had a salutary effect. Coverage of the next national calamity – the sinking of the cruise ship *Admiral Nakhimov* four months later, with the loss of almost 400 lives – was still slow off the mark, but remarkably complete in the end. At least there was no time – unlike during the Chernobyl crisis – for wild rumours to spread.

The tendency of rumours to proliferate whenever official news is lacking was one of the subjects which had been raised in the press at the beginning of 1986 in an unusual debate on the merits of reporting 'bad news'. *Sovetskaya Rossiya*, for instance, published a reader's letter which contrasted the full coverage in the Soviet media of the 1985 earthquake in Mexico (including regular film reports on television) with the reporting of an earthquake a short time later in the Soviet republic of Tadjikistan: this amounted to a brief statement, including the bald words, 'There are human casualties', and not a single picture on television. The covering up of bad home news, according to the writer, was a sign of lack of trust in the public – 'as if they might somehow misunderstand!' It was wrong, the letter concluded, for Soviet people to hear about 'unexpected or negative events' from 'foreign voices [i.e. radio stations] with anti-Soviet accents.'[4] For a while – until Chernobyl – it seemed the authorities had taken note.

Accidents apart, however, the press has become much more open under Gorbachov's rule. Articles on economic shortcomings and corruption in the Party ranks have grown more critical and adventurous. It was admitted for the first time that the Soviet Union has a drugs problem, and prostitution, too. The existence of food rationing in some cities and of special shops for the Party élite has been mentioned (and then, it's true, quickly forgotten again). *Ogonyok*, one of the boldest magazines, described in graphic detail a case of police brutality and printed previously unpublished poetry and memoirs. *Pravda* and other papers recorded instances of wrongful imprisonment and other violations of citizens' rights. Such ideas had hitherto been confined to dissident literature.

Newspapers began to depict the Soviet involvement in Afghanistan as a war rather than a charity event, and even raised the issue of draft-dodging, and the problems encountered by soldiers returning home. Openness itself became a major theme, with several articles describing powerful officials who used their influence to suppress criticism of their work – even to the extent of ordering already printed newspapers to be destroyed.[5]

How much of this new-found freedom was really intended by the leadership, and how much was merely due to individual editors experimenting to see how far they could go, is a matter for speculation. But there were certainly some public figures – especially writers – who took advantage of the generally more liberal atmosphere to raise their own pet subjects which had been suppressed in the past. Chief among these subjects was the very existence of censorship itself – especially in the arts and in writing about Soviet history. A number of articles named films made years ago and never shown in the cinemas, or described the time-consuming process whereby editors tinkered with manuscripts submitted for publication, or called for the belated publication of banned works such as

Boris Pasternak's novel *Doctor Zhivago*. It became almost commonplace to read that culture and the arts had suffered too long
under the dead hands of bureaucrats and mediocrities. The word
'censorship' – as far as this author is aware – was never mentioned in
these discussions, but the code-words used in its place ('Zalygin's
novel *After the Storm*', wrote *Pravda*, 'did not get into print
easily.'[6]) were not hard to understand.

Prominent among those who called for a reappraisal of Soviet
history was the poet Yevgeny Yevtushenko. He wrote in *Sovetskaya
kultura* that *glasnost* must apply to the past as well as the present: 'In
order to solve today's problems boldly, we cannot be timid towards
our own history, within which lie the roots of today's problems.'
Another writer, Vyacheslav Kondratyev, declared that 'the people
must know the entire history of their country—both its joyful
pages and the bitter ones.'[7] Since about the beginning of 1987,
without fuss or sensation, the names of Stalin, Beria, Khrushchev
and others have reappeared at last in the Soviet press, and a start
has been made to reassessing the tragic years of Stalin's terror.

A corollary of the concern with the past was the new vigour
injected into older campaigns – for the preservation of ancient
monuments, including churches, for example, or for the traditional
names to be restored to streets and cities renamed after dead
politicians or proletarian heroes. Ecologists became more vocal in
protesting about the pollution of Russia's lakes and rivers. And they
banded together with economists, writers, Russian nationalists and
scientists to launch the most successful independent press campaign
in Soviet history – against the government's plans to divert water
from north-flowing rivers in Europe and Siberia to irrigate the dry
plains and deserts of the south. Some feared disastrous consequences for the world's climate, others claimed that ancient Russian
villages would be swamped, and others still pointed out that local
land-improvement projects could do the job just as well. Bending to
public pressure – and also to the logic of its own new approach to the
economy – the government finally dropped the plans.[8]

Despite all this, the basic principles of Soviet journalism have
remained the same. The various press functions outlined earlier in
this introduction continue under Gorbachov to serve one under-
lying aim – to demonstrate the advantages of the Soviet system over
the capitalist one. This has obvious implications for editorial policy:
if criticism appears on the home news pages, it must be made clear

that the fault lies not in the system itself, or in the political leadership, but in, say, administration, or the imperfect implementation of correct policies, or individual incompetence. On the foreign pages, any favourable development in the West must be presented as the work of enlightened 'progressive' individuals or organisations, and in spite of the prevailing system. If any item of news does not naturally fit into this scheme, it must be given the correct 'interpretation', or – if necessary – ignored.

As a result, there are both severe limits to the criticism that can be voiced in *Pravda*, and also 'blank spots' – things that just cannot be mentioned at all. So before looking at what *Pravda does* print, it may be useful to examine what you will *not* find in its pages.

It is not known exactly what items remain on the so-called Index 7 of *Information Not To Be Published in the Open Press*, issued by Glavlit, the censorship agency. No copy of the Index (*perechen*) has reached the West, but at one time it reportedly included such items as details of the censorship system itself; advance itineraries of Soviet leaders; activities of the state security and intelligence organs; total crime figures; locations and conditions of labour camps and prisons; civil unrest or strikes; figures for Soviet economic and military aid to foreign countries; benefits enjoyed by athletes, including rates of pay; and much else.[9]

The list obviously includes scores of other subjects which never appear in the Soviet press, from Jewish emigration figures to the salaries of Party functionaries and menus available at the Kremlin clinic. But it has been reduced under Gorbachov. For example, it used to be forbidden to give numbers of people killed or injured in accidents, wrecks, fires or natural disasters in the communist countries (though not in capitalist countries); since Chernobyl that has changed. Statistics about numbers of drug-addicts, alcoholics and vagrants have generally been kept secret, but in 1986 one newspaper gave a precise figure (3,700) for the number of registered drug-addicts in Moscow.[10] And in December 1986 the press did report nationalist riots in Kazakhstan.

The Glavlit Index is concerned with *facts* which must be kept secret, not with ideology or policy. That is an area less easy to define, which has varied under different Kremlin leaders, and in which editors can exercise a limited amount of discretion. Here, it is a question of what may be discussed, or mooted, or argued about in the press – and that is directly dependent on the leadership's latitude or desire to encourage fresh ideas, filtered down to the press through the Propaganda Department of the Central Committee and the editors of the central newspapers. It is not enough for an editor himself to be open-minded: Viktor Afanasyev had to wait for the current of change at the top after Brezhnev's death before he could open up the pages of *Pravda* a little.

Afanasyev admitted in June 1986 that 'in the past' there had been certain 'prohibited areas' for criticism. Moscow Party officials and those who worked for the Soviet Interior Ministry, he said, had been 'out of bounds'. Now, according to Afanasyev, there were no longer such protected spheres. Anyone, regardless of office, from the lowest level up to a minister or leading Party functionary, he told the Czech newspaper *Rude pravo*, could be criticised.[11]

But under every Soviet leader, including Gorbachov, there have been firm limits to discussion in the media which are so broad that, were they applied to the Western 'quality' press, there would be little left other than straight news.

First and foremost, *the system itself* is absolutely sacred. Both its history and its existing social, political and basic economic structures can only be extolled and interpreted in the 'approved' manner. 'Deviations' from the accepted model may be criticised, but the model itself cannot. Similarly, 'mistakes' in the past (such as some of Stalin's so-called 'excesses') may be admitted, but only to the extent, and in the way, that the Party has decreed. Such mistakes must be seen as distortions of the system, and the possibility that they might be inherent in it may not be suggested. In June 1985 *Pravda* carried a long feature about the glorious history and traditions of the northern ore-producing town of Norilsk, on its fiftieth anniversary, which cast a veil of silence over its most significant feature: that it was founded and built in 1935 entirely by labour-camp victims of the Stalin terror.[12]

An extension of this is the silence observed on alternatives to *the prevailing Party policy* (as opposed to ways of implementing it, which can be discussed). It is important to stress the word 'prevailing': policies do of course change from time to time, but once the leadership has opted for a particular course it is generally impossible for *Pravda* or any other paper to contradict it. The one notable exception to this rule in recent times was the 'campaign' (albeit limited to half a dozen or so articles) against the grandiose river diversion scheme championed by Brezhnev and Chernenko and incorporated into successive economic plans (see above). But even this was only a partial exception: for although the scheme remained official Party policy for over a year under Gorbachov, its opponents evidently enjoyed his support.

A third area commonly covered in the Western press but totally ignored in the Soviet concerns the *personal qualities and private lives of politicians* and other public figures. (The personal qualities of selected workers, on the other hand, are the subject of many an article.) Linked with this is the non-reporting of disputes – or even discussions – within the leadership. It is for this reason that the speeches and published articles of individual leaders are scrutinised by Western experts: they are the sole basis, apart from the rare personal interview with correspondents, for any conjecture about shades of opinion within the Politburo. When a politician is sacked he is normally said to have been 'transferred to other work'. But even when he is promoted, his personal qualities are rarely dwelt upon. When Andrei Gromyko nominated Gorbachov for the Party leadership, his glowing tribute to his 'brilliance and erudition' was not reported in the press.[13] Politicians' families are subjected to none of the publicity of a Denis Thatcher or Nancy Reagan, and it signified a distinct, if slight, change in style when in 1985 Gorbachov's wife began to be pictured on *Pravda*'s front page in welcoming parties for foreign visitors and shown on TV taking part in various ceremonies. Another more 'human' touch came shortly after Gorbachov's accession to power, when *Pravda* carried a warm message of condolence to Politburo member Geidar Aliyev, signed by his colleagues, when his wife died.[14]

Another very large area of silence covers what may be described loosely as *the morality of 'progress'*, as defined by the Establishment. In the West the 'non-Establishment' view is promoted by various pressure groups, ranging from anti-vivisectionists to peace campaigners, from those against the building of a new airport to those against nuclear power. Their views are represented in the press. But in the Soviet Union, if the Party has decided that something represents 'progress', and is therefore an economic or political issue rather than a moral one, then it cannot be opposed in the press. That is why, even after the catastrophe at Chernobyl, there was no discussion in the Soviet media of the relative merits and disadvantages of nuclear power and other forms of power (even though *Pravda* indicated that it had received many letters from readers concerned about the dangers of nuclear power).[15] No journalist discussed the design of the Chernobyl reactor or suggested there could be faults in it: such things are suitable for discussion only in the relevant ministries and research institutes, not in newspapers.

The extent to which radically different approaches to *economic management* can be discussed in *Pravda* varies under different leaderships. There are in general many scholarly articles – by academics and specialists as well as by *Pravda*'s journalists – on the problems of running a planned economy. The problems are admitted and solutions are debated. But an article proposing a radical retreat from current Soviet policy (workers' self-management, say, or 'market socialism') could appear only after the Party leadership had, as it were, declared the debate open by at least adumbrating such change in policy in public. This was what happened in the first year or so of Gorbachov's rule.

Alternatively, a shift in policy may be foreshadowed in the press by a series of articles – or, especially, readers' letters – pointing out popular dissatisfaction and, perhaps, measures which should be taken. When the appropriate measures *are* taken, they are heralded as a response to public demand. Under Andropov, for example, the Politburo responded to the 'justified complaints of citizens' about the lack of discipline and public order by launching a campaign against corruption and crime. One of Gorbachov's first acts – to clamp down on alcoholism and drunkenness – also followed letters to the press on the subject. It is clear that the instruction to print such letters is given to newspaper editors in advance, presumably at the regular meetings in the Secretariat or Press Sector of the Central Committee's Propaganda Department.

Crime reporting is one of the staples of Western journalism. It is also one area most open to the charge of 'sensationalism'. *Pravda*'s crime reports are quite different from those in a Western newspaper, but they are also rather different from the rest of *Pravda*'s content.

Statistics are never given, and court proceedings are rarely reported. Even the types of crime reported are extremely limited: murder and robbery, for example, are virtually ignored, although their existence is occasionally admitted in the course of a general article. Rape, to judge from *Pravda*, simply does not occur in the Soviet Union.

The only crimes dealt with at length are economic: embezzlement, bribery, falsification of production figures, mismanagement and wastage of resources. The stress is always on the crime itself, not on the punishment. Even if the penalty is death, it is usually mentioned almost in passing somewhere towards the end of the article.

Very often, an article will encompass several crimes of similar types, but otherwise unrelated – committed at different times and in different places. The aim of such articles is not simply to keep the public informed of important court cases, but primarily to act as a warning to potential law-breakers. One piece, about a factory director sentenced to four years' hard labour after his factory was discovered to be non-existent, ended: 'So let this story, which ended for its heroes with a court sentence, serve as a warning signal to all those negligent, narrow-minded people, who try to conceal mismanagement and slovenliness behind the florid lines of a false report.'[16]

The most obvious difference between *Pravda*'s crime reports and the rest of its content is in their style. Most of the paper, especially its industrial and agricultural reports, but even its supposedly uplifting stories of model workers, is, quite simply, boring and dull. But many of its crime reports, particularly those under the heading 'Feuilleton' or 'With a satirical pen', sparkle with wit and irony. They are written up like short stories, with much direct speech, and a proper narrative structure, and even the most serious crimes may be treated with sarcasm and humour. Even punishments are treated lightly: one offender had spent time, according to *Pravda*, 'in places with an unfavourable climate'.[17]

With such a list of restrictions, one may well ask, what is there left to write about? *Pravda* is not a large paper by Western standards – only six pages, or eight on Mondays – but with no space taken up by advertising it can in fact pack in a good deal.

A strict internal 'protocol' governs where any item of news appears in the paper, and how it is treated. The West's 'front-page news', if it appears at all, will usually be on an inside page, and in a very different form.

Pravda's front page, by contrast, generally bears more resemblance to some sort of Court Circular or bulletin of royal proclamations than a newspaper. The names of Party leaders are endlessly repeated with their full, long-winded titles; and proceedings at Party plenums or sessions of the Supreme Soviet (parliament) are chronicled in painstakingly superficial detail, with leaders present listed in alphabetical order, and no indication of how the speeches were received, or indeed of what was said by any speaker other than the main one.

The decoration of a leader or cosmonaut might be reported in a Western paper under the headline 'Yuri gets top medal', but *Pravda* does not so much report it as promulgate it, in the style of a town-crier:

DECREE
of the Presidium
of the USSR Supreme Soviet
**On the decoration of Comrade N. A. Tikhonov
with the Order of Lenin**

Nikolay Aleksandrovich **Tikhonov**, Member of the Politburo of the CPSU Central Committee, Chairman of the USSR Council of Ministers, is awarded the Order of **Lenin** for his great services to the Communist Party and the Soviet state, and in connection with his eightieth birthday.

V. KUZNETSOV,
First Deputy Chairman
of the Presidium of the USSR Supreme Soviet.
T. MENTESHASHVILI,
Secretary of the Presidium of the USSR Supreme Soviet.

Moscow, the Kremlin.
13 May 1985.[18]

As well as official statements, decrees and resolutions, page one carries the leading article, and often some economic news, a picture-profile of a model worker or team of workers, and sometimes a few short items of foreign news (never the most important items, however).

Page two carries mainly Party news and discussion articles, and pieces on ideology and economics.

Page three concentrates more on aspects of Soviet society: education, culture, consumer affairs, the Soviet character, problems of discipline, and the like. There are often follow-ups to *Pravda*'s own critical articles, under the rubric: '*Pravda* spoke out: what has been done?' Generally, these indicate that the original article's criticisms were correct, and that individuals held responsible have been punished, or at least reprimanded.

Pages four and five are for foreign news and comment. Page four deals with diplomatic activities and the socialist countries or foreign communist parties. It will often contain a long commentary at the foot of the page (known as a *podval* or 'basement') on some aspect of foreign affairs. Page five is chiefly for news from the Western and developing countries.

The back page is devoted on different days of the week to cultural news, sport, travelogue-type articles about the Soviet Union and its peoples, history, nature, and other odds and ends. It also carries radio, television and theatre programmes, and the weather forecast.

Table 3 (on p. 277) gives some idea of the changing priorities in *Pravda*'s news coverage over the years since the war, as indicated by the proportion of space devoted to different groups of subjects. One remarkable feature is the predominance, 1956 excepted, of home affairs over international affairs, despite the overwhelming preference of readers for the latter (see below). Because of the small samples involved the figures can only serve as a rough guide to *Pravda*'s content, but certain trends stand out:

- The decline in space devoted to economic news and rise in 'public welfare' themes such as housing, social security and so on (though they remain a tiny proportion of the overall picture). The proportion of political news, including ideology and official materials, has remained fairly constant.
- The relatively high figures for 'history' in 1965 and 1985, coinciding with the twentieth and fortieth anniversaries of the end of the War, which were marked with many commemorative articles.
- The shift of focus away from Western countries, with a slight increase in coverage of most other areas of the world.
- A striking rise over recent years in the prominence given to questions of disarmament, peace movements and the work of the United Nations.

Pravda's appearance has also changed considerably over the years. Under Stalin, its pages were crammed with long columns of dense print, with scarcely a photograph to relieve the monotony. Nowadays its layout is based on blocks rather than columns, like most Western papers. It contains, on average, about two pictures per page (though these are often tiny and rarely connected with the news), and its headlines are larger than, say, those in the London *Times*. A greater variety of typefaces is used than in most serious Western newspapers.

In spite of this, 'skimming' *Pravda* to pick out potentially interesting articles is not easy, chiefly because the headlines, though large enough, rarely convey anything of the article's content. Domestic headlines on a typical day (5 January 1985) were: 'Unanimous support', 'Intensive methods of development for livestock-breeding', 'The honour of a brand-name', 'Waiting for wagons', 'Is the new crop thick?', 'Explosion at dawn', 'Among the sand-hills', 'We congratulate the victors' and 'The aroma of bread'. Foreign headlines on the same day included: 'May reason triumph', 'Wave of resistance', 'The two cats', and 'Condemnation of a conspiracy'. To find out who condemned what conspiracy, one must read on.

Since the headlines are so unhelpful, almost every article, especially on the home pages, also has a sub-heading, assigning it to a particular regular 'rubric', such as 'Pages of History', 'Party Life' or 'Problems of Culture'. Soviet journalists are rather obsessed by this concept of 'rubrics', and textbooks of journalism devote pages to discussing how rubrics and 'sub-rubrics' have changed over a paper's history, as though juggling with these headings were somehow a substitute for livening up the content.

Even with the help of a rubric, however, it is still only by actually starting to read an article that one begins to find out what it is about – and even then the main point will often not come until at least half-way through. (By contrast, the Western journalist's aim is usually to sum up the whole story in the first paragraph.)

While all Soviet newspapers share the same general aims, *Pravda* has the additional task of presenting Party policy, in the most unambiguous and authoritative form, both for domestic consumption and for the world outside.

One of the chief vehicles for publicising policy – though rarely for the initial statement of a *new* policy – is the *Pravda* leading article (*peredovaya*), printed every day in a broad column (since 1987 two columns) on the left side of the front page. Most of them are devoted to domestic affairs, and may be regarded as a set of standing instructions on current tasks, issued by the Central Committee to Party members and subordinate organisations. They are not normally topical, in the sense of dealing with specific events of the day or week, as in the comment columns of Western papers, but deal with the perennial problems of the Soviet economy, agriculture, Party affairs, and so on. Leaders on farming topics follow the cycle of the agricultural year; others deal with more general problems which concern the Party leadership at various times. Over the years the subjects – and style – of *Pravda*'s leaders have varied little. Their lack of immediacy is demonstrated by the fact that their subjects are decided in 'batches', two weeks at a time.

Usually, the front-page leader contains both a diagnosis of the shortcomings in the field under consideration, and a prescription of measures to be taken, with blame and praise apportioned where necessary.[19] Over the decades, a standard format developed:

1. Subject is named.
2. Quotation from incumbent leader.
3. Praise for towns or republics that are doing well.
4. Paragraph beginning 'However' (*Odnako*) or 'At the same time' (*Vmeste s tem*), mentions places that are falling behind.
5. Reminder of consequences of such shortcomings.
6. Remedies: the laggards are exhorted to pull their socks up. (Under Brezhnev they were told to adopt an 'integrated' (*kompleksny*) approach; under Gorbachov they are told to 'reconstruct' and 'accelerate'.)
7. The role of the Party is mentioned: 'It is up to primary Party organisations and/or ordinary members to play the leading role in seeing that things improve.'

The 'praise first, then criticism' format of Soviet journalism (and not just in leading articles) was satirised by Gorbachov in a speech to Siberian oilmen, in which he spoke highly of their achievements and told them in effect to enjoy the praise while it lasted because he was 'about to get down to the shortcomings!'[20] *Pravda* excised this remark from its account of the speech. Like the rest of the paper, however, the leading articles became livelier under Gorbachov's influence, and even the age-old format was partially discarded, though the moralising appeals in the final paragraph to 'remember one's obligations' usually remained. In the first days of Gorbachov's rule *Pravda*'s leading articles dutifully quoted from his first speech as leader, just as it had been used to quoting every other General Secretary. Gorbachov let it be known that this was not his style, and all references to him by name disappeared at once. His words were still cited, it is true, but were attributed vaguely to the meeting at which he spoke rather than to him personally.

More than any other part of the paper, perhaps, the leading articles perform the 'propagandist, agitator and organiser' roles of Lenin's oft-quoted prescription. Their prime purpose is to keep the Party apparatus informed about the current priorities of the central leadership, and to force any organisations criticised to take immediate action.

The occasional front-page leading articles on world affairs are always general re-statements of known Soviet positions on peace, arms control, cooperation with the other socialist countries, and so on. For *Pravda*'s official word on topical issues one must turn to the unsigned 'editorial articles' (*redaktsionnye stat'i*) on the foreign pages: these appear as and when required and do react to specific events such as a speech by the US president or a new diplomatic initiative. They represent not merely *Pravda*'s 'view' but the official (and often the first) reaction of the Soviet leadership.

In December 1982, on the personal initiative of Andropov, who perceived a public thirst for information about the deliberations of the leadership, *Pravda* and all the other papers began publishing accounts of the weekly Politburo meetings. But this feature very quickly lost its novelty. There was usually some indication of *some* of the topics discussed, but the most intriguing sentence was always the last one, which read: 'The Politburo also discussed other questions of domestic and foreign policy.' The vagueness conceals, of course, the most essential part of the discussions, while the bulk of the reports would have us believe that the Soviet Union's top policy-makers spend their time each Thursday chatting about 'winners of the socialist competition' or approving slogans for May Day.

Even when Gorbachov took over, proclaiming that the people could not be expected to work properly if they did not have access to information and to leading Party functionaries, the Politburo reports continued to conceal more than they revealed. In June 1985, for example, Gorbachov informed a Central Committee conference on the economy that the Politburo had 'recently' rejected the draft Five Year Plan for 1986–1990, but nothing had ever been said about this in the weekly reports of Politburo meetings.[21]

Of *Pravda*'s 22 editorial departments, the one dealing with 'Party Life' is considered the most important, and it has its own daily rubric. In this section the Party leadership explains how local and primary Party organisations work – or should work – and how individual Party members are expected to act and think. It is concerned with instilling what is known as the 'Leninist style' of Party work – that is, every good moral and organisational quality which a communist should possess, as exemplified by the myth-ologised Lenin: things like 'Party principledness', 'high responsibil-ity', 'collectivity', 'revolutionary scope and industry', 'links with the masses', and so on.[22]

Many of these virtues (quoted from a Soviet textbook on journal-ism) are good examples of the abstract phrase-mongering which all too often finds its way on to the pages of *Pravda*, especially the 'Party Life' section. It is hard to imagine how the modern Party member is supposed to evince 'revolutionary scope', whatever that may be, but Soviet journalists have a seemingly endless capacity to write bombastic, vacuous clichés like this, and it makes for very tedious reading.

And yet, when it gets down to brass tacks, 'Party Life' can be one of the most revealing sections of the paper. During 1983, for example, and again from 1985 onwards, it was used to set out what kind of Party the new General Secretaries – first Andropov and then Gorbachov – wished to see. And just as important, it began to show vividly what kind of Party they did *not* wish to see. So, instead of endless model workers to copy, readers got a glimpse of the cor-ruption, time-serving, careerism, protectionism and bureaucracy that goes on in the ranks of the Party. Reports of provincial Party meetings became less self-congratulatory, dwelling instead on failures, issuing reprimands, and mentioning sackings. *Pravda* was not, however, treating these matters like a Western newspaper in search of a 'good story': as Chernenko reminded the Party plenum in June 1983, 'For us, criticism is not a sensation, but a signal, the only aim of which is to eliminate shortcomings.'[23]

This is also the case with a fortnightly full-page feature entitled the 'People's Control Page', which exposes economic inefficiencies and crimes, often discovered during raids on enterprises by *Pravda* reporters or by the so-called People's Control Committees – watch-dog organisations which operate throughout the country.

The three economic departments – dealing with industry, agricul-ture, and 'socialist competition and advanced experience' – tend to provide some of the stodgier of *Pravda*'s articles, concentrating on detailed description of top enterprises and achievements, and on scholarly discussion of economic problems. But again, when times permit (usually in periods of flux following the death of a Party leader), these columns can be used to explore innovatory ideas on how to organise industry and manage the economy. So how much criticism is there in *Pravda*'s home news pages? Measured in column inches, the proportion of the paper given over to criticism has increased perceptibly under Gorbachov. A survey of fourteen consecutive issues in June 1985, three months after he came to power, reveals that some 19 per cent of the space available for domestic coverage contained open criticism, as opposed to only 14 per cent in a comparable period under Brezhnev, in 1982. By October 1986, the proportion had risen to 22 per cent.[24]

Overall, however, the stress in domestic reporting is still on exhortation and positive example, rather than criticism. Interestingly, even the *Banner of Labour*, a weekly paper for labour-camp inmates, the existence of which only recently became known in the West, concentrates exclusively on profiles of exemplary convicts who overfulfil their norms, and inculcation of 'communist morals' inside the Gulag.[25]

It is *Pravda*'s foreign pages, though, that are most popular with the readership, and it is fair to say that, within certain limitations, coverage of the world outside is both extensive and detailed. The limitations, which include both distortion and omission, are dictated by two quite separate needs: first, to impress upon domestic readers that life in the Soviet Union, for all the faults intimated on pages two and three, is better than life under capitalism; and secondly – a reason much underestimated in the West – to send the correct signals to foreign governments. It could be said that *Pravda*'s foreign correspondents and commentators have their hands tied, not just by their own bosses, but by the Western journalists and Kremlinologists who analyse their words. Because *Pravda* is the mouthpiece of the Soviet leadership, every word is examined for even slight shifts in nuance, so no writer can afford the luxury of idle speculation or even of personal interpretation of any government's policies (including his own). Imagine if a *Pravda* commentator 'wondered aloud' about the likely American response if Moscow were unilaterally to dismantle its medium-range missiles, or, on the contrary, to deploy some in Poland? Within minutes the lines to the White House would be buzzing about an 'imminent' Soviet initiative. Of course, this is not the 'fault' of over-eager Western analysts, but is the direct consequence of having a state-controlled press. For *Pravda*'s poor correspondents, however, it means that they can expatiate to their hearts' content about unemployment or poverty in the West, about peace movements, about US military build-ups and Israeli aggression, but when it comes to setting out Soviet policy they can do little more than repeat verbatim phrases from the latest official statement or speech.

There is a routine bias in coverage of Western countries, which slackens off only if relations with a particular country are warm. Sometimes these variations will simply evolve, because the writers sense the climate of relations, but sometimes they respond to a command from above. In 1984, for example, there was obviously an order to all Soviet correspondents in West Germany to write about 'revanchism' – the desire of some right-wingers, including, allegedly, leading politicians, to regain German territories lost to Poland at the end of the War. This followed West German acceptance of American missiles on its soil, and tied in with the celebrations of the fortieth anniversary of the end of the War by enabling the Russians to present current 'aggressive' intentions as a revival, or continuation, of imperialist ambitions which had been simmering ever since 1945.

Distortion also affects coverage of allied countries. During the Solidarity period in Poland, for example, there was never any indication of the immense popularity of the free trade union or of Lech Walesa, its leader (or 'ringleader', as *Pravda* put it). Afghanistan is presented as a country confident of its future, which is being built with the help of much-loved Soviet colleagues, despite the annoyance of deluded bandits funded by the CIA. Only since Andropov has any mention been made of Soviet troops actually being engaged in action there, and casualties are still rarely alluded to.

Some events, though, appear to be so embarrassing to the Soviet authorities that they are not distorted but totally ignored by *Pravda*, as if they had never occurred, even though they may have been front-page news in every Western country. The murder in Poland of Catholic priest Jerzy Popiełuszko and subsequent trial of the policemen who killed him went unreported until the final day: even then, a short report (see Part Two) merely said that four 'citizens' (the whole point that shocked Poland and the world was that they were not just citizens but secret policemen) had been sent to prison for the murder, and went on to explain the murderers' apparently noble motives and to attack the Catholic Church.[26]

When a stray Soviet cruise missile crashed in Finland in 1985, *Pravda* readers learnt nothing about the incident, although the news agency TASS carried an explanation and even an apology in its service for subscribers abroad.[27]

Even the Israeli rescue of thousands of Falasha Jews from drought-stricken Ethiopia in January 1985 – another front-page sensation in the West – never made it into *Pravda*'s columns.[28] Presumably it was considered embarrassing to Ethiopia, the Soviet Union's ally, which was then being shown as coping well with the drought.

The picture of life in the West which comes across in the Soviet media is one of almost unalleviated strife and poverty. The main 'heroes' are the unemployed and striking workers, the peace demonstrators and the anti-apartheid activists, most of whom seem to end up in capitalist jails. A favourite device of recent years, especially since Brezhnev's calls for more active 'counter-propaganda', has been what one might call 'giving the West a taste of its own medicine'. Phrases that crop up again and again in coverage of Western life include 'dissidents', 'human rights campaigners', 'political prisoners', 'censorship' and even 'concentration camps' and 'torture chambers'. Soviet readers are probably more familiar with 'prisoners of conscience' such as the imprisoned American Indian leader Leonard Peltier than they are with the real facts about Andrei Sakharov, the Soviet dissident scientist. The danger of such 'mirror image' propaganda is that it may also alert the Soviet reader to circumstances nearer to home – the long article on CIA espionage tactics included in Part Two of this book, for example, precisely echoes Western descriptions of KGB methods.

Although *Pravda* spends much time denouncing the Western press as anti-communist propaganda, it regularly quotes from it in order to lend credibility to its own reporting. This is a paradox which the Soviet reader is not expected to ponder over. Here, too, however, there is subtle distortion, with phrases shorn of their context, or mere quotations of a Soviet leader's words in a Western paper reproduced in such a way as to imply that the paper actually approves of what the Soviet leader has said. An almost daily feature on page four rounds up world press reactions to whatever the Soviet leader has most recently pronounced upon. Usually, this amounts to a rather clumsy attempt to 'show' that Soviet initiatives are 'at the centre of attention in the world's press'. But the experienced reader knows that the Western press highlights the most significant parts of a Soviet leader's speeches (a favour rarely done by the Soviet media), so he reads this column rather than the full text of the speech published on page one. For *Pravda*, it can be a way of slipping in remarkably frank comment. It quoted a Reuters report of one of Gorbachov's speeches on the economy as follows: 'The British news agency Reuters reports that the Soviet leader's speech, delivered in the hard-hitting style that has become his hallmark, was a detailed statement of how the CPSU intends to solve the country's serious economic problems.'[29] *Pravda* itself could never allow itself either to refer without further qualification to the USSR's 'serious' economic problems or to describe the 'style' of a leader. Even here, it inserted 'CPSU' for 'he' (Gorbachov) in the Reuters report: the Party solves problems, not one man.

In many instances, the idea of quoting the foreign press is to give Soviet propaganda the 'stamp of approval' of the Western media. In its attempts to justify the Soviet action in shooting down a Korean airliner in 1983, with the loss of 269 lives, *Pravda* published the initial TASS statements and a few articles by its own commentators, but thereafter relied largely, for many weeks, on selective quotation from the Western media, and managed to produce so much apparent corroboration of the Soviet version from so many sources that the impression was created that scarcely anybody disagreed with it. Here, too, the 'mirror image' tactic was deployed. Without specifically linking it to the Korean airliner incident, *Pravda* dug out a story about Nicaraguan CIA-backed 'contras' who had shot down a passenger helicopter carrying schoolchildren in a border area of Nicaragua. 'Of course,' it added, 'no condolences came from the USA.'[30] (The West was outraged at the time by Moscow's refusal to apologise for shooting down the Korean plane.) A few days later, it printed an article about the Israeli shooting-down of a Libyan airliner in 1973 which sounded like a parody of the KAL-007 disaster.[31] Having insisted for several weeks that no 'technical fault' could possibly have caused the Korean plane to deviate from its flight path into Soviet air-space, *Pravda* wrote that the Libyan Boeing 727's 'compass' had gone out of order: 'The pilot thought he was 40 kilometres from Cairo when in fact he had already crossed the Suez canal and entered air-space over Israeli-occupied Sinai.' Moreover, 'it was proved that the Israeli pilot did not fire a single warning shot' (just what the Soviet pilot was accused of)!

At precisely the same time, *Pravda* had the nerve (or was it

tongue-in-cheek, or even sabotage?) to print a 'feuilleton' beginning: 'There are some people who are persistently inclined to
ascribe their own shortcomings to others.' It went on: 'This applies
particularly to liars. The cheat is always on his guard. Whatever he
is told by all around, the liar calls into question. The more cock-
and-bull stories he makes up himself, the more distrustful he
becomes. . . . This is precisely the misfortune that has befallen the
US administration. They believe nothing and nobody. . . .'[32] This
was at the height of the Korean airliner controversy, when the
Soviet Union refused to believe a word from the West about the
incident! The writer went on to state that sympathy for the American administration had shrunk all over the world. Needless to say –
following the writer's own perceptive analysis – it was the Soviet
Union that was in the dog-house at that moment!

Pravda occasionally runs into trouble over speeches made in
Moscow by visiting statesmen, and messages sent to the Soviet
leaders, which the paper's protocol demands should be printed in
full. If a visitor is too outspoken for the Soviet reader's delicate
eyes, *Pravda* merely paraphrases the offending passage. At a
Kremlin banquet in June 1984, President Mitterrand of France
embarrassed his hosts by condemning their stance on human rights
and made an appeal on behalf of the banished dissident scientist,
Andrei Sakharov. Next day, *Pravda* replaced this passage in the
speech with the words: 'He expatiated in detail on the subject of the
need to observe human rights in all countries.'[33] (Under Gorbachov, the press overcame its squeamishness when publishing the
transcript of an interview given by the Soviet leader to French
television journalists who brought up the question of human rights
and named Sakharov and the then imprisoned Anatoly Shcharan-
sky – but there was little choice, since the interview had been shown
on French and Soviet television, and the 'trust me' image which
Gorbachov was projecting to the West depended on its being shown
uncut.)[34]

Even the Warsaw Pact allies can cause embarrassment. During
disagreements between Moscow and Berlin over East Germany's
close contacts with Bonn, which ended with the cancellation of a
planned visit to West Germany by President Honecker, *Pravda*
took the unprecedented step of rewriting a telegram of congratula-
tions which the East German leader sent to President Chernenko,
merely summarising its main points (other telegrams from Eastern
Europe were quoted in full) and even adding a few sentiments

which the Kremlin evidently thought *ought* to have been there.[35]

In general, *Pravda* tends to err on the side of caution, probably precisely because it is aware of the signals it sends abroad. In early 1985, for instance, it reprinted an article on the Second World War from the East German *Neues Deutschland*, but omitted a reference to Stalin's guiding role (which appeared, however, in the version carried by the Soviet political weekly *Novoye vremya* (*New Times*).[36]

Caution has also been the watchword in political cartoons. The West tends to be represented by symbols, most commonly Uncle Sam and anonymous figures in military uniforms. There was once an argument at an editorial meeting over whether the Statue of Liberty could be used in a cartoon: it was decided not to use it, I was told, because it represented the American people rather than their government (but in fact, it has been portrayed since then). Western politicians were taboo until President Reagan started calling the Soviet Union an 'evil empire', after which the most famous *Pravda* cartoonists – three men who work under the name of Kukryniksy – were allowed to draw a wrinkled old cowboy who closely resembled Reagan. The only unambiguously personal cartoon in recent times featured the right-wing Bavarian politician Franz Josef Strauss, identified by his name on his belt, and shown licking an American boot.[37]

For the Western reader there are hidden rocks in *Pravda*'s sea of officialese and carefully worded comment. Given the rigidity with which the paper observes protocol, it ought to be a simple matter to notice and interpret deviations from the established forms. Deviations are indeed important indicators of Soviet concerns and attitudes. Yet Western Kremlinologists often make mistakes, apparently because, while being aware that the Soviet press is state-controlled and therefore a reliable barometer of official opinion, they fail to understand that the whole press system – from news values right down to presentation – is quite different from the Western one. It is not enough just to point out that '*Pravda* is the mouthpiece of the Soviet Communist Party' and then to read it as one would *The Times*.

In November 1984, for instance, almost all the British papers reported that opposition leader Neil Kinnock had been given a 'muted welcome' in Moscow because news of his arrival there was 'hidden away on page four of *Pravda*'. In fact, page four is the only place, according to *Pravda*'s protocol, where the announcement could possibly have been, and in itself indicated nothing about the Kremlin's attitude towards the visit. (Nor did the fact that he was met at the airport 'only' by Boris Ponomaryov: meeting foreign opposition leaders was part of Ponomaryov's job.) When Kinnock met President Chernenko the talks were reported (or, in Western parlance, 'splashed') on the front page of *Pravda*, even with a photograph.[38] But again, this said little about Kremlin attitudes: all foreigners' meetings with the Soviet Party leader are front-paged. The real indications come in the precise wording of the reports.

Sometimes, the Kremlinologist is 'too clever' – or just too lazy to check up the precedents. In April 1986 *The Guardian* divined Kremlin dissatisfaction with the Afghan Party leader, Babrak Karmal, in the fact that a 'formal message of congratulation from the Soviet Central Committee was addressed to Mr Ali Kishtmand [the prime minister] as well as to Mr Karmal – a step with little precedent in Party protocol.'[39] In fact, it had happened every year since the Soviet invasion in 1979. (Moscow was indeed unhappy with Karmal at the time, and he lost the Party leadership a short time later, but seeing the portents in that particular telegram was just wishful thinking!)

In the light of this, it is worth examining in more detail what *Pravda*'s own protocol actually is. The following 'check list' may enable significant deviations from protocol to be spotted more easily.

THE PARTY LEADER. Anything at all to do with the Party leader is reported on the front page: this includes meetings with him, messages sent by him, statements made by him, his replies to correspondents' questions, reports of his own visits or even of his leaving on holiday.

The Prime Minister's meetings and movements are also reported on page one, unless displaced (to page two) by more significant material (such as Central Committee decrees, Plenum reports, etc., which must appear on page one.)

FOREIGN VISITORS. The position and prominence given to arrivals of and talks with foreign guests depends on the visitor's status and rank.

- *Heads of state and government*, whether communist or not, tend nowadays to be met at the airport by the Prime Minister rather than the Party leader. The announcement of the arrival goes on page one. He will normally have talks with the Prime Minister and/or President (page one) as well as with the Soviet Party leader (page one, generally with a photograph).

Recent deviations: The arrivals in Moscow in 1984 of the leaders of Ethiopia and South Yemen (*Pravda*, 17 December and 2 November) were reported on page four (they were met by Ponomaryov, then Secretary in charge of the Party's International Department, rather than by the Prime Minister). Both met President Chernenko, however, and this was reported on page one with a photograph. The low-key welcome for the Moscow-allied South Yemeni leader contrasted starkly with the normal protocol accorded to the non-communist leader of North Yemen on his arrival only eight days later.

- *A Western or non-ruling communist party leader* is met by the Secretary in charge of the International Department (now Anatoly Dobrynin) (reported on page four), with whom he will also have talks (page four). He will not always have talks with the Soviet Party leader (in 1984 the British and Luxembourg CP leaders did not), but if he does (e.g., the CP leaders from Greece, Portugal and Japan in 1984) it will be reported, with a photograph, on page one.
- *The leader of a Western opposition party* will be met by Dobrynin (page four). If he has talks with the Party leader they are reported on page one.
- The arrival of a *foreign minister* is reported on page four. He will normally only have talks with the Soviet foreign minister (page four).
- All other meetings with *foreign delegations or ambassadors* are carried on page four, as are all statements, movements and meetings of the Soviet foreign minister, even if it involves a major new statement of Soviet policy.

PRE-VISIT PHOTOGRAPHS AND BIOGRAPHIES. On the eve of a visit by a foreign head of state or government, *Pravda* normally prints a short biography of the leader, with a small photo, in the lower right-hand corner of page one.

Recent deviations: the January 1982 *Pravda* significantly accorded this treatment to Lucio Lara, head of the pro-Moscow faction of the Angolan ruling party, the MPLA, but not head of state, thereby indicating its support for him.[40] Similarly, in May 1986, it carried a photograph and biography of the visiting *deputy* leader of Libya, Major Abdel-Salam Jalloud.[41] During talks with Jalloud, Gorbachov issued a subtly worded warning that Libya had provoked the US bombing raids on Tripoli the previous month by its association with terrorist acts. It could be, therefore, that the 'head of state' honours for Jalloud on *Pravda*'s front page were also meant to indicate some disapproval of the Libyan leader, Colonel Gadaffi.

By contrast, no biography of East German leader Erich Honecker was printed before his visit to Moscow in May 1985, although this was done for his Bulgarian and Czechoslovak counterparts only weeks later.

SIGNING OF DOCUMENTS. Routine messages (on birthdays, anniversaries, national days, etc.) to foreign heads of state and government, Communist Party leaders, and congresses of foreign Communist Parties, are signed collectively by the Presidium of the Supreme Soviet, the Council of Ministers and the Central Committee of the CPSU, as appropriate, but not by the individuals who head these bodies.

- Greetings to international conferences are generally signed by the Council of Ministers.
- Greetings to special forums (peace gatherings, youth or cultural festivals, for example) are signed by the Party leader personally.
- Messages of congratulation to foreign leaders on their election or re-election to office tend to be signed by the Presidium of the Supreme Soviet; communist Party leaders, however, may be congratulated by the General Secretary personally.
- Supreme Soviet decrees are signed by the Chairman (i.e. President) and Secretary – currently Gromyko and Menteshashvili.

TITLES. Soviet officials are invariably given their full titles in all communications (except in long lists of those present at gatherings, or of signatures after obituaries, when the following order is adhered to; the General Secretary; full members of the Politburo; candidate members of the Politburo; secretaries of the Central Committee – all in alphabetical order within their groups.) All the more intriguing, therefore, was the appearance on 30 June 1985 of a decree signed by 'M. Gorbachov, Secretary of the CPSU Central Committee' (see page 54). When Brezhnev suffered the same apparent 'fall' in protocol on 30 November 1969, this was also interpreted as a sign that he was in political trouble or perhaps being admonished in an oblique fashion by a powerful faction opposed to him.[42]

Another problem encountered in interpreting *Pravda* is the relative importance which should be attached to various writers, statements, and so on. Clearly, anything signed by the Party or government leader is an authoritative statement of Soviet policy, every word of which may be analysed for nuances since it will be the product of much collective agonising in the Propaganda Department of the Central Committee and probably in the Politburo too. A 'TASS Statement' carries equal weight, and often includes the words 'TASS is authorised to state . . .' These are reproduced in all the central newspapers.

An unsigned *Pravda* article is also an official statement of Central Committee or Politburo opinion. Other articles originated by *Pravda*, however, must be seen as very reliable indicators of the leadership's views rather than authoritative statements. The daily 'Commentator's Column' on foreign affairs, for example, is written at relatively short notice, by ordinary journalists on the staff, and though it is approved by the editorial board, its 'status' is fairly low. Kremlinologists have in the past attached special significance to articles by 'I. Aleksandrov' and 'A. Petrov', assumed to be pseudonyms used by senior Party officials.

'Political commentators' and 'observers' are senior figures (the latter sit on the editorial board), in theory free to express their opinions – or at least, the prevailing opinion in their own way. They are important because many of them are also influential advisers to the leadership. In *Pravda*'s case, most of them are dull and conservative. But others – Aleksandr Bovin on *Izvestiya*, or Fyodor Burlatsky on *Literaturnaya gazeta*, for example – often offer glimpses of the thought processes behind Soviet policy-making, and make interesting reading for this reason. After the Korean Airlines jet was shot down by the Russians in September 1983, for instance, Bovin felt free to *open* a long and thoughtful article in *Izvestiya* with his regrets and horror at the tragedy, whereas *Pravda* commentators were, if anything, even less apologetic than the official TASS Statement.[43]

5

Pravda and its Readers

Pravda has twice carried out extensive readership research – once in 1968, and once as part of a study of all newspaper readers in 1977.[1] (Lenin also carried out a rudimentary study as far back as 1913, which showed that nine subscribers out of ten were workers, but this was never published and, according to his wife, was 'probably thrown in the wastepaper bin' by Chernomazov, then the paper's secret-police editor.)[2]

The most recent research reveals the following facts:

- *Pravda*, with sales of 10 million has a total readership of 39.5 million. But a confidential report noted that 54 per cent of those who claimed to be 'readers' turned out not to have read the previous day's issue, suggesting the paper is actually read each day by some 18 million.[3] (The population of the Soviet Union is 280 million.)
- Women account for 40 per cent of readers.
- A quarter of the readers are under 30 years old.
- *Pravda* is virtually obligatory reading for Party members: over 90 per cent of them are readers, and almost all subscribe to it rather than relying on finding it at kiosks.
- The average *Pravda* reader has had 11.5 years of education, considerably more than the national average of 8.5 years. By comparison, readers of *Izvestiya* have had 10.8 years, of *Trud* 9.6 years, and of *Literaturnaya gazeta* – the 'intellectuals' paper' – 13 years. (See also Table 4, at end of book, for social composition of *Pravda*'s readership.)

Some of the fullest information available concerns the likes and dislikes of *Pravda*'s readers. One subject – foreign news – emerges as the most popular in every survey, followed by questions of 'morals and upbringing' (i.e., loosely, human interest) and 'housing, pay and social security'. Soviet internal affairs, including the all-important 'Party Life' section, attract relatively little interest (see Table 5 p. 279).

Soviet journalists, it turns out, have – or had – a wrong impression of their readers' interests. *Pravda*'s staff imagined these to be 'pyramid-shaped', with most interest in 'man', then the country, and lastly the world. In fact, readers order their preferences differently: the world, man, the country.[4] This misconception must, in part at least, explain the disproportion between *Pravda*'s content and its readers' preferences.

Although the foreign pages are most popular, many readers – particularly young ones – are not satisfied with the coverage. They would like *Pravda* to publish more on practically all aspects of life abroad, especially politics, literature and the arts.[5] Some look for alternatives: the confidential study referred to earlier noted that '*foreign* sources of information influenced the opinion of the audience about certain elements of the conditions of life in capitalist countries'.[6] The influence of foreign films was found to be especially great, but radio broadcasts are clearly seen as a major threat, since the authorities have at times spent over $150 million a year – and employed some 15,000 people – jamming them.[7]

Jamming of Russian-language broadcasts by the Voice of America, the BBC and Deutsche Welle ceased under Khrushchev in 1963, but was reintroduced after the Soviet-led invasion of Czechoslovakia in 1968. It stopped again at the height of détente in 1973, but was restarted during the Solidarity crisis in Poland in 1980. In early 1987 jamming of the BBC's Russian Service, and a few months later of the Voice of America, was suddenly lifted—a sign of the new leadership's confidence in allowing its views to compete more freely with Western ones. (The more overtly anti-communist Radio Liberty looks likely to remain jammed, however.) Even with jamming, it is estimated that some 30 million Soviet citizens tune in at least once a week to the Voice of America alone.[8]

Soviet propaganda theorists believe that the greatest ideological effect is achieved when reading of *Pravda* and the other papers is backed up by discussion of certain articles at various meetings and discussion groups held at places of work. S. Tsukasov, formerly *Pravda*'s responsible secretary, claims that 62 per cent of readers attend such meetings, while 31 per cent of readers take part in 'propaganda work, political information sessions, lectures, and classes in the system of political and economic education'.[9] The present writer's observations, and conversations with Russians, however, suggest that such meetings, which are by no means as voluntary as they are claimed to be, have the opposite effect: that is, they generally bore the audience and, if anything, 'depoliticise' them. Attendance at political meetings tends to result from a sense of duty or fear of 'unpleasantness' at work.

It is, indeed, the depoliticisation of Soviet society – the population's lack of interest in politics – that is striking, and this is partly shown by the actual reading practices of *Pravda* readers. Although they are the most politically active section of society – generally well-educated and including almost all Party members – Pravda's readers are primarily interested in non-political subjects such as 'morals', 'housing, pay and social security', 'sport' and so on. The main exception is 'international life' – the most popular topic of all – but that too is significant, suggesting that what political interest there is is almost exclusively directed outwards, not to Soviet internal political affairs. No published research has yet revealed whether the *glasnost* of the Gorbachov era has stimulated more interest in home news, but it seems probable.

Pravda's most recent readership survey was carried out in 1977. In 1980 *Pravda*'s responsible secretary wrote: '*Pravda*'s experience testifies to the fact that it is advisable to carry out such large-scale studies once every five or six years.'[10] But six years after the last audience research was done, *Pravda* had no plan for a new study in the near future.[11] And when all is said and done, what changes can really be said to have taken place as a result of the previous studies? The head of the 1968 research team says the idealistic sociologists who undertook the work were disappointed by its results. In general, the study 'gave back what the paper "put in" to its readers,' he says, and this had the unfortunate effect of bolstering the position of conservatives on the staff such as Yuri Zhukov, who was named as the most popular journalist – simply because he was the best known.[12] (Zhukov, incidentally, had opposed the very idea of audience research.)

The 1977 study, too, produced no obvious changes in *Pravda*'s approach or coverage. When the press did finally become more open and critical, under Gorbachov in 1985, this was due to a conscious decision by the new Party leadership, not because of sociological research. It is clear that Soviet readers are given what the Party thinks is good for them, whether or not this coincides with their own preferences.

To create the illusion that readers' wishes are paramount, however, *Pravda*'s audience is also 'consulted' at Readers' Conferences, held periodically throughout the country. At these, journalists meet the public, listen to criticism and suggestions, and answer questions. But the published accounts of such meetings suggest they are of limited value. There inevitably seem to be people present who call for more of exactly what they are already being given, or whose pet subjects happen to coincide with the Party's latest initiative, or who simply wish to read more about their own particular line of business or part of the country.

If little notice is taken of polls and conferences, readers' views do at least arrive in abundance in the form of letters to the editor, and these cannot be ignored – by law. All communications must be answered, and any complaints are forwarded to the organisation or person criticised, who is also obliged to come up with a written reply. *Pravda*'s correspondents investigate particularly interesting cases. Reports of action taken following readers' complaints are regularly printed in the paper, but it is part of the Letters Department's job to make sure that faults are remedied whether or not they choose to print a particular letter. To this end, the department also compiles regular reviews of letters received, concerning a particular subject or institution or part of the country, and passes them on to the appropriate authorities. Between eight and ten of these reviews are prepared each month.[13] Other 'thematic reviews' are also written for publication in the paper.

In short, as one Soviet journalist put it, unlike in the West, where a newspaper sees its job as over once it has published a reader's letter, in the Soviet Union this is only the start of the story.[14] The fact is that given the general powerlessness of the citizen in a one-Party state with non-competitive elections and an unresponsive bureaucracy, Soviet people turn first and foremost to the newspapers to air their grievances and call for change. Asked in an opinion poll what were the most effective and desirable means whereby public opinion influences local organs of administration, a majority replied that it was the role of the newspaper in publishing 'requests, remarks, suggestions and demands of the population'.[15] By contrast, they were sceptical about the usefulness of speaking or writing to party officials, and the fact that the volume of letters to newspapers far exceeds the numbers addressed to party and state bodies speaks for itself. Letters to the editor, in the words of one Western specialist, play an '"ombudsman" role of some significance in Soviet politics in dealing with the wide variety of individual problems and grievances which occur throughout the USSR and which are capable, at least in principle, of resolution within the existing political framework.'[16] The qualification – 'within the existing political framework' – is crucial, of course: the range of issues which the public feels free to bring up is strictly limited – few souls are brave enough to write in support of dissidents or to call for Soviet missiles to be dismantled – but the fact remains that Russians regard letters as the best means they have to voice their opinions.

The postbags of the central newspapers are accordingly very large. *Pravda*, *Izvestiya* and *Trud* each currently receive over half a million letters a year.[17] To cope with this avalanche, *Pravda* employs some seventy people in its Letters Department: ten of these form a 'Literary group' which edits material for publication and writes reviews; the rest belong to the 'technical group' which sorts and registers incoming mail, and makes the initial decisions about where to send a letter and whether it is worth printing. Each letter (and its envelope) is filed with a registration slip on which are written a serial number, the writer's name and address, and a brief summary of the contents. Special code-numbers are also entered to indicate the part of the country concerned, the social group of the writer, and the 'theme' of the letter. A small number of anonymous letters are received, and occasionally even referred to in published reviews. All this information is regularly collated, and monthly and annual analyses produced for internal use.[18] *Pravda* declined to supply the present writer with any concrete data about letter-writers and the subjects that worry them, but analogous information about other newspapers is available.

Those who write to the press are not representative of the population as a whole. Soviet men, for example, are much more active letter-writers than women: 70 per cent of letters to the press in general come from men.[19] The occupational spread is unusual, too, with pensioners, 'engineering and technical workers' and 'the intelligentsia not engaged in production' (teachers, doctors, etc.) over-represented among letter-writers, and workers – though forming the largest single group – under-represented. (See Table 6 on p. 280.)

College-educated readers are most inclined to write to the press: 17 per cent of letters come from this group, which comprises only 8 per cent of the population.[20] Finally, authors of letters to the editor tend to be 'socially and politically active', with a quarter of them even holding elected posts in Party, trade union or Komsomol organisations.[21]

No precise data is available about the subjects of letters sent to *Pravda*, though one of the paper's letters' editors said in 1983 that 'moral' themes were common, and that 'almost half' of the letters concerned the 'struggle for peace': the vast majority, of course, supported Soviet policies, but 'a very small number', he admitted, compared unfavourably the money spent by the state on weapons instead of, say, housing. It appears that waves of related letters tend to come in the wake of government initiatives – about discipline, for example, after Andropov's clampdown on idlers and wastrels – or in response to the paper's own articles. Many readers offer advice or suggestions on how to deal with problems.[22]

At least half of the letters received by most Soviet newspapers, however, contain complaints of one kind or another. A study of *Izvestiya*'s mailbag discovered that the most common concern was housing (19 per cent of letters), followed by social security (13 per cent), legal matters (12 per cent), industrial production (9 per cent), transport (6.5 per cent), and family matters, health or leisure (4–5 per cent each).[23]

The letters chosen for publication – only about one per cent of the number received – are not necessarily representative of a paper's mailbag as a whole. A study of letters to one Soviet local newspaper found that the editors gave greater weight to letters on industry and construction than was merited by the content of those received, whereas letters on transport, retail trade, services, town planning and housing were under-represented on the pages of the paper. Some 69 per cent of the letters printed were generally favourable in character, compared to only 25 per cent of those received; and negative or hostile letters – 67 per cent of the paper's mailbag – accounted for only 8 per cent of those chosen for publication.[24]

Citizens who write to *Pravda* to complain about the wrong-doings of their superiors take a certain risk, of course, and although victimisation is prohibited by law, *Pravda* itself has occasionally reported instances of this – usually ending happily with the vindication of the complainant and dismissal of the rogue. But one Western writer has calculated that more than half of those who 'blow the whistle' are sacked or otherwise penalised at some time during the dispute arising from their complaint, whereas only one in ten of the offending managers receives serious punishment. Not only that, people who complain about abuses at work lose friends too, since work comrades tend to have few scruples about receiving undeserved bonuses because their production results have been massaged upwards.[25]

Pravda's chief feuilleton writer, Ilya Shatunovsky, justifies the efficacy of writing to the press, however. He claims that more than 500 critical letters were directly used in *Pravda*'s articles in 1984, and adds: 'In a preface to a collection of my satirical articles a couple of years ago, I calculated that 246 of their "heroes" had been committed for trial and sentenced to an aggregate term of 1,123 years in prison.'[26] He does not say over how many years this happened.

As well as writing to newspapers, citizens may also approach one of their 'public reception offices'. *Pravda* runs thirty such offices throughout the country. Each one employs 10–12 people, two or three of whom are on duty each day. In most cases they are pensioners, but in the Moscow office there are two full-time employees. The work of the public reception offices is varied: partly, they perform a task similar to that of the newspaper's letters department – allowing people to air their grievances, and collating the information thus received and passing it on to the appropriate authorities. Visitors' complaints, like readers' letters, may also act as signals to the editorial departments of problems to be investigated. Often visitors seek advice on legal matters.[27] When this writer met the head of the Moscow reception office, someone rang up to complain that he had been unjustly sacked. She patiently explained the relevant laws to him and tried (in vain, it seems) to convince him that although she could advise him where to turn next, it was beyond her powers to have him reinstated. On the bench in the corridor outside, several people (all women) waited their turn: apparently there is no lack of Soviet citizens who – usually, I was told, after having tried and failed elsewhere – find it worthwhile going in person to *Pravda*'s public reception office in the hope that there at least their grievance will be redressed.

6

Getting the Message Across

'Words, words, words . . . Just try to imagine what concrete sense lies behind them. It's a waste of time.' When *Pravda* thus lambasted some Tadjik provincial papers in February 1986 for filling their pages with generalisations not backed up with facts, one can imagine the editors of those papers shaking in their shoes and taking urgent measures to avoid a repeat visit by *Pravda*'s two special correspondents.[1]

The dullness of the Soviet press is so notorious that *Pravda* takes up the theme once or twice a year. In 1983 it admitted that it receives many letters complaining that too many publications are 'filled with materials with no human interest, written in grey, unexpressive language.'[2] The criticism, of course, was aimed at the rest of the press, but much of *Pravda* suffers from the same ailment. If *Pravda*'s 'resonance' and effectiveness are less than they are intended to be, then its sheer dreariness is certainly partly to blame.

Another complaint, which comes up at readers' conferences and in letters, is that it is too difficult to understand: one reader said it used 'many words understandable only to specialists'.[3] According to a Soviet scholar, now in the West, a 'secret poll' discovered that almost 85 per cent of *Pravda*'s readers cannot understand it all, both because of its language and because of constant allusions to unfamiliar concepts or people.[4] At first sight this seems exaggerated (and how or where the 'secret poll' was conducted is not explained). But official Soviet figures about the readership of *Literaturnaya gazeta* suggest it may be less farfetched than it seems: 40 per cent of them said they did not always understand the paper's articles on internal affairs (and three-quarters of *Literaturnaya gazeta*'s readers have higher education, compared to only one-third of *Pravda*'s).[5] This suggests that a fairly large proportion of *Pravda* readers may also find the paper difficult to understand.

Both its dullness and the difficulty of its language undoubtedly diminish *Pravda*'s potential power. But both are merely symptoms of a much more serious debility in the structure of Soviet propaganda as a whole, namely, its failure to appreciate the *psychology* of propaganda and persuasion, its unwillingness, in other words, to copy the much more successful advertising – or, if you will, 'propaganda' – techniques of the West. It has been observed that the art of persuasion in the West is manipulative, whereas in the USSR it is coercive.[6] In the West it is treated as a branch of the social sciences, in which highly developed opinion survey techniques are used, and the target audience's wishes and prejudices carefully exploited, whereas a Soviet propagandist sees himself purely as an ideologist, much more concerned with 'correctness' and questions of organisation. Like managers of their respective economies, in other words, the West's persuaders are consumer-oriented and judged solely by their results, while the Soviet Union's are plan-oriented and often satisfied with merely formal fulfilment of their obligations. How else can one interpret the reaction of sections of the Soviet mass media to Gorbachov's anti-alcoholism drive in 1985, when, with total disregard for the usefulness of such items, dozens of reports were printed and broadcast about, say, Caucasian factories bottling fruit-juices (rather than turning them into alcohol), or about how members of some teetotallers' club had sipped tea instead of vodka at their wedding. Were the propagandists actually aware of the dreary stupidity of the first item, or the laughable sanctimoniousness of the second? The answer is: probably they were – but at least they could formally report that they had 'done something' for the campaign.

The results of this contempt for public relations can often be ludicrous. Take, for example, the official silences about the health or whereabouts of Presidents Andropov and Chernenko during their long illnesses: was the ordinary Russian really supposed not to be interested in the reasons for such a prolonged absence of the country's leader? Is it surprising that rumours abound? Or take the death of Defence Minister Marshal Ustinov in 1984: this came as second item on radio and television news, after the text of a Central Committee greeting to the Soviet republic of Turkmenistan on its sixtieth anniversary had been read out. The propagandists should count themselves lucky that anyone bothered to stay tuned long enough to hear the second item! Even the assassination of Indira Gandhi, one of the Kremlin's close friends in the Third World, although reported fully, never made the front page of any Soviet newspaper or the lead item in the television news.

In general, the home news sections of the press and broadcast media are filled with tedious official communiques, statistics about over-fulfilled plans (often even referring to a single work-team), long-winded profiles of miners and weavers who have performed stupendous feats, and never-ending reports of work collectives which have solemnly promised to fulfil some special pledge, precisely stated in tonnes or hectares or kilowatt-hours, 'in honour' of the next great event on the Soviet calendar – the Party Congress, Revolution Day, May Day, whatever. . . . Simple slogans and generalities may have been suitable for inspiring the semi-educated 'masses' of the Twenties, but today they are an insult to the intelligence of a sophisticated and diverse population. On the one hand, Russians are being asked to computerise for the twenty-first century; on the other, they are treated like illiterate peasants. Back in December 1982, an academic wrote in *Pravda* that radio listeners find home news boring and stereotyped. 'Listeners are particularly dissatisfied with economic news. . . . "Fulfilled . . . over-fulfilled . . . competed to fulfil . . . put into operation . . . commissioned . . ." – these turns of phrase and figures are constantly heard in news bulletins, often giving no idea of the scale of the successes or of the ways they have been achieved.'[7] How did journalists react to such criticism? Well, now they add on every possible occasion: 'This success was achieved by the introduction of intensive technology' or 'This success was achieved by the widespread introduction of the team-contract system of payment.'

Soviet journalists cannot conceivably believe that all these mind-numbing items are truly 'newsworthy', or that anyone reads or listens to them – far less finds them interesting – or indeed that they can have any effect whatever, apart from making people shut off and sink into apathy. And yet they still continue to churn them out, as they have done for decades. Why? One is forced to conclude that the reason for this is simply that Soviet journalists and propagandists are judged primarily by the assiduousness of their efforts to follow up Party initiatives, not by their success in actually persuading people. No attempt is even made to assess this: it is assumed that if a journalist has told the world how many litres of fruit juice a certain factory has bottled, he has contributed to the anti-alcohol campaign. He can, in the Russian phrase, enter a 'tick' in his record of work. The other problem is that Soviet newspapers do not compete in any meaningful way, so there is no incentive for radical improvements to try to win new readers. (In industry and agriculture, by contrast, great stress is currently laid on material incentives to work harder.) Furthermore, the Soviet media work in a vacuum,

with no real clash of ideas, whereas the successful Western techniques ·of persuasion developed originally as a direct result of
competition: governments, political parties and pressure groups
use methods derived from commercial advertising, and many
even employ established advertising agencies to manage their
campaigns.

All this is really an argument for freedom of the press and
freedom of expression. It is probably inevitable that without an
opposition, without competition of ideas, Soviet journalists will
always find it easier to lapse into merely formal fulfilment of their
tasks, with little regard for their impact. And yet, whatever one
thinks of the 'message', it is not inherently 'unsellable'. Any top
Western advertising agency could make a better job of 'pushing'
Soviet policies than the Soviet news media do, especially if they had
the tremendous resources that the Kremlin pours into propaganda.
For all the planning and organisation and central control, the return
on this investment is not high.

It is, perhaps, above all as a 'mobiliser' in domestic affairs that the
Soviet press fails – that is, it can claim little success in inspiring the
people to perform the current tasks of 'socialist construction' to
which so much newsprint is devoted. But what about the longer-
term aim of propaganda – the moulding of the 'New Soviet Man'?
Here, a measure of success may have been achieved in the slow but
thorough indoctrination of the population with certain moods and
attitudes: anti-Israeli feeling, for example; distrust of American
foreign policy objectives; support for the Soviet Union's 'super
power' status; a general awareness of economic and social problems
in the West; and even acceptance – by the majority of the population – of the basic tenets of the Soviet system. But even these
'desired' attitudes cannot be assumed to be purely the result of
successful propaganda. In many cases they are rooted in tradition or
patriotism (forces not to be underestimated in Russia), and merely
reinforced by propaganda. In the words of one British scholar,
'Soviet citizens remain overwhelmingly the product of their distinc-
tive historical experience rather than of Marxist-Leninist ideological training.'[8] As the constant stress on exhortation and reproach in
the Soviet mass media amply demonstrates, the New Man – selflessly working for the good of the collective – does not yet exist.

The above criticisms apply chiefly to domestic propaganda.
Significantly, the opinion polls referred to earlier show that Soviet
readers find world news (precisely that area where there *is* a clash of

ideas) more interesting. But is Soviet foreign propaganda much more successful than the domestic?

At best, the Soviet media's depiction of Western life is only partly credible. Where it succeeds, it is by dint of endless repetition of images of Western strife and poverty, in what for the majority of the population, who do not turn to foreign sources, is a news vacuum. Where it fails, it is because, as with domestic propaganda, it shows not reality as it is, but an 'ideologically correct' version of it – reality honed to fit Marxist precepts – which only the naïve can believe in. A country obsessed with Western electronic gadgetry and fashions cannot be expected to accept the image of a West consisting *solely* of unemployment and misery, any more than people who put up with chronic shortages of basic goods can be expected to believe that the Soviet Union 'leads the world' in every conceivable field. In one Soviet joke, a man asks at a hospital reception desk for the Eye and Ear Department. 'Surely you mean the Ear, Nose and Throat?' says the receptionist. 'No, no, the Eye and Ear,' says the man. 'I keep hearing one thing, but see something quite different.'

As for the influence abroad of Soviet propaganda, this tends to be greatly exaggerated in the West. Soviet propaganda is said to be 'splitting the NATO allies' over such matters as cruise missiles or space weapons, when in fact the NATO allies are split without any help from Soviet propaganda – which in any case reaches the West only through the filter of the Western news media. The Soviet image abroad improved dramatically after Gorbachov came to power, with his 'walk-abouts' among the people turning him into a television personality, and his relaxed, candid interviews with Western news organisations making front-page headlines. President Reagan's advisers were said to be seriously concerned that Gorbachov was 'winning the propaganda war' in the arms debates. But significantly, all this was due entirely to Gorbachov's adoption of Western-style publicity techniques, and was even conducted almost exclusively through the Western media (it was they, certainly not *Pravda*, that turned his wife Raisa into a 'star' who softened the traditional Russian image). He also put forward several headline-catching arms-control proposals – whose appeal, however, owed nothing to their presentation in the Soviet media and everything to Gorbachov's personal image of reasonableness and, again, to Western coverage. (For all the obstacles put in the way of Western correspondents in Moscow, the Kremlin *needs* them to present its policies in a digestible form.) The Soviet press, meanwhile, continued to reproduce the leader's speeches and interviews in yards of densely-packed small print, and even occasionally censored the country's greatest propaganda asset, cutting out remarks considered too daring for public consumption.[9]

The Soviet propaganda machine fails to serve the government as much as it fails to serve the people. Of course, the Politburo has access to vast amounts of secret information about events at home and abroad – from confidential TASS bulletins, embassies, and dozens of research institutions inside and outside of the Party apparatus – but Western governments have such sources too, yet they still rely heavily on a free press to inform them quickly about what is going on in the country and the world. They rely on the press to give them many alternative views of events, not tailored to suit *them*. The press provides options, discusses issues and analyses problems not because the government has asked it to (that is the Civil Service's job) but because it is in touch with the political, social and economic climate. In the USSR the leadership has in effect only two Civil Services – the official one and the press, both pleasing the same bosses and both constricted by the same ideology. It is likely as a result that there are still those in the government who seriously believe – as Gustav Husak, now the leader of Czechoslovakia, did in 1968 – that on 'capitalist' television no communist is allowed to express his views, or that no Westerner can criticise his government in the media.[10] With only blinkered sources of information, governments, like people, are condemned to be ill-informed.

So what effect has Gorbachov had on the Soviet media? What does his campaign for openness really amount to? At the time of writing it seems premature to assert, as one British newspaper did, that 'access to knowledge has ceased to be an attribute of leadership and is increasingly seen as the right of a citizen'.[11] Rather, it is simply that the new leadership has redefined the boundaries of information to be divulged to the public. The right to set those limits is still very much the prerogative of the leadership.

Gorbachov has already moved his own appointees into key positions in the Party propaganda apparatus, in radio and television, and in the major newspapers. He has held several meetings with representatives of the mass media at which he called, not just for openness and constructive criticism of shortcomings, but for their help in mobilising the population to his goals of 'restructuring' the economy (and the mentality of the people) and 'accelerating' growth and development.[12] The different media have responded unequally: television has undoubtedly become livelier, bolder and more interesting; newspapers have become more investigative; radio has changed little. Certainly, more problems can now be aired in public, high-ranking officials are less protected from criticism, and the Soviet citizen is more likely to learn about accidents and disasters inside the Soviet Union. The old idea that if the media pretended all was well, all would be well, has been discredited, and (partly) discarded. Under Gorbachov, Western politicians and journalists have been given access (sometimes censored, but not always) to Soviet newspapers and television, where they were able to criticise the Kremlin's foreign policies quite openly. At the time of writing, yet more former taboos in Soviet journalism look likely to be broken in the future.

Pravda, in short, has become more believable. But *glasnost* is selective, and there is still no guarantee that the *whole* truth is being told. Dozens of lives were lost when a dare-devil pilot 'testing his skills' crashed his Aeroflot plane in October 1986, but this was not reported until June 1987, and then only by one newspaper, *Sovetskaya Rossiya*. Gorbachov revealed in a speech that a crucial meeting of the Central Committee in January 1987 had been postponed three times because of disagreements in the leadership, but *Pravda*, the Central Committee's mouthpiece, did not report these postponements at the time or ever discuss what disagreements lay behind them.

Moreover, the basic Soviet concepts of propaganda and news, and the structure of the propaganda apparatus, are unchanged. It remains to be seen whether Gorbachov's 'overhaul' will yet encompass more subtle psychological approaches to replace the failed old methods of mobilising the public. If not, the danger is that new slogans will merely be substituted for old. Gorbachov's watch-words—'restructuring' (*perestroyka*) and 'acceleration' (*uskoreniye*)—have already been repeated so often as to render them virtually meaningless, leaving them as targets for after-dinner witticisms, but rather ineffective as means of engaging a largely apathetic population in putting Gorbachov's ambitious plans into practice.

Part Two

SELECTIONS FROM
PRAVDA

NOTE

Unless otherwise indicated, the extracts from *Pravda* have been translated in full. Any substantial omissions within an article are indicated thus: [. . .].

Certain liberties have been taken with Soviet nomenclature, however, to facilitate understanding for the non-specialist reader. 'Regional executive committee of the soviet of people's deputies', for example, is rendered simply as 'regional council', where a more precise translation is not crucial.

The following rough guide to the structure of the Soviet government and Party system may prove useful when reading the first section of extracts, on domestic affairs (these have generally been provided with more background information than the foreign extracts). The Soviet Union is divided into 15 republics, the largest of which is the Russian Federation (or RSFSR). Many of these republics are subdivided into regions (*oblast*), provinces (*kray*) and autonomous republics or regions. They in turn comprise several districts (*rayon*). (The larger cities are also split into districts.) At each level there are corresponding government bodies (soviets, translated here as 'councils') and party organisations (committees). In each case the party committee supervises the work of the corresponding council (in effect an executive body) and is consequently 'more important'. Thus, the first secretary of, say, Leningrad regional party committee wields far greater political power than his local government counterpart, the Chairman of the Leningrad regional council. Tension between party committees and councils and overlapping of their responsibilities are at the root of some of the conflicts described in the extracts.

1

Domestic Affairs

Party Life

[The three articles included here from *Pravda*'s 'Party Life' section illustrate some of the changes taking place in Soviet political life in the Eighties.
The first piece, written by V. Krushevsky, the director of a furniture factory
in Chardzhou, in the southern republic of Turkmenistan, contains a
remarkably frank description of the stifling atmosphere that reigned at
Party meetings during the Brezhnev period. It was published in the summer
of 1982, a time when impatience with the complacency of the Brezhnev era
was mounting, and the more energetic leaders grouped around Yuri
Andropov were already bidding for power.]

The article by the Astrakhan worker, A. Stakhanov, published in
Pravda on 3 January, gave me much cause for thought. I'll begin
with something that I often hear myself: 'Why has Krushevsky
always got to be speaking out about something? Does he feel he's
got more to say than anyone else? He should just keep his mouth
shut for a change. . . .'
    . . . A meeting of the town's Party activists was in progress. All
those who had put down their names to take part in the discussion of
the report had spoken. 'Who else wishes to speak?' asked the
chairman. . . . They were discussing the work of certain enterprises
which, because they were behind with their own work, were holding
up the whole of Chardzhou's industry. I had thought out earlier
what I was going to say on this matter. I was making my way to the
platform, when I heard a comrade, also a manager, say behind my
back: 'There he goes again, pushing himself forward!' And in such a
tone of voice as though he were accusing me. I wanted to turn round
and say: 'You'd think I was pushing myself into your home!' But I
held my tongue. And although an amendment was included in the
resolution after my speech, my colleague's words left me with a
bitter taste in my mouth.
    I experienced something similar at another meeting of the Party
activists. The draft resolution was read out. A few days before, the
collective of one of our town's enterprises had come up with a good

initiative. The local paper had written about it. I proposed that the resolution should include a point about the need to spread the initiative to every work collective. 'That's true. We've overlooked that,' said the chairman in support. The proposal was adopted. But again I heard a familiar whispering behind me. I could have ignored it, of course – you can't stop tongues wagging. But this was a different situation. These were communists, my comrades in the town's Party organisation, who were making remarks about me. That is what surprised and dismayed me more than anything.

When A. Pirkuliyev, the first secretary of the town Party committee, announced during the plenum that Ch. Vapayev and R. Svirskaya had requested to be relieved of their duties as secretaries of the committee, the members of the audience were bewildered, exchanged glances, shrugged their shoulders. '. . . In connection with their transfer to other work. . . .' This cliché clearly satisfied no one. However, nobody asked any questions. I decided to break the silence. I asked for an explanation as to why it had suddenly become necessary to relieve two secretaries of their duties at once. Pirkuliyev looked at me disapprovingly and said: 'I'll explain to you later.' You will agree that he ought to have explained it to all the participants of the plenum. But they merely deferred to 'Number One', and voted that that request should be granted. Yet on my way out of the hall, some of my comrades came up to me and told me that I had done the right thing.

'So why didn't you support me?' I asked.

They answered: 'It's better not to interfere. They know better.'

Who are 'they'? It was we, after all, who elected the members of the committee, and entrusted them with running the town's Party organisation. We ought not to be indifferent to how they develop.

Incidentally, although Pirkuliyev promised to 'explain' to me, he never did get around to doing so. The real reason became known later. It turned out that the two secretaries were absolutely opposed to his style and methods of work. It had reached the stage when they simply could not work with him, and they put it to a higher body: it's either him, or us.

I myself was later to experience A. Pirkuliyev's 'exactingness'. The town's Party committee asked me to join a commission specially set up to look into the state of personnel work at a chemical factory. When we arrived at the factory, the director, A. Laryanovsky, was not there. We set about our business. Then Laryanovsky suddenly appeared, shouting, 'Why are you noseying about here? Who gave you permission?' In short, he insulted us. During our inspection of the factory, several workers complained to us 'in confidence' about his bad temper.

Then, lo and behold, at the next plenum of the town Party committee, A. Pirkuliyev started showering praise on Laryanovsky for his . . . sensitivity towards other people. I expressed my bewilderment. 'This isn't the place to settle personal accounts,' declared the speaker. I had to prove that this was not a question of 'personal accounts'. But it was to no avail. Moreover, I was later 'carpeted' by the secretary: 'Why do you always have to be the odd man out?' he asked. I spoke my mind, of course. But later I began to feel that the clouds were beginning to gather above me. Fortunately, a commission from Moscow arrived in Chardzhou. They were checking the work of many enterprises, and named our furniture factory as one of the best. Only then did the first secretary leave me in peace. And later he himself was dismissed.

Our present First Secretary is Bakhtiyar Astanovich Ishankuliyev. I knew his late father, and worked with him. In his later years his father headed the regional Party committee and the Turkmenistan People's Control Committee. He was a businesslike man, with great initiative, and an honest and principled communist. It was good to see that his son had taken his best qualities. And not without reason, a thorough reorganisation in the workings of the town Party committee was begun. The peremptory, commanding tone is no longer heard. Members of the committee are constantly consulted, and our opinion is listened to. Even the content of the speeches at activists' meetings has changed. Indiscriminate criticism has disappeared, and constructive criticism increased. There are fewer meetings and conferences. The leaders of the town's Party committee now meet only once a month.

It is not easy to eradicate the shortcomings which have accumulated as a result of a previous first secretary's unworthy style. They were particularly evident in the work of the law-enforcement organs and trade. The council executive committee was used to letting the town Party committee do its work for it. But now things are changing. The selection and placing of personnel is improving.*

I see, however, that not everything is working out the way

---

* Freed of jargon and understatement, this paragraph means that under the previous Party chief, corruption had become rife in the town's militia, or police force, and in the shops, and that now many of the corrupt had been sacked.

Bakhtiyar Astanovich – and all of us – would have liked. But he is genuinely trying, and spares no efforts for the cause. Is he taking on too much? Well, a communist ought to take on as much as needs doing, he must show initiative, and firmly carry out the Party line.

It is well known how highly Lenin rated people who were independent in their judgments, who 'would not say a word against their conscience', and would not be afraid of 'any struggle to achieve their goals'. The Party has always supported such people. I cannot help wondering: why is it that you nevertheless sometimes come across a different reaction to a person's desire to express his opinion or disagree with something? Take, for example, these activists' meetings or the plenums of the town Party committee. Sometimes the participants' role amounts to merely voting for a resolution hatched behind closed doors. And it is not just their fault. Also to blame is the manner in which these meetings and plenums are prepared and conducted.

The custom here in Chardzhou is that once those who have put their names down have addressed the meeting, 'a line must be drawn'. But it is well known how they usually 'put their names down'. The town Party committee knows the names of two or three 'reliable' comrades in a factory. They lift the telephone, and dictate the names. Some of these 'staff' speakers have a store of speeches for every occasion, and even keep their old ones. The names of the latest model workers are inserted, and your speech is ready!

You sit and listen to identical speeches. There is nothing particularly *wrong* with the content. But it's all figures and positive statements. Empty barrels make the most noise. But that's all they do! You hear the same old things time and time again. The people in the hall quietly talk among themselves, or read, or daydream. And if anyone other than those on the official list asks to speak, it is sometimes regarded as an encroachment on their time, too much of which has already been wasted. Perhaps the person wishing to speak has something interesting to say, something important or useful for everyone. But the empty verbiage has tired the audience, and all they want now is to get out of the hall.

Such a highly organised exchange of opinion only serves to encourage passivity. It is also time to make sure decisions are carried out. Some leaders repeatedly speak from the platform about pressing problems. Each time they are promised help, and that the problem will be looked into, and each time it all comes to nothing. The more persistent among them will not be satisfied with this, and will take the matter further. Others will simply give it up as a bad job, and sink into indifference.

I have no respect for 'yes-men', and get depressed when I meet them. Especially in our factory. A team-leader – a Party member – comes to see me in my office. He complains about the foreman, calling him this and that. What he says surprises me. Because the team-leader has always spoken well of him at meetings, agreeing with him about everything. But it turned out that the foreman had always been very indulgent towards the team-leader. And as soon as he stopped showing indulgence, the team-leader suddenly remembered all his faults. 'Why did you choose to forget them before?' I asked him. He had nothing to say.

I often say to my subordinates, especially the Party members: 'If you ever feel that any of us is wrong, never be afraid to say so.' No one in our factory has ever been reproached for offering just, helpful criticism. On the contrary, they are thanked. And people are changing, becoming more responsible, and more principled.

It sometimes happens that you put forward proposals during Party meetings, and you turn out to be in the minority. Well, what of it? It only means that you were not convincing enough, or have not worked it out properly yourself. And your comrades put you right. I should like to name the following communists: R. Nigmatulina, G. Akshayeva, R. Kurbanov, M. Ulyanova and R. Sakhatov. They will never remain silent, and will always express their own opinion, without looking over their shoulders at the authorities. It is a fine thing, when someone puts forward his own ideas. And I know that because of this we shall always find the best way to solve our problems.

[14 July 1982]

[The next article, by the *Pravda* correspondent in Turkmenistan, profiles the 'new type' of Soviet leader, a man in the Gorbachov mould. Indeed, although most of the events here evidently took place towards the end of the Brezhnev era, the 'hero' is almost allegorical, acting exactly as Gorbachov has acted since he came to power. The article was published under the headline 'Flowers for the First Secretary'.]

Everything was going well! Bairam Amanovich Ovezov had devoted eleven years to Iolotan District, as first secretary of the Party committee. Under him the district grew and flourished in every way.

Delegations flocked there to learn from his experience. It seemed that all that was left for him now was to reap the fruits of his labour. And suddenly . . .

Three hours ago he left the office of the first secretary of the Turkmenistan Party Central Committee. And now, on the plane travelling home, the first secretary's words came back to him: 'We know you, Bairam Amanovich, as an honest, principled and experienced leader. We are proud of people like you. We value them. . . . The Turkmen-Kala District is not an easy one to handle, things are in a mess. There is no order there. People have forgotten the meaning of the word 'discipline'. . . . It is you we want to take charge there. I know – it will be very difficult. But we are sure that you will cope. Please do your best. I am asking you as a father. . . .'

Bairam Amanovich had not expected this turn of events. He had heard of the ill-fame of Turkmen-Kala District and of the 'tricks' of the local leaders.

'Can you imagine?' he said to me. 'I got ready to go to the plenum of the district Party committee, and was seized by an unpleasant trembling. I couldn't calm myself down. Who could say how it would all turn out?'

In fact, there was nothing to worry about. The Party members understood that the district needed a real boss, who would be concerned not about his own prosperity but about ordinary workers and the common good. One who would inspire others to work conscientiously not just with words, but by personal example, by his honesty and by being a true communist. The district had not been blessed with such a leader for many years.

'Where did you start, Bairam Amanovich?' I asked.

'You won't believe this. When I went to the first two collective farms – the "Zhdanov" and the "First of May" – not a single tractor was in working order. They were either broken or had no fuel. The farms were in debt and had run out of credit. To be perfectly honest, I wasn't quite sure what to do to begin with.'

'And how did you find a way out?'

'I took the simplest way out. I went straight to the farm workers – I visited them in the fields, on the livestock farms, I went to many people's houses, I went to see the shepherds on remote pastures. . . . I wanted to understand why these people were working so badly. In what way were they dissatisfied? What was preventing them from working? They wanted their hard work to be appreciated, they wanted people to listen to their opinions. But this was not happening. What was needed was a complete change of psychology in the work collectives. . . .

Bairam Amanovich's wife, Sheker, probably knows better than anyone what this cost him. She told me 'in confidence': 'He would go out to work at five or six o'clock in the morning, and appear again at midnight. I would peep into his room and see him pacing up and down, as though he were arguing with someone.'

The loafers and money-grubbers had it easy in the district. Even some of the people in charge had forgotten what discipline was. Ovezov called his first meeting of managers and Party activists. One in three of those invited arrived twenty to thirty minutes late. Later, he spoke to each of the latecomers individually. He pointed out that the Party activists were the district committee's mainstay, and if *they* were so lax in their attitude, how were they ever going to pull up the district? They stopped arriving late. Well, what else could he have done? The 'educators' had to be educated.

Ovezov began with the apparatus [bureaucracy] of the district Party committee itself. Here, too, things were in a state. Many district Party workers spent all their working hours sitting in cool offices 'twiddling their thumbs'. Or solving personal problems. Ovezov made it quite clear to them that the time for warming seats was over: they had to involve themselves fully in the problems of the work collectives, and to help them in every way possible. Some people were none too pleased with the secretary's demands: prolonged inactivity had become a way of life. They had to be ushered out.

Those for whom the personal plot took precedence over the farm, and for whom the market had become a source of profit and the sole meaning of their lives, were also firmly dealt with. In the 'Moscow' collective farm, for example, about twenty people had not worked anywhere for between five and ten years. But each had a quarter of a hectare of land, given over to a pomegranate orchard. These businessmen took their fruit to various parts of the country to sell, even to the Far East. And no one stopped them. Ovezov asked the public prosecutor to investigate. But first of all he had to find out what the public's position was.

. . . The village gathering on that collective farm was at first like a disturbed beehive. Finally things quietened down. In the dock of the collective farmer's public court sat an unpleasant character by the name of Taganov, who had not worked for the past ten years. Next to him was Agadzhanov, whose sole passion in life was to make money by selling the produce from his vast private plot. Also sitting there, hunched up and hiding behind each other's backs, were fifteen healthy men who did not even know the way to the fields or the cattle-sheds.

Every word spoken by M. Yailimov, an honoured veteran of labour, expressed deep concern about the affairs of the collective farm. 'We need to wash out the soil without further delay. Just look at what has become of it – it's completely covered in salt. What has it done to deserve this? It's shameful, unforgivable. And what state is our equipment in? The buildings on the stock-farm are falling down – they should have been rebuilt long ago, and a kindergarten should have been set up. . . . And if some don't want to work, let them go somewhere else to make their big money – they've been blinded by it.'

After Ovezov spoke, one woman tried to defend herself and her husband, both speculators: 'You district committee workers are no better than us! We know what our leaders are like. They build themselves houses – just like mansions! And not with their own money, of course. They take produce from the collective farms for free, they hand out the best jobs to their relatives, and they don't say no to bribes, either. Don't worry, we know all about it. And their children behave like hooligans – and get off scot free. The best goods from the warehouses go straight to them. That's the kind of workers we have in the district Party committee. Only they hide behind their Party cards. They don't want for anything. And they've got the nerve to tell others how to behave. . . .'

It pained Ovezov to listen to this. Others would have been outraged, or would have tried to avoid answering. But Bairam Amanovich broke the deathly silence that had descended: 'Yes, there have been people like that. But there will be no more! And don't dare to blacken the names of all the district committee officials. Most of the people there are decent and conscientious. If wormy apples appear on a tree, and are not noticed at first, they fall anyway before they ripen. . . .'

Three days later he went to a similar gathering at the 'Zhdanov' collective farm. There were 447 farmworkers here, of whom 220 actually worked. And of them, 163 were not fulfilling their work minimum.

Here are some short extracts from the speeches:

'There are two people in the Nurmetov family. The husband works on a geological expedition, and the wife stays at home. They make 14,000 roubles a year by selling the produce from their personal plot. What's the collective farm to them?'

'People go to work in our farm when they feel like it or when they are asked to. When will this matter be put to rights? Why doesn't the Party committee do something?'

And once again Bairam Amanovich had to give an answer to a difficult question. He hid nothing.

'Thank you for speaking the truth. You don't blather like the others,' said a grey-bearded old man.

People understood the secretary. His frankness was the key to their hearts that was needed in those circumstances. They believed him. And that was already a big step forward.

'There was a time when I went to work every day as though I was going into battle,' said Bairam Amanovich. 'One day I discovered that the doctor from the district hospital, I. Tokgayev, and two of his relations had a flock of 500 sheep. They even hired a shepherd and paid him a wage. They kept the sheep on the collective farm's land, and even stole fodder for them. . . . On the 'Red October' collective farm three families had 600 sheep and goats and 30 camels above the statutory limit. One 'farmworker' had three cisterns of diesel fuel and car oil, and was speculating in them at a time when fuel was in short supply.

The district Party committee held village meetings on all the farms. Then a district meeting was held. Orazmuradov Dovlet-aga, a war and labour veteran, spoke movingly at it: 'Our district has been lagging behind long enough! It's shameful, comrades, to hear nothing but ill spoken of the people of Turkmen-Kala. Is it that we are not able to work? Do we not live on our own native soil? We have wronged the land which feeds us, and it is longing for the labour of our hands. Where is our pride? Where is the honour of the farmer? I did not expect to live to see such shame in my old age. . . .'

It was difficult to make the break. But in the end it came. In 1983 for the first time in many years the district fulfilled its state plan in every sector. Last year's results were also good. Only the production of cotton was very slightly down. But, says Ovezov, they will make good the shortfall this year. And the most important thing is that people have taken heart, have started to believe in their own strengths, and in the future. . . .

Behind this success I see Bairam Amanovich's sleepless nights. His constant state of nervous tension, his heated arguments with stubborn people and pessimists. . . . This success could be called the first secretary's finest hour.

Bairam Amanovich has very many friends. People occupying high public offices often visited him without telling the Mary regional Party committee. This made the regional first secretary rather jealous of Ovezov, and he started trying to find fault with him, picking on him, and even giving him undeserved dressings down. A sensible leader would have been proud to have in his region such a warm-hearted man who attracted others to him. But the regional Party secretary (he was dismissed not long ago) was not even pleased that Ovezov had sorted out the backward district – he was probably expecting something different. Of course, Bairam Amanovich tried not to take all this too much to heart. But it all mounted up . . . and his health gave way. Illness overtook him at the beginning of this year, and confined him to bed for two whole months.

Bairam Amanovich woke up one morning and saw a beautiful bouquet of flowers in a vase standing next to his bed.

'Who are they from?'

'Three women and some men came. They said they were from a collective farm, but that their names were not important. They asked me to get you better as quickly as possible,' answered the doctor.

After that there were always flowers. They were brought not only by 'delegations' from various organisations, but also by individual workers and farmers who happened to be visiting the district centre.

'You see, people would come to visit me: "Greetings! How are you feeling?" And I would never have seen them before. It was winter, yet they brought flowers. That was the best medicine.'

Flowers . . . But how many 'bouquets' of thorns he had received! Many people had openly expressed their disapproval of his activities. Anonymous complaints were written: 'He's too strict.' 'He's chasing staff away.' 'He's making fun of honest workers.' 'We demand that the first secretary be replaced.' He was even threatened with violence. But that is all in the past now. Although everything leaves its mark.

Recently, during one of my regular trips to that district, I asked Bairam Amanovich: 'What did you consider to be the most important thing when you came to work here?'

He answered without a moment's hesitation: 'Trust. I had faith in people, I relied on them. And they did not let me down.'

And my second question: 'What do you fear as a Party leader?'

'Compromising your conscience. If you do that, then you can consider yourself no longer a Party leader. Not even a communist. . . . You are probably thinking – "here's the first secretary sounding off again with his high words." I apologise if you are. I don't know any other way.'

[7 August 1985]

[In the months before the Party's 27th Congress in February 1986, the Soviet public was invited to discuss the drafts of three documents which were to be approved at the Congress – a new Party Programme, new Party Rules, and the Five Year Plan. Many of the letters to the press at the time were outspoken. But one review of letters – certainly the most controversial publication in *Pravda*'s recent history – went so far as to call for an end to Party privileges (whose very existence is normally denied). That was too much for conservatives in the leadership, and caused Yegor Ligachov – regarded as Gorbachov's deputy – to criticise *Pravda* at the Congress. Entitled 'Weeding Out', it is published here in slightly abridged form. (The sting comes in paragraph eight.)]

In the lead-up to the Party Congress, thousands of readers' letters have passed through my hands. And in many of them, behind the words of sincere and ardent approval of the Party line on accelerating economic and social development, there is a hint of concern: will we all have the strength and commitment to continue what has been successfully started, and to see it through to the end?

Indeed, the restructuring of our life is far from simple. The path approved at the April (1985) Plenum of the Central Committee [shortly after Gorbachov came to power] is thorny, steep, and difficult. What is required is painstaking work – day in and day out – by the entire Party and the entire nation. Standing in the way are retrogrades and windbags, bureaucrats and extortioners. While they pay lip-service to the Party decisions, in fact they fear change and therefore strive any way they can to retard our forward movement.

People see this and understand the implications. That is why they write of the need not to let up in the struggle against alien phenomena, of the need to observe the Leninist norms of Party life, right across the board, and to uphold the moral purity of the Party member. [. . .]

V. Kuzovlev of Sverdlovsk writes: 'When I learnt from the papers that in the Caucasus the Party secretary at a militia [police] station had turned out to belong to a gang of poachers, that at Domodedovo in Moscow Region the secretary of the Party organisation in a restaurant had accepted bribes from her subordinates, and that the head of a department of the Rostov city Party committee had not been above receiving gifts, I seethed with indignation, not so much at the rogues themselves, as at the people who accepted them into the Party and blessed the appointment of crooks and thieves to high posts, who protected them and pretended that everything was fine.'

'I am not a Party member,' writes O. Zelentsov, a metal-worker from Kursk. 'I have been reading *Pravda* since the war years, and took out a subscription in 1962. At that time the paper printed a letter of Lenin's that disturbed me. In it he inveighed against the Moscow Party committee, which in the spring of 1922 tried to protect certain leaders who had committed abuses in the allocation of housing. Lenin viewed this as indulgence towards "communist criminals" and stressed that "the courts much punish communists *more harshly* than non-communists". And he added, furiously: "It is the height of shame and disgrace when a party in power protects 'its own' scoundrels!" I note with pleasure that the "scoundrels" in our life are now beginning to find it uncomfortable. The Party is naming, for all to hear, those who have forgotten their honour and conscience and are violating Lenin's behests. That, for example, is how I personally took the short report in *Pravda* about the Chairman of the USSR State Committee for Petroleum Products, T. Khuramshin, who has been removed from his post and expelled from the Party. As a worker, I am ashamed of such – if I may use the word – leaders. They should be punished severely, by an open court, for they cause enormous damage – and not just material damage, but moral too: people often judge the whole Party on the strength of the behaviour of its individual representatives.'

That is the view of other *Pravda* readers, too, who write about the need to tear out of our life the poisonous roots of the bureaucratic mentality, abuse of official positions, nepotism, and love of the 'good life' at the state's expense. [. . .]

'I get the impression,' writes V. Ivanov, a worker from Shchokino, Tula Region, 'that between the Central Committee and the working class there is still a slow-moving, slothful, sticky layer of Party administrators, who are none too keen on radical changes. Some just carry their Party cards, but ceased to be communists long ago. All they want from the Party are privileges, and they are in no hurry to devote any of their strengths or knowledge to the people.'

From Kazan writes N. Nikolayev, a Party member since 1940: 'When discussing social justice, we must not close our eyes to the fact that Party, government, trade union and even Komsomol leaders sometimes objectively exacerbate social inequality by making use of all sorts of special canteens, special shops, special hospitals, and so on. Yes, we have socialism, and each must receive according to his labour. Let it be that way, without any egalitarianism: a leader should get a higher salary, but otherwise he should have no privileges. Let the boss go to an ordinary shop and stand in a queue the same as everyone else – maybe then the queues that everyone is so fed up with would be eliminated more quickly. Except that the beneficiaries themselves are hardly likely to give up their privileges of their own accord. What is needed is the force of law, and a fundamental purge of the [Party] apparatus.' B. Alekseyev, a Muscovite and a member of the Party since 1919, is of the same opinion: 'As an old Bolshevik I believe a rule about periodic purges has to be reintroduced in our Party.'

The Party is undertaking a huge task at the moment, not least in weeding out its own ranks. But it is just that – a weeding-out, not a purge. We renounced mass purges long ago, and for weighty enough reasons, which were detailed in the resolution of the 18th Party Congress [in 1939, at which Stalin cynically admitted 'grave mistakes' in the purge of the Thirties, while putting the blame on over-zealous local organisations]. Even then, quite rightly and justifiably, the need for a strictly individual approach to the question of Party membership was recognised. And that is the approach we need today as well.

'Every application to join the Party must be scrutinised more closely. Then there would be no need later to expel the pseudo-communists,' say the brothers Sharov from Oryol. 'But often acceptance into the Party is too much of a formality. In some institutions there are waiting lists stretching years ahead. What are they after, these people who join this strange queue? Is it not those selfsame privileges that we are so vehemently condemning these days? A queue to join the Party is absurd. The Party is not a supermarket. Its strength lies not in the number of people paying dues, but in its ideology and in the might of its ranks.'

'We are too easy on offenders, as regards Party membership,' thinks A. Ototyuk of Petropavlovsk-Kamchatsky. 'A person who commits a serious misdemeanour should be drummed out of the Party – but instead we "censure" him, "rebuke" him, "issue a reprimand". But everybody knows that a reprimand leaves not a trace a year later. No, in a Party such as ours, wishy-washy liberalism is impermissible. Being nice to everyone is to show one's weakness.'

Readers note that by no means everywhere or always is use made of openness – that effective means of instruction. Lenin called it a sword which itself heals the wounds it inflicts. But how many communists have the courage to use this 'healing sword' properly? Here is what A. Terekhov from Krasnogorsk in Moscow Region writes: 'I read a note in the local paper: "A plenum of the Party's town committee released Yu. Vorontsov from his duties as second secretary in connection with his transfer to other work." Such vague wording gives rise to all sorts of discussion and guesswork. These reports should be more definite and should give reasons.' [. . .]

Criticism and self-criticism – that is the Party's keen, tested weapon. A. Karagodin from Saratov recalls Lenin's words to the effect that the building of socialism is the use and maintenance of criticism, for criticism is one of the chief components of social progress. A healthy weeding-out of the Party's ranks is inconceivable without it.

[13 February 1986]

Town and Country Life

[Many of *Pravda*'s articles about the problems of town life concern housing. It might be hard to find fault with Soviet housing policy as such, with its aim of providing a separate flat for every family, but the rate at which new buildings are put up inevitably brings problems of quality, which are widely reflected both in letters and in articles. Half-completed houses are handed over by the builders; thereafter they are maintained by ill-equipped or indifferent Housing Offices; and to cap it all, it may be months or even years before adequate local services are provided.

The first report reveals the findings of a study by the USSR People's Control Committee, a body designed to investigate failings in the economy and root out inefficiency, wastage and corruption.]

Since the beginning of this year the USSR People's Control Committee has received many signals from various regions, all along the same lines.

From Tula: in two districts a number of blocks of flats have been put into service with no heating, and many flats have no doors or windows.

From Armenia: in the capital, Yerevan, 18 blocks of flats and kindergartens have been deemed suitable for occupation despite a multitude of defects and omissions. Back in September of last year a kindergarten with 320 places was built in the Sovetsky district of the city, and a little later another went up, but mothers are afraid to take their children near them because they are dangerous: the ceilings leak, the floors are lopsided, and the doors are all askew.

Teams of People's Controllers investigated these and other warning signals. What did they find?

In Orsk, they were still laying the floors, installing toilets, and painting walls and ceilings of flats, which, on paper, were completed long ago. The kindergartens which had frightened off parents in Yerevan last year were still empty in February this year. In ten supposedly finished blocks of flats there was not a single occupant. In others, on the other hand, work was in full swing, as the new owners refitted their flats, relaying or evening up floors, glazing windows, replacing doors and bathroom suites . . .

And in Tula. . . . In Tula the People's Controllers came across some puzzling phenomena; in buildings passed with no windows or doors, many of the openings for the windows and doors were still empty. But at the same time, according to the documentation, the builders had contrived to fit doors and window frames in other houses which did not even have walls yet!

But there is nothing supernatural in this sleight of hand. The builders were merely 'combining'. In violation of the regulations they presented incomplete buildings and managed to have them passed. But one deceit leads to another. The buildings had to be finished somehow – and where could they get extra money and materials when they were all used up already? By dipping into resources earmarked for other buildings, which have yet to be started.

Of course, the builders have their own difficulties to cope with. Enterprises supplying prefabricated parts for buildings produce components with such defects and deviations from the required sizes that they have to be repaired and brought up to standard on the building sites, at a great cost. Joinery products are a headache: door and window units are faulty and deformed, the wood for the parquet floors is damp and badly worked.

Most buildings (in Tula, 60 per cent) are completed in December, in a great rush [to fulfil the annual plan], and in poor weather conditions.

On the 30th, or more often the 31st, of December, the Building Inspection Commission appears on site. Officially, this is a state commission, but in fact it often turns out to be part of the local bureaucracy. As experienced people, the members of the Commission can see from a mile off that the building is not ready. The heating pipes do not reach the house; the underground systems (electricity and gas supply, hot water supply, plumbing, telephone lines) are unfinished; the floors are uncovered; the windows have no glass. . . . In a word, there is still a mass of work to be done.

What should they do? Pass it or not? To be frank, for the Chairman of the Commission the question does not even arise. The day before, the Chairman, I. Slipchenko, was called to the Executive Committee of the City Soviet [Council], and was asked a simple question: 'Do you want to work with us?' After which he signed all the documents approving the buildings as suitable for occupation.

The chief architect of the town of Shchokino – also the head of a Commission – was called to both the town council and the Party committee. There they listened patiently to his long list of gaps and defects in houses awaiting approval. And then they recommended: go ahead, sign the documents!

Perhaps in Yerevan, Orenburg and Stavropol things were a little different, but the result was the same: there too, state commissions accepted poor-quality, unfinished houses as ready to be lived in.

Asked why he had resorted to fraudulence, falsification, and violation of state discipline, the head of the Yerevan Capital Construction Board replied: 'It was in the interests of the city.'

The Chief Architect of Shchokino answered the same question: 'To meet the working people's wishes to obtain housing as quickly as possible.'

And the Chairman of the Tula Commission: 'We took account of the people's interests.'

Nobody, it turns out, was saving his own skin, or thinking of personal interests, or trying to please local bosses. They went in for eye-wash and deception motivated purely by good and noble intentions.

[15 April 1982]

[For all their good and noble intentions, the guilty partners received 'severe reprimands' from the People's Control Committee and were warned that they would be dismissed if the same thing happened again.

Readers' letters to *Pravda* are a particularly fruitful source of sad tales of urban life. . . .]

In May we received a surprise from the builders. While preparing the ground for a new block of flats, a road was destroyed. As a result our fruit and vegetable processing factory, and also the nearby storehouses and distribution points, were left without an approach road. Neither vehicle nor pedestrian can get near. On top of this, we are all amazed by this strange picture: the foundation pit has been dug, but for many months now no more building work has been done. The foundation pit is used as a rubbish dump.

We have already approached the local councils several times about this matter. The local paper, *Taganrogskaya pravda*, has publicised the destruction of our road. But nothing changes.

[Letter from group of workers at a fruit and vegetable processing factory, Taganrog; 14 October 1982]

The inhabitants of our block of flats have grown used to the 'tricks' of our communal services. Particularly annoying is the frequent absence of hot water. Usually this is explained away by 'technical reasons'. We heave a sigh, and gather our patience for another week or two.

Recently a notice went up informing us: 'For the purpose of saving heat, the hot water supply will be turned off from 24 to 31 January. (Signed) Head of Heating Dept. Yelizarov.'

We wonder who will receive a bonus for this economy measure? *[Letter from residents of block 14/16, Kirov Avenue, Saratov; 17 December 1982]*

[While the lack of heating is explained in Saratov as an 'economy measure', in Aktyubinsk (Kazakhstan) there are other excuses, as this piece by a local journalist reveals. Its title is 'Involuntary Walruses'.]

The door was opened by a man in a coat. 'I don't advise you to take off your coat,' he said. 'The gas burners are lit, and there is an electric fire on, but that's not enough to heat up the frozen walls. . . .'

I had gone to A. Reve's flat in response to a letter, signed by many of the people in his block, No. 169 Kurashaiskaya Street. 'Our flats have not been heated for two years,' it read. 'Our children are often ill, and the adults don't find it exactly pleasant. And where haven't we sent our complaints to: the city council, the district council. . . .'

The year before last, Aktyubinsk Civil Aviation College, which owns the block of flats, accepted the completed building from the builders. As is normal, they entrusted the service of the block to the City Housing Board, and the appropriate document was signed by the deputy head of the college, the chief engineer of the Housing Board, the Kazakhstan Deputy Minister of Housing, and the USSR Deputy Minister of Civil Aviation.

This document stated: 'Central heating in the building: 100 per cent. Hot water supply: 100 per cent.' In fact, this was complete hogwash (100 per cent).

The communal services workers claim they did not receive enough money from the College to service the building properly. In such cases it is normal to ask the State Arbitration Agency to help. But the deputy head of the Aviation College's accommodation department preferred 'not to involve himself'. (He lives somewhere else.)

Alas, the 150 families in block No. 169, Kurashsaiskaya Street are not the only 'involuntary walruses'. No. 20, Moldagulovaya Street: indoor temperature – 4 degrees. No. 2, Proletarskaya Street: heating turned off.

'We don't have the parts, the mechanisms,' say the head of the City Housing Board and the Chief Engineer, trying to justify themselves. The reason, however, lies above all in the laxity and low discipline of workers in various services of the Housing Board. Absenteeism and lateness have become almost the norm here: in a single year more than a thousand working days are lost. *[1 March 1983]*

[There are three ways to have a flat repaired or redecorated, according to *Pravda*'s correspondent in Ufa, capital of the autonomous republic of Bashkiria. The local service agency can do a decent job, but they lack the basic materials and facilities; the city Housing Board also do repairs, but they were allocated only '1½ tonnes of whitewash, five bathtubs, two mixer-taps, ten sinks, and not a single square metre of wallpaper' for a whole year (and that in a city of a million inhabitants). In any case they have too much other work on their hands to care about repairs; in six months they repaired only 300 flats. The citizen is left with the third way – to do it himself.]

The third way. This begins with trips to the shops in search of materials – whitewash, floor varnish, glazed tiles, linoleum, wall-paper. All of these things are in very short supply. People who manage to buy them consider themselves to be very fortunate. But they are a minority. This year the *Khozmebeltorg* shop got in only 1,700 taps, although they asked for 10,000, and only half the required quantity of wallpaper and one-third of the whitewash. And it is a struggle to wrest even this meagre amount from the suppliers.

And so, just when you are about to give it all up as a bad job, worn out from hunting down scarce goods, a knock comes at the door. A polite man offers to upholster your doors.* 'Thirty roubles! Quality guaranteed!' 'Do you need new wallpaper, or new tiles in the bathroom? That's no problem, we will help you!' And they do help. And they do a lot of it. Several times as many flats are repaired and redecorated by these enterprising moonlighters as are by all the [official] specialised organisations put together.

Furthermore, the moonlighters do not experience any difficulty in getting hold of the building materials, tools, and so on. All this they buy up in bulk from the shops, or simply filch from building

*The main doors of Soviet flats are commonly upholstered with padding and leatherette.

sites. And hundreds of thousands of roubles, which the public could be paying to the state, goes instead to line their pockets.
[30 August 1985]

[Modern blocks of flats are built in groups, or 'micro-districts' (*mikrorayony*), theoretically equipped with all the shops, services and amenities required for everyday living. Each 'micro-district' has its own school, kindergarten and nursery. Normally it is situated near a main road, but within the 'micro-district' itself there are only narrow lanes, for access by car or on foot.

Sociologists made a comparison of life in two of Moscow's 'micro-districts' – Belyayevo, a well-established district, though not particularly old; and Yasenevo, a popular, fast-growing new area. Their findings were published in *Pravda*.]

Yasenevo has the advantage over Belyayevo that its flats are modern and better planned. Another important feature is that it has a greater proportion of young people among its inhabitants, who are keen to make use of any public services that are available – laundries, dry cleaners, repair shops for domestic appliances, and so on.

Yet only 21 per cent of those questioned in the new micro-district [Yasenevo] said they made use of laundries, while 49 per cent in the older district used them. Only 23 per cent of those polled in Yasenevo used dry-cleaning facilities, whereas 74 per cent used them in Belyayevo.

The reason for this is the lack of essential services. At the time of the research there were few domestic services and good shops in Yasenevo. To obtain such services and do their shopping, people had to travel into the city centre. And that is a long journey, using a poorly developed public transport system. Yasenevo's nearest metro station is at Belyayevo, to which it is linked by only a few overcrowded bus routes. The people of Yasenevo spend an average of three to four hours per day travelling to work, college, or for other reasons.

This is a most serious problem. The inhabitants of the new micro-district waste a considerable part of their free time. Hence the alienation among them, which is caused not so much by their personal qualities as by their conditions of life.

According to our survey, some 58 per cent of the population in the established district spent most of their free time at home, while in the new district the figure was even higher – 72 per cent. And yet the population of Yasenevo is much younger, as we have said, and therefore in principle more 'communicative'. Naturally, people would always find an hour or two to spend in a club, or library, or in some sport or leisure group, where there is company, and interesting activities. But in the new micro-districts there are usually none of these things.

The conclusion would appear to be obvious: *all* aspects of development must be borne in mind. Every deviation from the integrated development plan is a cause of annoyance, whether it is an unbuilt kindergarten or shop, cinema or laundry, or an open foundation pit, or rubbish left lying around after construction work is over.

How does the public envisage the model micro-district? Above all, they want comfortable homes, with an extensive complex of social, cultural and sports facilities. And these should not be scattered around, but concentrated in a sort of economic and cultural centre. Such centres are planned for new micro-districts in many cities, but too often they remain on paper.

A good 'micro-climate' depends largely on the pulse of social life. During our investigations in Yasenevo, however, this pulse was pretty sluggish. And here is one impartial index of this: a large proportion of the population, according to their responses to our questionnaire, encounter hooliganism and other social disturbances. This is bound to cause concern. There were only half as many complaints of this in the older district. There people find themselves less often in stress situations – long waits in queues in shops, fighting to board packed buses – and have more opportunities for civilised leisure activities. [. . .]
[2 March 1982]

[The above article was part of a series published throughout 1982 under the title 'The micro-climate in the micro-district', to which journalists and readers contributed. Among the issues raised was the feeling of insularity and alienation experienced by many flat-dwellers. The vast majority of Soviet townspeople live in blocks of flats, and this has brought unexpected problems into a society which is collectivist not so much by political decree as by tradition. The following contribution to the 'micro-climate' debate came from a reader in Alma-Ata, capital of the Republic of Kazakhstan.]

I'm not the only one to have noticed this: arriving at work, you hear greetings all round – 'Hello!' 'Good morning!' Warmth and cordiality everywhere. People are united not only by their work, but also by strong feelings of comradeship. Yet half an hour earlier, as you are leaving home, the atmosphere is quite different, I'm afraid. Neighbours, living in the same block, in the same micro-district, walk to the same bus-stop, and most of the time don't even exchange greetings. Why should that be?

One sometimes hears it said that self-contained flats disunite people. A great many multi-storey apartment blocks are put up every year; but the people moving into new areas are in no hurry to get to know one another. Can it be that separate flats – that social benefit which has been sought after for decades – have a negative side to them: that they set people apart?

It is not an idle question. Soviet man is a collectivist, who knows from his experience – togetherness makes life jollier and problems easier to solve. And there are no few problems.

Take our children. One feels sorry for them. A year ago the youngsters of our micro-district got into an almighty brawl. There have been instances of a motorbike or a car being stolen. Last autumn a group of ten-year-olds climbed through a kindergarten window: they thought they would try some fruit juice! But that is theft . . . !

It seems that in our efforts to care for our children we forget the most important thing – the collective care of neighbours and passers-by for our youngsters. But how can we achieve that if the grown-ups hardly see each other?

Surely it would not be a bad thing if we were to spend our leisure time together, in an interesting, fruitful way? As it is, it is only the young people who play on the volleyball pitches, never adults; and handymen do their sawing and soldering in their kitchens. Why not do it in a workshop, which would surely be easy enough to set up in the basement? I'm afraid the most 'sociable' people in our micro-districts are often those who like to get together over a bottle.

The yard, as they say, is an extension of the home. It is not hard for the occupants of an apartment block to improve the surrounding area – by planting flower-beds, or preparing a space for games and other recreations. But what is our attitude? The flat is our responsibility, it's nice and comfortable – and the Housing Office can look after everything else.

Naturally, the municipal workers and local councils are not idle onlookers. But at the same time, some of the streets in our micro-district are impassable in rainy weather unless you wear gum-boots, and there is no lighting on Ushakov Street, Rudnev Street, Artem Street, Gaidar Street, and others. For more than a year now there has been a gaping foundation pit, full of dirty water, in the middle of the housing scheme; if it were cleaned up and planted with grass, it would make a marvellous recreation area.

There is no polyclinic nearby, nor cafeteria, nor any basic services. The people waste masses of time queuing and travelling all over town, when they could be spending it reading, going to the cinema, doing something interesting outside or in the company of others with similar interests.

Thinking of how to solve these problems brings me back to the contrast between groups of residents and work collectives. How are these questions dealt with at work? A collective agreement is discussed, possibilities and priorities are weighed up, and the management and work-force take on mutual commitments. So why can't residents and their Housing Offices conclude 'social agreements' – on what they can do by themselves, and what they require help for? But before this can be done, people have to meet their neighbours. Residents' meetings are infrequent, and usually boring. Sometimes residents don't even turn up at them – and this is why: serious questions are discussed, and suggestions made, but nothing is done about them. The meeting breaks up, and things are left to take their old course.

So what is my personal position on this? It seems to me that very little can be done alone. We need to get together. Come on, neighbour, let's get to know each other!
[1 February 1982]

[A more serious problem, affecting town and country alike, is alcoholism. The following hard-hitting article took the form of a review of *Pravda*'s mailbag on the subject.]

We are not afraid to speak out loud about drunkards, and that is as it should be. Our newspapers print articles about them, and radio stations broadcast warnings. The price of an overnight stay in a sobering-up station is going up. And yet there is no reduction in the use of vodka.

There are queues for the restaurants; orders for weddings,

jubilees, or promotion banquets are taken many weeks in advance. And if you try to order a table without vodka and other strong drinks, they won't accept it.

'The custom of giving bride-money,' writes R. Nurmuhamedov from Samarkand [Uzbekistan], 'still survives, though it has been condemned a hundred times. Weddings here are accompanied by many days of celebration, often with the participation of the state farm or even district council bosses. And, what is worst, people cling to the view that unless you get all your guests blind drunk (and sometimes there are a hundred guests or more), then you are a bad host.' The same perception of a good and bad host is current in the North, too, according to a reader from the Arkhangelsk area.

Everyone agrees that dipsomania is an illness. So why is it that we always feel sorry for invalids, but merely despise drunkards? After all, is there anyone who is glad that he drinks, glad that his hands shake, that children run away from him, that he has to beg for a few kopecks to buy a bottle of hawthorn syrup, so as not to die from the unbearable tightening of his arteries? Where is the person who would enjoy being in such a state? The wife growing old before her time, the downtrodden, retarded children – nobody benefits.

'I know what should be done with alcoholics,' writes a woman from Magadan categorically. 'Women have the right to leave their drunken husbands. And so they should! What trouble I had with mine: I even forced him to sign up for work over here on the Kolyma River [in the Far East] to get him away from his mates, but he just carried on the same as ever. Then I left him, for the sake of the children (I have three). I forbade him to come to our house, and though he fell at my feet I stood firm. My children grew up, and each now has his own family, flat and car. They respect me, invite me to visit them and even to live with them. When they were still young I told them their father was dead. To this day he still drinks away all his money and sleeps in garrets. Now he himself probably wouldn't dare tell his children that he is their father. And they wouldn't believe him. If he ever asked them for money for a drink, they would not give him it. I have brought them up to hate alcoholics too.'

Without comment, let us compare that letter with another, also from a woman, but unsigned.

'My husband used to get so drunk that the militia would pick him up. He would come home without a kopeck. But I always had faith that he would see reason. Now he says that without me he would never have pulled through. We went through it all – arguments, tears, deceiving the children ("Don't go near Dad, he's tired, let him sleep"). And the terrible screams in the night when he imagined somebody was trying to smother him. . . . I thought of sending him for treatment, but everywhere you looked there were cases where treatment had not helped, where the people had sunk even lower afterwards. I went to the militia, and applied for a divorce, but then decided to try "once more". I cursed myself for being weak and called myself a fool, but now I am glad I saw it through. Nowadays I am trying to restore his standing in our children's eyes. And do you know the most important thing? Many of those with whom my husband used to have his binges, far from laughing at him, are actually following his example. . . .'

It is hard to overrate this woman's actions. To force oneself to love again the father of one's children, to forget his unattractiveness – only a woman strong in spirit, loving, capable of enduring almost unbearable suffering in order to save a man, could do that.

This complex illness can be cured only if the ill person himself desires it. If he has given himself up, no amount of treatment will help. The first and most important thing is to inspire him with that desire. And that requires the patience and help of his wife, comrades and work-mates.

There is something else I would like to say. Sometimes one is ashamed of those popular singers who literally stupefy young people with their debauching songs: 'The clash of swords, like the clink of glasses, has caressed my ears since I was a kid(!)' or 'Let's make hay while the sun shines – a girl, a glass, and a happy blade. . . .' (In other words, primitive love, drunkenness, and fighting.) Such songs, sung, moreover to the beat of drums, poison the mind.

All sorts of ways out of the situation are proposed in our mailbag. Some suggest severer measures against alcoholics, including compulsory treatment (this is already done, by the way, but to little effect). Many readers advise that sales of vodka should be limited to certain hours and to specialised shops. There are special television programmes about alcoholism, but, as some readers note, they tend to be accusing towards alcoholics instead of treating them as ill. More and more snack-bars selling vodka are opened (our trading organisations are always keen to do that). A beer-bar may even be opened next to a school or kindergarten (for example, school No. 773 in the Lyublino district of Moscow). Vodka is more expensive in the bars than in shops, so 'three-man collectives' are formed [to share a bottle], usually beside children's play areas and stadiums, at the entrances to blocks of flats, or in cafés. . . .

Drunkenness has reached such a pitch that machines stand idle in factories, and building-sites come to life not on Mondays but on Tuesdays, and fall silent on Fridays. On pay-days women stand waiting for their husbands at the factory gates to stop them drinking away their earnings.

Receipts from vodka sales are considerable. But the damage it causes, as economists have calculated, far outweighs the revenue. Count up the days of work lost, the fall in productivity, the sick-leave of drunkards, paid for by the trade unions. Add to that the cost of crimes committed by drunks, the premature ageing of wives and mothers, the orphaned children. What more proof do we require of the need to fight the infection by all means possible?
[11 December 1982]

[The following letter, purportedly from a Saratov worker, R. Goryunova, was printed in March 1985, just two weeks before the Politburo announced that stringent measures were to be taken to combat drunkenness and alcoholism. The letter foreshadowed many of the measures later adopted, and indeed its headline, 'Sobriety – the Norm of Life', became the motto of the whole anti-drink campaign.]

Yesterday was a fairly ordinary day. Everything went well at work, and there was nothing to annoy me at home. But nonetheless I felt up-tight and jaded. I had been unsettled, and my mood spoiled, by drunks.

I bumped into one of them in our factory yard. Wobbling along on rubber legs.

'Aren't you ashamed? Other people are working, and you. . . .'

'Whassol the noise about? Bugger off!'

I felt sickened. What on earth is happening? These soaks have grown impudent!

Then after work last night when I went into a shop I was completely put out. There was a great crowd around the wine counter, all shoving and swearing. I tried to intervene and reason with them to behave themselves decently. Some hope! They just told me to shut up . . .

And so I decided to write this letter. I cannot keep silent any longer. How much longer are we going to put up with drunkenness?

Above all, of course, it is the drinkers themselves who suffer: they lose their health, their prestige, their families. At the same time they do enormous damage to society, and production. Here is a simple example. Suppose just one worker fails to turn up at an assembly line producing fridges. Fifteen to twenty minutes pass before a replacement is found. Not much, you might think, but in that time 40 to 50 fridges could have been produced. Or say a fork-lift truck driver doesn't deliver materials to the shop on time: he was 'busy' looking for booze. And again production has to stop. Many alcoholics, after a hard binge, work a couple of days and are then off 'sick' for a long time.

And how much sorrow they bring to those around them. I remember an incident at our enterprise. A lift-truck driver who wasn't sober ran into a worker. The driver was put in the dock, and lost his job as head of the lift-truck department. But even the severest punishments will not bring back to life the man who died as a result of this dreadful incident. Drunkenness causes family dramas, official misconduct, and hooliganism. Spirits burn up a man's moral principles, make him stupid, and deaden his higher feelings.

At our factory a good deal is done to fight against this vice. Last year the number of cases of absenteeism and public order offences fell considerably. I know quite a few people who have given up alcohol and have not drunk for five to seven years. But still progress is not so gratifying that one can relax. Suffice to say that in 1984 hundreds of our workers spent time in the sobering-up station.

What is wrong, then? I am firmly convinced that preventive work is still carried out very feebly. You don't have to look far for the facts. A welder called Aksyonov works in our workshop. He carouses, and has brawls in his family. Recently he came to work after a three-day drinking session, and his hands were shaking. And what did management do about it? They deprived him of his bonus payments and told him to come to his senses. And that was that.

Sometimes at meetings efforts are made to take the drunkards in hand and stricter penalties are proposed, but usually some soft-hearted ones make a different suggestion: let's give them one last chance, let's not take drastic measures. The fitter Uranov ended up in the sobering-up station last year. His behaviour was discussed at a trade union meeting, which took a decision to . . . give him a public reprimand. Katyshev, who works machine punch, for the same misdemeanour was given nothing more than a warning by the shop-floor council for the prevention of offences. These 'measures' yielded no results whatsoever.

One may ask: why not dismiss workers like these? But they will only drink in some other collective instead. You may say: there is a way out – send alcoholics to the work-and-treatment clinic. But here too there is no certainty of a successful outcome, because the drunkards still carry on drinking. The work-and-treatment clinic is inside the city limits, and it is no great problem to get hold of liquor. These clinics, in my view, if they are set up at all, then they should be far from the vodka counters. It is essential to create an atmosphere in them that can be of real help. At the moment we are a long way from that.

Conditions for drinkers should be made unbearable everywhere, and the worst offenders should be excluded from the trade union. It is impermissible that drinking bouts – as often happens – are logged as 'earned' days off, or repayment for overtime, or visits to villages or building-sites sponsored by the firm. From whom are we hiding the evil?

Many of the people who run shops and public eating places deserve a severe reproach. Sometimes it is hard to find milk or soured cream in the shops, but there is any amount of wine and vodka. On Tverskaya Street there is a café which, aptly, in my opinion, is popularly known as the 'Three Piglets'. This is why. They drink [vodka] straight from the bottle there. Near the house where I live, on Zagorodnev Street, a private sale of vodka starts up after seven each evening, at ten roubles a bottle. And nobody gives a damn about it.

Go into my food shop, and you'll see various wines and brandies on sale from early morning till late in the evening. In specialised shops you can buy vodka under the counter even after closing-time. . . .

How do the militia and voluntary patrols react to all this? After all, it is their job to keep order and put a stop to infringements of the law. Alas, it has to be admitted: the men in militia uniforms often turn a blind eye to these disgraceful scenes.

Like other mothers, I am particularly worried by the fact that so little care is taken to protect juveniles from the alcoholic environment, with its pernicious effect on the unformed minds of boys and girls, who sometimes start drinking and smoking out of blind imitation.

In Saratov many people know about the jogging club, which has over 200 members. It is noteworthy not just because it is invigorating and healthy, but also because all its members are teetotallers. For several years now they have celebrated New Year and other holidays in their own way: first in the woods (in winter on skis), then in the sports hall. Instead of bottles of vodka and wine they have mineral waters and fruit-juices on the meal-table. This initiative deserves to be supported and spread in every way.

I have heard of teetotallers' clubs in Gorky, Dnepropetrovsk, and Nizhny Tagil. They don't just have conversations there about the evil of alcohol – they organise sensible leisure activities, hold interesting events, and are reviving the old customs of dry celebration meals. And what talents are found in the people! One is a fascinating raconteur, another is a dancer, a third sings satirical songs. . . . And what groups and choirs are formed! It's a pleasure to hear them. I am certain that you only need to get rid of this alcoholic drug, and people will start going to the houses of culture and clubs. Amateur arts, technical clubs, and art and craft circles will gain a new impulse. It's obvious that a sober head has sober, cultured interests.

At present, however, I'm afraid we have no few other 'traditions' which we must decisively get rid of. Take school-leavers' parties – they're never held without spirits these days. There is a custom among factory foremen to celebrate their workers' first pay-day, or birthdays, with a bottle – at the work-place. Tipsy people walk through the entrance gates, and nobody challenges them.

This is no coincidence, I think. Some managers see nothing shameful in holding official 'celebrations', banquets and other 'comradely' binges, under any pretext. People know about these 'customs' and copy them blindly. I believe we should clamp down harder on such liberties, and especially on Party members, whatever post the lover of the bottle might hold. It is probably necessary to think of new rules which would allow this work to be carried out to greater effect.

And can it be normal that there is rarely a movie without a drinking scene? And this is often shown with great relish. One never ceases to be amazed at what the talent of directors and actors is channelled into.

There exists a Decree of the Russian Federation's Supreme Soviet on measures to step up the fight against drunkenness and alcoholism, and other laws, but the situation is not improving. The point seems to be that the laws are by no means always applied in practice. Nor do they particularly affect those who carouse, or show indulgence towards the consumption of alcohol in public places, or encourage under-age drinkers.

To be quite frank, I am deeply convinced that the time has come for a sharp reduction in the production and sale of spirits. Sobriety should become a norm of our life. The sooner the better.
[23 March 1985]

[The following contribution to the anti-drink campaign, a letter from A. Yegorov, deputy editor of a local newspaper in Kazakhstan, is a good example of *Pravda* at its patronising, scoutmasterish worst. The headline was 'What fun the wedding was'.]

They had a wedding at the Tyumen-Aryksky state farm – a joyful, jolly affair. The traditional *dastarkhan* [sheet spread out on the ground, serving as a table] greeted the guests with abundance: Kazakh national dishes, heaps of golden pastries, and *tapanan* pancakes. The painted cups were filled with fruit-juices, sparkling mare's milk *koumiss* and camel's milk yogurt.

When preparing for the feast, the groom's father, Abdrashit Zhapenov, a state farm herdsman, sought counsel with the whitebeards, the farm managers. The young couple had decided to celebrate their wedding without alcohol. It seemed rather strange. Still, they decided that the young people's idea was a good one.

The farm's Komsomol members applied all their skill and inventiveness to make the wedding a real celebration of youth and beauty. There were stirring dances and jaunty songs, and young bards competed with verses. . . . There were proverbs and choruses, semi-jocular eulogies of the bride and groom – it was all perceived as part of a fine tradition.

The guests were pleased, and the couple were splendid. Isakhan has served in the army and graduated from a telecommunications college; Gulnar is a teacher.
[23 September 1985]

[Linked to the problem of alcoholism is the question of crime, especially hooliganism, which, though less in evidence than in many Western countries, certainly exists, as a candid article by the USSR Procurator General, A. Rekunkov, demonstrates.]

The vast majority of citizens conscientiously obey Soviet laws. However, there are still those who have not acquired the habit of conforming to the law. Disorganisers of production, hooligans, drunkards, speculators, bribe-takers and thieves fill the Soviet people with indignation by their anti-social behaviour. In many letters sent to the central authorities, the working people justifiably point to the need to step up the struggle against those who violate work discipline and the rules of a socialist community, and to apply the force of the law against them quickly and consistently. Citizens are particularly worried by the unsatisfactory state of public order in certain towns and villages.

The Public Prosecutor's Office recently checked a letter from a group of residents in the Moskovsky district of Gorky, in which they complained about the state of public order and discipline there. 'It is often dangerous for us returning from work in the evenings,' they wrote. 'There are attacks on citizens and even on the *druzhinniki* [voluntary police helpers]. Many of these hooligans and rowdies go unpunished.'

These facts were confirmed. The local forces of law and order were lax in their fight against breaches of the law and ignored citizens' reports of hooliganism. The district prosecutor showed leniency, and was not sufficiently vigilant over the work of the militia. Several officials in the militia and prosecutor's office have been punished for neglecting their duties.

[9 January 1983]

[Rekunkov went on to outline measures taken to improve the work of the police in their fight against crime and anti-social behaviour. But another article, almost three months later, was equally critical of the police. Here, a Leningrad writer, Stanislav Rodionov, responds to a letter from a woman who complained that policemen often walk past drunks and hooligans without so much as a comment. 'Is that order?' she asked. 'Who is it that the police are supposed to be protecting?']

I too have seen many such scenes . . . Six men were standing near the wine store on the corner of Basseinaya Street and Gagarin Avenue. Their clothes were neither clean nor pressed. They were unsteady on their feet, and spoke loudly, using unprintable words. Then a militiaman appeared on the scene, and I thought, 'You've had it now, chaps,' for I was sure he would give them a good ticking off. The militiaman went up to them, and . . . shook the outstretched hand of one of the drunks. I thought: a local militia officer ought to know them all by sight, but to shake their hands . . . ? That, after all, is how one greets people one respects.

And how come six hooligans, drunk and disorderly, show not the slightest concern for a representative of authority? The answer is simple: the militia in some places have relaxed and lost their educative power, and exchange greetings with 'winos'. They should be dealt with according to the law: then they would not loaf about near shops in the middle of the working day, embarrassing people with their appearance and language.

[21 March 1983]

[In May 1982 the Central Committee of the Communist Party adopted a wide-ranging Food Programme which was intended to boost the country's agricultural output. Apart from massive investment in the farming sector and related industries (known in the Soviet jargon as the 'agro-industrial complex'), plus the introduction of new supervisory bodies in every district, the Food Programme laid great stress on improving the conditions of life in the countryside in order to stem the population drift – especially of young people – from the villages to the cities. Some of the following extracts illustrate why the concept of 'living in the country' is less idyllic in the Soviet Union than it is in the West.]

Our team, number seven, is based 20 kilometres from the centre of the state farm. We work on a livestock farm [part of the state farm], which has 94 milch cows. We have a lot of good pasture-land, a decent farmyard and cowshed. But the trouble is that when it rains in summer, and in spring and autumn, we often cannot get the milk to the collection point, which is four kilometres away, because the road turns into impassable mud.

The director of the state farm, Comrade Kapran, knows about this but does not take any action. This year again, the road is still unrepaired. Who is supposed to answer for this?

We don't have a shop. For bread we have to go to Chadkovo station, but even there not much bread is delivered, only for the railway workers. So often we have to drive more than 20 kilometres, to Lyubytino or Nebolchi – which takes a whole day.

Our electric power lines have broken down, and the [wired] radio hasn't worked for two years.

In the autumn of 1981 we wrote a letter to the Lyubytino district

Party committee, then to the regional committee. We have still not had a reply. And our letter was signed by 18 members of our team and two members of the Khirovo village council.

[Letter signed by A. Ponomaryov on behalf of his team-mates at 'Mstinsky' State Farm, Novgorod Region; 20 September 1982]

'How many kilometres is it from Staiki to Medenevichi?'

'Eight as the crow flies, but 40 by road.'

Staiki is the main village in the centre of the 'Lenin's Way' collective farm, in Brest region [Belorussia]. The above conversation could have been heard only two years ago. But now, an 8-kilometre surfaced road crosses the marshland between Staiki and Medenevichi.

The opening of the new road has transformed the village of Medenevichi. Houses are being refurbished, and the daily life of the collective farmers is improving.

I went to the 'Zarya' [Dawn] collective farm with the chairman of the Belorussian Collective Farm Building Organisation, A. Kichkailo. A 12½-kilometre road was recently built, linking the nearest main road to the farm. Before that, in bad weather the only way to reach the centre of the farm – the village of Podgornoye – was by landrover: it is surrounded by forests and marshes. And now we could see lorries from every republic here. They had come for the mushrooms which the farm produces in abundance every summer.

'We would have been left sitting with all our mushrooms and other fruits of the forest if they hadn't built the road,' remarked the farm's deputy chairman, V. Nesterovich. 'You should have seen how the people rejoiced when the first cars arrived!'

These villagers are lucky. They have now become part of 'the outside world', something which cannot be said of the inhabitants of many Belorussian villages.

An institute belonging to the Belorussian Ministry of Agriculture drew up an inventory of all the internal roads in collective and state farms. There turned out to be 120,000 kilometres of roads, but only 18,000 of these had a hard surface.

According to experts, transport costs in collective farms, state farms and districts which do not have good roads are two-and-a-half times higher than in those where surfaced roads have been laid. Fuel costs for vehicles using gravel roads are 70 per cent higher than for vehicles on surfaced roads, and on earth roads the costs are 150 per cent higher. The service period of vehicles which have to use these roads is reduced by forty per cent. During the bad weather in spring and autumn cars and buses get stuck in the mud. As well as all this, a large part of the harvest is wasted every year.

Of course, it is a very expensive business building roads. But the costs of 'roadlessness' are even higher.

Statistics cannot describe the social effect of this. The inhabitants of hundreds of large and small villages, cut off by the lack of roads, are deprived of the most essential conveniences. If someone falls ill or a fire breaks out, there is no point in waiting for the emergency services. Everyday services do not get through either. You have to go many kilometres on foot to buy even the most necessary items. As a result, the villages with no roads are emptying of people.

These problems are worrying the Belorussian Party Central Committee and Council of Ministers. They are being examined as an inseparable part of the Food Programme. Three main elements have been identified: the building of housing, cultural establishments and public amenities in the villages; the mechanisation of labour on the livestock farms; and the building of roads. The last point is given top priority – but one of the biggest headaches is the lack of building materials. [. . .]
[28 August 1985]

[Most families living on state or collective farms have private plots of land on which they grow fruit and vegetables and rear animals. The plots are small – normally only a few '*sotki*' (a *sotka* is one-fortieth of an acre) – but they are the most productive sector of Soviet agriculture. Official attitudes to the private plots have swung between hostility and encouragement throughout the years of Soviet power. At present the government is even encouraging town-dwellers to cultivate plots of land in the countryside – though there is no sign that faith in the ever-inefficient state and collective farms is wavering.

The following article is based on what the writer says is *Pravda*'s growing post-bag on the subject of private plots. One collective farmer asks for help: he and his wife wish to buy a piglet to rear on their plot, but the farm chairman refuses, saying they had the chance to buy one earlier and did not take it: 'It's too late now.' A retired teacher explains that she has inherited a cottage on a state farm; she wants to keep hens, turkeys and a piglet, but the farm management has given her only a third of the land which used to belong to the cottage, a patch too small to rear livestock on: 'I don't know if it becomes an old schoolmistress to go begging for a few more *sotki* – what would people think of me!' she writes. 'But on the other hand, is it right to live in the country and go to the town shops for food?'

A group of readers complains about the size of private plots and the difficulties of getting materials to put up a shed. They insist that they only want to feed themselves and are not thinking of selling what they grow. The reviewer mocks them for this: 'As if it is bad to provide one's daughter's family, living in the city, with pork or vegetables. Or as if it wasn't permitted to sell surplus milk to the neighbours or take it to the district market!'

A fourth letter is from a villager who keeps sheep but does not know how to shear them. He does not have the knack that people had in the old days, and modern shearing machines are unavailable.

The reviewer continues:]

The letters, of course, are all different, each concerned with its own problems. And perhaps they are not all equally correct. But their authors are unanimous in one thing: that personal plots are establishing themselves ever more firmly as an important additional source of food, that everywhere people are trying to participate with their personal labour in fulfilling the Food Programme approved by the Party – on collective and state farms, and also on their modest personal plots. [. . .]

Here is another letter. 'I am 28. My name is Gennady Rossikhin. I am a factory foreman. I used to live in Ivanovskoye village, Istra district, near Moscow, but now I have a well-appointed flat in the town of Dedovsk, in the same district. With me live my father, mother, wife and five-year-old son. My brother Aleksandr is in the army and will soon be coming home. We seem to have everything, but I believe that one essential thing is missing. Where we used to live we had a little plot, about three *sotki* [300 square metres], on which we grew potatoes, berries, apples, and kept rabbits. Now the old house is in ruins, the plot lies empty, and we live nearby in a multi-storey block. For several years now I have been asking the village council and Istra district council whether we could not work those cherished three *sotki* to which our hearts have been tied ever since childhood. Answer: you have no right. But these *sotki* are lying empty! Is that sensible? They tell me: 'If you're such an enthusiast and so keen on farming, you're welcome to move to the countryside.' But I can't leave the factory. It needs me, I'm useful there. And there are lots of us in the same situation. Soviet laws are just, and we deeply respect them, but if some article or other is obsolete and needs changing, why dally over it? The only garden plot the factory could offer me is way beyond Volokalamsk – two hours' journey from Dedovsk. Meanwhile, right next door, land is lying empty and getting covered with weeds. . . .'

To give a person a proper explanation and reply, and not palm him off with formal excuses, is always essential. To help young people like Gennady Rossikhin to start up a personal garden plot means enriching and embellishing their leisure, their lives, and of course it means obtaining extra hundredweights of vegetables, potatoes and meat – which is absolutely vital. It is not out of the question that some young townspeople will actually want to return to the country. But as for the right of a towndweller to devote his spare time to working on the land – that is indisputable.

There are more and more letters about personal plots. They convincingly confirm the vitality of the measures taken by our Party and government. The letters show that there are still frequent traces of those days, now gone, when the owner of a kitchen-garden or a hen-house was branded a capitalist, and a privately owned piglet was considered almost a sign of immorality. Now things are going the other way: soon people will probably condemn those who live in the country but go to town to buy meat and potatoes, cabbage, beetroot or onions. That is what will become immoral. The letters are a reminder of how great are the possibilities of personal plots, of how great their reserves are. But they also demand constant attention and unwearying care. Because in every district there are not only successes but also difficulties, which have to be overcome as and when they arise. And because behind every personal plot stands a personality, a person.
[16 May 1983]

Consumers

[The furious industrial expansion of the Stalin years provided the Soviet Union with the foundations of a modern economy: electric power, dams, iron foundries, heavy industry. Since then, successive Soviet leaders have stressed the need to develop the production of consumer goods. The population, it was felt, needed at last to see some fruits from their hard labour, and they were becoming more and more aware (and envious) of the flourishing consumer society in the West.

As far as most household articles and leisure goods are concerned, the Soviet Union still lags some twenty years behind the West, both in quality and range, and in 1985 a special programme was adopted which aimed to bring Soviet consumer goods up to world levels.

The following letters to *Pravda* illustrate the inability of the central planning agencies to respond to consumer demand. The first is from a design institute which cannot get hold of its most basic tools – pencils!]

There is a constant lack of pencils for sale in the shops of Tashkent [population 1,779,000]. The shop assistants always have the same answer: the manufacturers let them down. Whenever anyone from our Institute travels to another city on business, we beg him to try and find various items of stationery. But usually nobody brings anything, because there is a shortage of them everywhere. And anyway, no shop assistant would dare to sell one person, say, a thousand pens and pencils. Even if you did manage to persuade a store manager to sell them to you, just try to explain that to your head accountant: his instructions forbid him to accept receipts for goods over the value of 5 roubles.

[Letter from deputy director of a design institute in Tashkent, Uzbekistan; 17 March 1983]

In our small town more than half the population have private plots. They keep rabbits, goats, piglets and cows. All this, it would seem, is good, useful, and necessary. But feeding individually-owned livestock is not so simple. This year the grass grew so fast it was possible to cut it several times in the summer. We could make hay at the sides of the roads, in ditches, on marshes, and in the forest plantations. But what are we supposed to mow it with? There are no scythes or sickles in the shops either of our town or of any nearby town. Three households have to share one sickle.

Then the grass has to be transported home – and there's the next catch. What can we carry it on? Bicycles have not been on sale for many years. And what happens if you try to buy a small or medium-sized motorcycle on credit? They tell you: 'We do sell motor-cycles on credit, but only after they have been in the shop for three days!' But after three days there is nothing left: they are all bought up.

[Letter from reader in the Ukraine; 15 August 1982]

I recently bought a three-litre samovar, made at the 'Shtamp' factory in Tula,* in an ironmonger's shop in the village of Makhmudly. The very first day, the tap began to leak. Within a week the plastic handles on the lid cracked with the heat and fell apart, so that now you can't lift the lid.

Perhaps I wouldn't have bothered writing about such a trifle. But the 'Shtamp' factory is supposed to have 'improved' the old model of their samovar, and even won a Mark of Quality for it. At the same time its price went up by almost 15 roubles. And now look at the kind of workmanship being sold! Everyone who bought a samovar in our ironmonger's at the same time as I did is complaining about it.
[Letter from reader in Azerbaijan; 3 November 1981]

It is difficult to buy ordinary writing paper in the shops. On the other hand you can buy all sorts of 'writing sets', with brightly ruled sheets, and various vignettes and ornaments in the left-hand corner. It is bad enough writing a letter on them, they are so pretentious and vulgar, but an official application is impossible.

These articles are produced by the Perm paper factory. One wonders why they cannot produce ordinary writing paper as well as their colourful sets? Apparently that would not suit the Perm papermakers: ordinary paper costs only a few kopecks, so it is more profitable to cover it with drawings!
[Letter from a reader in Moscow; 14 October 1982]

[As if shortages were not enough, customers have to put up with unhelpful, bad-mannered shop-assistants, as the next article shows.]

I recently observed the following scene in a shop. In a small department, partitioned off by a counter, a new, highly popular article appeared on sale: a non-stick frying-pan. A specimen frying-pan was displayed in a cabinet behind the salesgirl's back, and it was hard to see it. People would come up to the counter, have a look round, and go away. Then one sharp-sighted customer spotted the new utensil and asked to see it more closely. There came a shower of questions from others too: 'What is this wonder-pan?' 'Show it to us,' 'Put it on the counter, or at least let us see the specifications.'

---

* The town of Tula has long been famous for its samovars.

And how did the shop-assistant react?

'If I put it on the counter it will nicked in no time. And as for the specifications, they're inside the boxes and we don't have any spares.'

I am sure that many readers will recall something similar from their own experience. You ask the assistant a question, and he replies grudgingly, and monosyllabically: 'Yes,' 'No,' 'Don't know.' And yet, the ability to deal with people, to hold a businesslike discussion, is the most important qualification for anyone working in the service sector.

Here is another scene, witnessed recently in the Moscow shop 'Biryusa'. A young couple were buying cloth for curtains. Having chosen their fabric, they asked the assistant to cut the required length. But just as the last snip of the scissors was made, the young woman exclaimed: 'Oh, I'm sorry, we'd forgotten that when you hang the curtains, you have to match the pattern. We've taken a bit extra, but probably not enough. Could you cut another piece for us?'

'You should have thought of that earlier. I've already cut it. Who's going to buy that?'

The young couple were about to admit defeat when another junior assistant entered the conversation. 'Just a minute,' she said, taking the cloth and laying it out on the table. 'Let's try matching the pattern. How much do you need? Eight metres. But here you've got eight-and-a-half. That will be quite enough to match up the pattern, you know.'

A conflict was avoided; a purchase took place. The shop received 119 roubles. But it could have received a complaint. So you see, good service and commerce go hand in hand.

[2 October 1982]

[And the shortages, it seems, may even be contributing to Russia's low population growth. . . . The following letter came as part of a discussion about what size of family is advisable.]

I have three children – a boy aged twelve, a girl of six, and baby Anya, who is not yet one year old. I have plenty of work to do with them around. We live in a house with few amenities. Most of the houses on our street are old and tumbledown. Eventually, of course, they will be knocked down and new, well-appointed ones will be built. But when will this be? My neighbours are thinking twice about adding to their families. And the years are passing by.

There are other problems too. I have a large family, but washing-machines are not to be found in Zaporozhye's shops. I find it hard to believe that our industry is incapable of producing the required number of washing-machines. A washing-machine or a sewing-machine is not just a trifle – and this is a social problem, not a technical one. As for a good self-service laundrette, such as I have seen in other towns – that is just a dream.

We don't lead a particularly rich life-style, but our children have toys and books. It's not necessary, I feel, to shower them with expensive things. I don't want to turn them into little aristocrats.
[From V. Veshchikova, Zaporozhye, Ukraine; 4 March 1985]

[So what can be done to help Soviet consumers? The following review of letters to the editor, entitled 'What's in the shop today?', includes a stream of readers' complaints together with their analysis of some of the reasons for the shortages. Note that, although a number of remedies are put forward, the selected letters skirt round the one solution which almost all Western economists would suggest: allowing the free market to become the vital link between producer and consumer.]

The rigidity of the plan and the fluctuations of consumer demand: sometimes these are seen as incompatible concepts, as opposites. Nonetheless they co-exist in the field of trade. On the one hand, both the production of consumer goods and the turnover of money in the shops are regulated by the plan. On the other hand, we are free to use our pay, our ready money, to buy or not to buy the goods on sale. So we don't touch the unattractive articles that lie gathering dust on the shelves, and at the same time we wear ourselves out in queues for the notorious scarce goods.

How can the plan be reconciled with consumer demand? This problem, which has been discussed in our regular feature, 'Industry – Trade – The Customer', is one which concerns our readers. Many people have written to us about it. The letter-writers not only analyse the present situation, but also put forward proposals as to how to improve the supply of goods to the population.

The same idea runs through many letters: the plans of the manufacturers of these goods and the plans of the retailers often do not match the demands of the population. As A. Kirillov from

Syktyvkar correctly points out, these plans are not scientifically based. He explains: 'The plans do not always include the things that people queue up for in the shops. Year in, year out, the articles that customers are interested in are not produced in sufficient quantities or variety.'

'I am writing to you from Pyarnu on the Baltic coast, where I am on holiday,' says G. Shevtsov. 'I have just sent a parcel of nails home to Tolyatti. And it's not just in my home town that nails are scarce. There was a woman sending off a parcel of nails at the same time as me. Where do you think she was sending them to? To Magnitogorsk, the capital of the iron industry. How do local industries devise their plans? Why do they not ensure that nails of every size are available in every town?' 'Can it be right that knitting needles, darning needles, drawing pins, refills for pens, and flat enamelled dishes are in such short supply? All these items are unobtainable here in Odessa,' writes I. Milgram. F. Tertychny writes from Makeyevka about the shortage of batteries, pens, and jam-jar lids.

The USSR State Planning Committee and other central bodies are responsible for the planning of only the most important and complex goods. The work quotas of factories producing millions of other articles are expressed only in terms of money: which articles they produce is regulated by contracts with the trading organisations. Here the plans lose their rigidity, and become more elastic. It is not so much demand which determines their content, as various 'objective' factors – hold-ups in supplies of materials and parts, difficulties involved in putting new ideas into production, and so on. Expressed in terms of money, a factory may appear to be up-to-date with its plan or even overfulfilling it. But what are the results of the work 'in real life', as it were? 'That concerns very few of us here,' complains D. Sattarova, a factory worker from Kazan. 'Our pay and bonuses are dependent on the amount of raw materials, energy and semi-manufactured products we use up. It is advantageous to produce expensive articles, which use a lot of material. "Gross figures" are all that matter.'

Anyone who goes into a shop can see the consequences of the 'gross figures' approach to planning. 'It is assuming the proportions of a natural disaster', says G. Sivak from Dnepropetrovsk, 'when our shops are being stocked with dowdy jackets made from poor-quality material. No one wants to buy them.' 'You know,' says V. Petrenko of Bryansk, 'I get the impression that it suits everyone to produce unmarketable goods. Industry manages to fulfil its plan without much effort, and so does the retailer: he sells the goods, if only at half-price; and the customer, too, gets the goods – not when they first come out, but cheaply, at least, by waiting for the price to come down. But this is economics back to front! It should only be profitable to produce goods which are in "hot" demand.'

A matter of even greater concern to our readers is the shortages and the fact that you never know what will become scarce tomorrow. Here is a letter from I. Didenko in Kemerovo. 'Towels have not been on sale here for several years, and cotton and linen fabrics have disappeared. You can only find dresses, underwear, stockings and socks made from synthetic materials. In the shops there are no spare parts for domestic appliances, you can't even get vinegar essence or baking soda.' P. Dementyev, a veteran of the Great Patriotic War from the village of Gordeyevo in Altai province, has had his name down for a washing-machine for three years now. A. Kashkina of Barnaul cannot buy sandals for her children, or a coat for herself. 'There are five of us in our family,' she writes. 'Money is tight, but even when you save up to buy something you really need, it is no joy to go the shops: there are plenty of goods there, but nothing worth buying.'

There is a steady improvement in the availability of clothes, footwear and household items. The customer is becoming more discriminating in his choice of goods. The impossible question being posed is: where can I get what I need? Can industry and trade carry on working in the same old way, given these conditions? The answer is simple: no. V. Sklyarov of Pyatigorsk, Ye. Kuznetsova of Sterlitmak, A. Polyakov of Kaliningrad region, I. Zinkovsky of Kiev, and other readers all believe that radical improvements are needed in the way that industry and trade are run, and in the economic mechanism, which is not yet geared towards the most important thing – satisfying the needs of the public. Yes, today there is no alternative but to stop planning in 'faceless' roubles, and to make *choice* the main priority.

Meanwhile the planning of the production and sale of consumer goods based on scientific study of the state of the market is still, according to F. Zevriyev, an economist from Alma-Ata, 'virgin territory'. It would appear that consumer demand *is* being analysed – thousands of specialists in trade and industry, including hundreds of doctors of science in research institutes, are all engaged in this. But the return is small. 'We need an effective interdepartmental coordinator to study demand,' says F. Zevriyev. 'This could come under the USSR State Planning Committee or the State Committee for Science and Technology, and its recommendations should be obligatory for all planners, manufacturers and trading organisations.'

Sh. Magomedov of Odessa develops this line of thought: 'Because demand is not properly studied, because of the lack of coordination between the wholesale organisations and industrial ministries, and because of gross miscalculations in the orders submitted by trading organisations, there have often been fluctuations in the production of electric irons, mincers, light-bulbs and other articles. Either there are too many on the market, or none at all. These ups and downs continue. Was it so long ago that there were queues for bed linen? Now the shops and warehouses are overflowing with it. It is high time production settled down at the optimum level.'

Many readers who have written about this have brought up the question of the personal responsibility of people involved at every level. 'It seems to me that the lack of punishment is the basic evil which gives rise to such disgraceful mismanagement,' writes L. Tsiryulnikov from Yessentuki.

It is also felt by some readers that more firms should have their own specialised retail outlets, so that they would have a better understanding of how the customer rates their goods. I. Vlasov, from the Komi Autonomous Republic, goes even further. He proposes that 'industrial-trade associations' be set up, which would both manufacture and sell their own goods. This, of course, is no easy matter. There have been gross miscalculations even in the organisation of specialised trade outlets. 'In Saratov,' writes K. Ionov, 'premises were provided for a shop run by the "Volzhanka" ["Volga Girl"] association, but in a year and a half they have still not sorted out the sale of light summer dresses and underwear. Even by the most modest estimate, some 2,000 roubles have been lost.'

To understand consumer demand right down to the finer details, and to make this the point of departure in formulating plans – this is the unanimous request in our mailbag. But perhaps it is more difficult to understand consumer demand than it is for weather-forecasters to make sense of cyclones and anti-cyclones? We have all heard about the vagaries of fashion. It is undeniable that the tasks facing the modellers, designers and technologists who have to put new ideas into production are considerable. Every article has to be attractive and right up-to-date. The difficulty should not be minimised.

However, to judge from readers' letters, trade and industry have simply been ignoring large sections of the population. Yet gearing your product towards a particular consumer group means opening up new, wider sales markets. 'We older people', writes M. Levin, a war and labour veteran from Moscow, 'have more modest requirements than the young ones. We only ask that things are durable, not easily stained, that the colours are muted, and that they suit our figures (one's shape changes with age).' How easy it ought to be to please such an obliging consumer. Yet he, and other readers too, claim that trade and industry are ignoring them, that it is almost impossible to get hold of suitable clothing and footwear.

I. Blazhchuk wrote to *Pravda* on behalf of 'large' men. 'Even in the "outsize" department of the Omsk department store, which ought to sell size 60–62, there are only empty shelves. I needed a raincoat, a winter coat, a suit, boots – so I wrote to the higher management of the trade organisation. Do you think I found an answer to my problems? Nothing of the sort, there is no need to look for help in that quarter – they just fobbed me off with formal replies.'

Every article has its own 'address', and nobody's requirements should be forgotten: neither the Siberian living in severe conditions, nor the southerner with his own national traditions, nor the amateur sportsman, nor the gardening enthusiast. Nor, of course, those people with low incomes – large families or pensioners living alone. N. Morozov of Kiev makes the following suggestion: that fashionable Soviet and imported goods, which are in great demand, should be sold in specialised 'luxury' shops.

V. Dyakov, a serviceman, raised an important problem in his letter. He bought two colour television sets in Yuzhno-Sakhalinsk, one after the other: both were defective and had to be returned to the shop. In Leningrad he bought an ultra-modern stereo radio. He went round three shops, and chose carefully. His 'top quality' machine worked for . . . precisely one hour. A stereo unit made in Riga, which he bought later, lasted even less time – only thirty minutes. Just one unlucky customer? But he is not alone. Many of our readers criticise the poor quality of radios, some fridges, and other domestic appliances. G. Oshin from Mogilyov believes that radical measures need to be taken in the struggle against defective goods. He and many others think that the quality control departments should be subordinated to the State Standards Committee instead of to individual ministries. They also point out that the administrative organs [i.e., courts, etc.] have the authority to stop defective goods from being produced. So what is holding things up? The whole range of penalties foreseen by the law for shoddy workers must be applied.

We have tremendous resources of raw materials in our country. And there is surely no shortage of talented designers, modellers and skilled workers. The 'Made in the USSR' stamp should be a guarantee of high quality, top fashion, and world-beating consumer-satisfaction, say N. Kadilov of Novosibirsk, M. Tsvetkov of Kaunas, A. Nikolayeva of Kuibyshev and I. Minchenko of Shakhty, Rostov region. If that is achieved, shopping will become a pleasure for everyone.

[21 August 1985]

We had to wait a whole month for our application to get married to be accepted. The fact was that the banqueting hall where our reception was to be held could only fit us in on 25 June – all other dates were already booked. It was no easy matter trying to get the ceremony at the register office to coincide with the reception date. Our application was eventually accepted at the Palace of Weddings on Leningradsky Avenue – after we had queued for over three hours. We had to queue for another hour and a half to order a taxi.

We really wanted to go on a honeymoon. It turned out that the demand was very high, but tickets scarce. Places on these tours are allocated once a month by the Moscow Travel Agency, and to get one we had to start queuing the night before. Then we had to stand in another queue to buy our return tickets. A few days later we got a phone-call from the Travel Agency. The Riga office had not accepted our hotel booking for the days we wanted. We had to cancel the trip.

Surely the Agency should have to honour its commitments to its customers? After all, you don't go on a honeymoon every year.

[Letter from O. Yurasov, an engineer from Moscow; 1 July 1982]

Inverted Comfort
A feuilleton by Yu. Kirinitsiyanov

I fell victim to an advertisement for comfort and speed, just like the other passengers on the Ilyushin-62 airliner which took off from Aktyubinsk for Moscow one frosty, sunny day.

There we were, flying along, looking forward to seeing the capital. Then came the announcement: fasten seatbelts for a landing in Ulyanovsk. Annoying, of course, but what could one do. . . . Moscow was in the grips of a blizzard.

All right. We landed in Ulyanovsk. The fact that there was nowhere to sit in the airport, or even put down your briefcase, and the fact that the cafeteria served up only a murky apology for coffee – all that was nothing. Soviet air passengers are the most hardened in the world. . . .

At about eight o'clock they announced the start of boarding. Excellent! We boarded. We sat for a while. And we got out. . . . Some of the weaker-willed ones started grumbling: other planes had just taken off for Moscow. But the information desk explained that the weather was changeable, and nothing could be done about it. The night was spent on a little stool begged from a tender-hearted cleaning-lady. Naturally, no proper seats were anticipated in the foreseeable future. Anyway, it was no great tragedy. In the morning boarding was announced. We got into the plane longing for it to take off . . . this time! And again, fears began creeping in. . . . We sat for an hour, two hours. . . . Wasn't it time we got out again? Especially since the airport radio was blabbering about 'weather conditions . . .', 'delays . . .', and 'we apologise for. . . .'

And suddenly a baritone voice rang out in the aeroplane: 'Citizen passengers! This is the captain speaking. I'm not going to apologise to you. We pilots are not to blame. We are sitting here because of the negligence of the airport workers. The weather is perfect, and the crew is ready to take off.'

What did we discover? The pilot, Captain N. Seifullin, had been requesting a towing tractor to pull the plane out to the runway ever since the previous evening.

In the morning a towing tractor was found, but no tow-rope with which to attach it to the aircraft.

The Ilyushin-62 had not been filled with water or nitrogen, and the passengers had to push up the boarding ramp themselves. Evidently the workers of Ulyanovsk airport had adopted the principle of self-service flying. But we had nothing with which to replace the tow-rope – unless we all took off our trouser belts and tied them together. Or used them for another purpose. . . . They say that in pre-Aeroflot times the belt was prescribed as a medicine – for lazy schoolchildren. But alas, it was we passengers who were given a good lesson. . . .

For several hours they hunted for the notorious tow-rope. Finally it was found nearby, at the pilots' training centre.

Our airliner gained height, pursued by the words, 'Delayed . . . because of weather conditions . . . we apologise for the . . .' But for some reason these polite words evoked a feeling of irritation.

It has not died away yet, that feeling, and I have to go back to Aktyubinsk. I grow nervous reading about 'speed and comfort'. I'm off to the railway station.

[20 January 1985]

The Economy

[The following front-page leading article (printed here in full) was entitled 'Taking account of the customers' wishes'.]

Every day tens of millions of people go shopping. Can they purchase everything they need? Are they always satisfied with the quality of goods? These questions are certainly not minor ones, for they bear directly on the interests, needs and demands of the Soviet people.

The shops offer customers a reasonable choice. Last year, for example, more than 316 billion roubles' worth of goods were produced in all. But in that case why do people often leave shops without having bought anything? The main reason is because industry still takes scant account of the changing market and consumer demand. Articles are often produced and ignored by the public, while production of goods which people actually want is erratic. The result is a glut of some items and shortages of others. This is what has happened, for instance, with footwear, especially children's: in a number of places shop shelves are either empty or packed with out-of-season goods. Measures are now being taken to increase production and improve the quality and choice of footwear.

Some consumer goods are unavailable because of mistakes made in compiling orders [to manufacturing enterprises]. And this happens largely because the level of study of the population's requirements is inadequate. Managers in commerce, industry and the planning organs must know precisely what kinds of article, and in what quantities, to produce today, in a year, in two years, in five years. Experience shows that where trade and industry work 'in unison', there is success. In Belorussia, for example, the trade organisations, together with the rural cooperatives and the ministries of local and light industry, carried out a comprehensive study and forecast of demand for various goods. Last year, as a result, dozens of articles for which there was no demand were taken out of production, while output of popular goods was greatly increased.

A key role in providing the population with goods lies with industry. Today, enterprises of all ministries are joining in this task. It must be made easier for them, together with the trade organisations, to react more quickly to changes in consumer demand. This was the subject of a letter from a group of USSR Supreme Soviet deputies which was published in *Pravda* under the title 'What shall we spend our pay on?' It raised the urgent question of improving the quality of goods being produced and of raising the standard of work of the trade organisations.

In order to satisfy the market more active and fuller use of local resources must be made, and managerial flexibility and initiative shown. The reserves of the cooperatives are great. But is proper use made of them everywhere? It is easier, of course, to send to the centre for goods than to exert efforts locally. In Armenia, for example, every second enterprise in the cooperative union fails to fulfil the plan, and in the Russian Federation last year a third of local enterprises did not cope with the plan. It is the duty of the local councils to improve their monitoring of the production of goods needed by the population.

People often waste a lot of time searching for what they need. Not all shops and services are open at times convenient for those who work during the day. Party, local government, trade union and management organisations must seek an improvement in trade and domestic services for working people, and develop services directly at the factory.

To speed the flow of goods from factory and farm to the market place much will depend on those who work in trade organisations. They should be able to defend customers' interests, and be more demanding towards industry as regards range and quality of goods and the dispatching of orders on time. Knowing how to make efficient use of available goods is also important, as is a deep knowledge of demand. And of course, the standard of service must constantly be raised. From year to year the work of shop assistants is growing more complex and diverse. Today more than a million different articles are on sale in the country's shops. It is clear that consultant-salesmen, commodity researchers and managers of departments and sections require more and more knowledge, skills and abilities, and that everywhere rational organisation of labour should be introduced and precision, order and good organisation be achieved.

It is the job of researchers into consumer demand to orient industry and services towards the production and sale of goods which are wanted. It is a barometer which should work constantly, taking in both the results of 'low-level' demand research and data from scientific-research institutions. Yet in a number of places this new service has still to come into its own. This is what happened in Kazakhstan, for example. On paper the research service here looks all right, and has a large staff, but in practice it has not yet become an integral part of planning and commercial work, and feedback is not great. It is weakly linked with industrial enterprises and advertising organisations. Workers in the field are waiting for well-founded recommendations and advice from the All-Union Scientific-Research Institute for the Study of the Demand for Consumer Goods and the Trade Market, and also from the coordinating councils.

There are a fair number of communists employed in industries connected with the production of consumer goods, and also in trade and in services. The most important duty of the Communist Party member is to make his work an example to others, to be sensitive to customers' demands, to observe discipline strictly, and to display a creative approach to his task.

Party organisations are expected to show constant concern for the fulfilment of plans in the production of consumer goods, the retail trade, and the services. To this end it is important to step up organisational and mass-political work in collectives, and to raise the responsibility of staff for carrying out their duties.

Preparing a worthy welcome to the 27th Congress of the CPSU, labour collectives in trade and services are competing to give a high quality of service and fuller satisfaction of people's requirements. And if people leave a shop satisfied with their purchase, and with spirits raised, then that is the best sign of appreciation of the collective's work and efforts.

[4 April 1985]

[This short article, entitled 'To Moscow for a besom?' deals with the over-centralisation of the Soviet economy and the resulting inability of local industries to respond to local needs.]

History has handed down to us a simple but instructive story of managerial practice. When kerosene ran out in the town of Okhansk in 1918, the local council immediately took the decision to lay in 6,000 . . . wooden torches to light government offices. Such a quick solution was found, perhaps, because at that time local government was still manned by not-very-literate people who didn't have thick address-books of Moscow offices, or direct-dial telephones.

Otherwise, they could have gone about it differently. As happened recently in Udmurtia, for example. When the local collective farms needed some ordinary packing fibre – in other words, the waste material from the flax which they themselves grow – the Balezino district council sent to Moscow for permission. And what happened? At first Moscow refused, and only after many months of red tape did they finally give back a wagonload of fibre which had been sent away from Balezino station. . . .

It is time to widen the managerial independence of local authorities and production units. Independence and responsibility are inseparable concepts. . . .

But it can often be quite different from this. Many items which people need can now be manufactured locally, but the local Party and government authorities prefer to send dispatches to the USSR Planning Agency or Supplies Agency, or to ministries and government departments, asking for this or that to be 'allocated' or 'supplied'. You should see the telegrams that go flying to Moscow! 'Send us gravel. . . . We need besoms. . . . There aren't any spoons or matches on sale here.' There is no end to this kind of helpless pleading.

As was noted at the November 1982 Plenum of the CPSU Central

Committee, 'It cannot be seen as normal that the question of producing a number of simple goods is decided virtually at the level of the USSR State Planning Agency. This task must be taken on by local authorities, who should be fully responsible for carrying it out.'

[During key periods in the farming year *Pravda* publishes a daily 'Agricultural Review' about country-wide progress in ploughing, sowing, mowing, harvesting, fodder-procurement, and so on. This Review appeared in August, when food shops ought to be brimming with seasonal produce. It explains why, in most places, they are not.

A brief (and greatly simplified) note about the 'bureaucracy' of food distribution may be useful here. State and collective farms are financially autonomous units, and *sell* their produce to the state. The produce goes first to a local procurement and marketing depot, which sends it out to consumers in urban areas – either to factories, flour-mills and so on, for re-processing, or to 'fruit and vegetable associations' (serving districts within cities) whose distribution depots send it the shops. In rural areas, buying, distribution and selling are carried out by 'consumers' cooperatives'.]

Nowhere are the hiccups in the food industry so clearly in evidence as in the supply of vegetables. This is borne out both by statistical information and by local reports. Compared with last year's figures, sales to the state of fruit and vegetables by 12 August were down by 56,000 and 299,000 tonnes respectively. Farms in the Ukraine, Uzbekistan and Moldavia, and in a number of regions in the Russian Federation, have been particularly disappointing in this respect. The situation is not good as regards the supply of fruit and vegetables to towns and industrial centres.

Often, poor-quality tomatoes, cucumbers, cabbages and marrows are dispatched to the shops. For example, the Ashkhabad marketing depot sent three wagon-loads of tomatoes to the town of Bakal in Chelyabinsk region. And what happened? Out of 47 tonnes, one-third had to be thrown away. The Kasan district cooperative society in Kashkadarya region 'rejoiced' the inhabitants of Irbit (Sverdlovsk region) with water-melons – half of which turned out to be unripe. Customers in the town of Pushkino near Moscow were also 'unlucky' when a refrigerated lorry from the 'Zapadny' state farm in the southern province of Stavropol arrived with a whole consignment of apples which were fit only for processing. One cannot help wondering why lorries are sent on fool's errands from one end of the country to the other.

Four railway wagons of spring cabbage arrived at the Aleksinsky district co-op in the region of Tula this summer. They had been sent from Gardabani in Georgia. Imagine the surprise when the doors of wagons No. 8734828 and 8734829 were unsealed, and there were no cabbages inside! The wagons were empty. And this is not an isolated incident. Empty wagons that should have contained cabbages were also sent to Tula, by Charkha and Lenkoran marketing depots in Azerbaijan. This cannot just be called mismanagement. . . .

The answer is not new; to avoid wastage, the path to the shop counters must be made as short as possible. The more points there are along the chain, the worse will be the condition of the fruit and vegetables when they arrive at the shops, and the more will be wasted. Unfortunately not everyone has accepted this simple truth. On 10 August barge No. ST-1302, bringing tomatoes from Astrakhan, dropped anchor at a jetty on the Moskva river. The tomatoes were bound for the Leninsky and Zelenograd fruit and vegetable associations. They were transported in an experimental type of polythene packaging, and arrived in excellent condition. To send the tomatoes straight to the shops where the customers were crying out for them would seem to have been the obvious thing to do. But alas, most of the tomatoes were sent to . . . distribution depots – which were already full to overflowing with tomatoes! At depot No. 1, more than 600 tonnes of tomatoes had accumulated, although no more than 20 tonnes are dispatched from there to the shops each day. It is not hard to imagine what state the tomatoes are in after a week's storage.

The situation is even more disturbing at the Volgogradsky [district] fruit and vegetable association in Moscow, where about 700 tonnes of tomatoes, almost 2,000 tonnes of potatoes and 260 tonnes of apples are 'waiting their turn' to be sent out to the shops.

And what is happening in the shops themselves? Moscow green-grocer's shop No. 20 is right across the road from distribution depot No. 1 at the Leninsky [district] fruit and vegetable association. The shop's vegetable counters are bare. The manager, R. Allyamov, complains about his suppliers' careless work: this is the second day that they have failed to deliver his order. Where are they bringing the produce from? From the Gagarinsky fruit and vegetable depot – which is in Tostopaltsevo, 40 kilometres from Moscow! Why send lorries all that way, when hundreds of tonnes of vegetables are 'languishing' in the storerooms of a depot only 40 metres from the shop?

Pravda has written about the shortcomings in the organisation of the sale of fruit and vegetables twice of late. However, it would appear that the Chief Moscow Fruit and Vegetable Organisation (whose manager is N. Seregin) is incapable of improving the situation. Not even its enormous computer centre, where a large number of people are engaged in collecting information about the availability of produce in the depots and shops, is able to help.

The time for laying in fruit and vegetables for the winter is just around the corner. By the beginning of September the warehouses should have been put in order. But are they ready to receive the produce everywhere? The basement of the Leninsky depot is waterlogged, and in a number of rooms in the Volgogradsky depot No. 3, which were hastily whitewashed, condensation from the refrigerated batteries along the ceiling is dripping on to the floor. It does not look as though they even intend to store vegetables in the Kievsky depot in Moscow. In one of the rooms of the fruit and vegetable depot on Ryabinovaya Street, about 1,000 tonnes of salted cucumbers – written off long ago – have been 'in store' since 1978! Meanwhile next door, peaches, grapes and other fruits are all 'sweating' in the August heat, unprotected under open canopies.

Not enough work is being done to prepare storage facilities for the new harvest in Azerbaijan, Armenia, Moldavia, Latvia, Estonia, Bashkiria, and elsewhere. We have also been let down this year by the food-processors. The seven-month plan for the production of tinned fruit and vegetables has not been fulfilled in the Russian Federation, Uzbekistan, Kirghizia, Tadjikistan and Turkmenia.

The season for marketing fruit and vegetables is now in full swing. We must not lose time, we must organise things in such a way that the produce gets straight to the shops and the processing factories.
[22 August 1985]

[When *Pravda* criticises, it expects something to be done about it. Normally, measures taken in response to a *Pravda* article are reported under the headings '*Pravda* spoke out. What has been done?' or 'After criticism'. And the response is not always satisfactory. . . .]

'One potato, two potato. . . .' Under this headline, on 10 January, *Pravda* published a report about a meeting of the USSR People's

Control Committee with a commentary by our correspondent. The article told of the criminally negligent attitude of the workers at the Volgograd fruit and vegetable association towards the unloading and storage of potatoes harvested in 1984, which led to the rotting of almost 9,000 tonnes of potatoes.

A large number of readers responded to the paper's report. 'I read it twice,' writes L. Kasyanova from Moscow, 'and just couldn't take it in: how could such a thing happen? How could officials in high positions justify their actions by saying that "the situation is no better in other regions?" Forgive me, but they are – to put it mildly – too comfortable in their jobs.' The same conclusions were reached by E. Sazhin (Leningrad), N. Potanin (Krasnodar province), I. Yevdokimov (Yalta), V. Guryev (Uzbekistan), N. Lokhova (Chelyabinsk), P. Biryukov (Rostov on Don) and others.

In contrast to the readers, the USSR Ministry of Fruit and Vegetables took over two months to respond to the article. The heads of the Volgograd association, deputy minister I. Kholod informed the newspaper, had indeed been slow in taking measures to unload, sort and store the potatoes.

The deputy head of the association, A. Chekashkin; the director of the city fruit and vegetable trading organisation, Yu. Onishchenko; the manageress of the Tsentralny distribution depot, G. Yevdokimova; and other managers, have been released from their posts for the offences committed by them.

Concrete measures to safeguard the quality of the undamaged potatoes have been taken. This year it is planned to put into operation potato stores with a capacity of 4,800 tonnes. In the next few years it is planned to construct a cold store for 8,000 tonnes of fruit and vegetables. For this year the Volgograd association has been allocated 10,000 containers for storing potatoes. Unfortunately, I. Kholod had nothing to say about making wider use of the experience of the Kurgan farms and other innovators, whose recommendations help to preserve potatoes for long periods.

Several months have passed since the disgraceful case in Volgograd. But the paper still does not know what the reaction of the Volgograd regional Party committee is to this case of flagrant mismanagement – nor what conclusions have been reached by the investigation agencies, who were sent our findings.

There is one other bewildering thing. In his reply the deputy minister reports that the head of the Volgograd fruit and vegetable association, V. Sulatskov, was released from his post and fired.

In fact, it turns out, he has been transferred to the post of deputy head of the association. A manager who – as was noted at the meeting of the USSR People's Control Committee – has displayed serious shortcomings in his work over many years, proves to be indispensable.

[4 April 1985]

Social Services

[In the summer of 1985 *Pravda*'s reporters went out to study health care facilities in a village, a 'worker's settlement' and an average-sized town, representing, it said, three typical 'cross-sections'. The picture painted was so appalling that the editors felt obliged to append the following cautionary note.]

Of course, readers of *Pravda* will not be misled by the critical stance of these accounts. The correspondents could have said far more that was good about medical treatment in the localities. But the tremendous successes of our country in the field of health care, achieved in the years of Soviet power, are widely known. We already take them for granted and look ahead. We must and can do even more so that the people's health service in no way lags behind the requirements of the day. It is this that the Party aims for. Consequently, it is necessary to concentrate attention on the short-comings, of which unfortunately there are still many.

[One of the reports, from a 'typical district centre' with 23,000 inhabitants, half of whom are oil-workers, contained the following description of the main hospital.]

'Our hospital has all the necessary equipment,' says head doctor F. Gaisin. 'It is staffed by specialists in every field. We can provide any kind of medical assistance.'

A spacious hall, spotless corridors, stairwells and operating theatres create an impression of order and good patient care. But take a look in the wards and this impression is immediately shat-tered. The beds are standing so close together that it is often difficult to move between them. Water taps and sinks have been removed, and the pipes sealed up. For the whole floor there are only three working taps and one shower which no one wants to use, as it is not even screened off from the ward. The lift was also out of order.

'The wash-hand basins in the wards often used to get blocked up, and it's difficult to get hold of a plumber,' explained Gaisin. 'The lift? It was working yesterday. Yes, the wards are crowded, but what can we do? The hospital was designed for 240 beds, and we have 370. But things will ease off a little this year. Oilmen have helped to build a new 120-bed wing.'
[14 July 1985]

[Another report, from Buzuluk, a town in Orenburg region, is printed here in full.]

In a remote village a sick man was waiting for a doctor – he needed help urgently. Grankin asked a young woman, who was known to be a decent doctor, to go. Her reply was unexpected: 'I can't go, I have personal matters to attend to,' she said, and then added in an irritated voice: 'And please, I don't want any lectures!'

He was about to remind her of her duty, and of the Hippocratic Oath, but bit his tongue. How can you send a doctor in a mood like that to a sick man? He immediately set about finding a replacement from one of Buzuluk's other medical establishments. It was no easy matter – he needed a specialist in a narrow field, one that was in short supply. Eventually one was found, and he set off to the patient. . . .

Having phoned to say that help was on its way, Grankin sank back into his chair, and was suddenly overcome with tiredness, as though he had spent several hours over the operating table. It is painful and unpleasant to see a doctor betraying her duty. It is doctors like that who undermine people's faith in the beneficence of medicine.

It was ten years ago as a young surgeon that he had come to the ancient Russian town of Buzuluk. He grew used to its streets, old and new, and to its parks. And he came to love the measured, unhurried pace of life, the people, and the picturesque countryside.

Now much of his time and energy is taken up with his duties as head doctor at the local oil and gas directorate's medical unit. It is the largest medical complex in the town, serving over 30,000 adults and children. The consulting rooms are well-equipped, and there is provision even for special operations: recently, two surgeons, G. Subtelya and A. Khizhnyak, successfully operated on the heart of thirteen-year-old Olya Titova. Olya has made a complete recovery, feels fine, and can now go back to school.

Doctors are perfecting techniques of diagnosis. Treatment, after all, is directly dependent on timely and accurate diagnosis. In the past, patients with medical complications were sent to Orenburg for treatment. Now, the medical unit has bought and put into operation the first fibre-optic gastroscope in the town.

In view of Grankin's authority and experience, he was asked to deputise for the head of the local health board, when the 'chief' himself, A. Melnikov, was on holiday. Grankin, a conscientious man, immediately got down to tackling the problems of health care in the town. And problems there were a-plenty.

Buzuluk – a typical medium-sized town, with a population of 80,000 – is served by seven hospitals. That ought to be sufficient, but materially several of them are not up to scratch.

Take, for example, the town's main hospital, which is supposed to carry the greatest 'load'. Unfortunately, it is not coping with its task. The staff are, of course, trying not to fall behind the times, and are keeping abreast of the latest developments in medical practice and equipment. But it is difficult, you will agree, to provide full medical assistance in ramshackle, wooden huts which are waiting to be pulled down. There are 375 beds in the hospital – considerably fewer than are required. Twice the existing number of beds are needed in the therapy department.

Talk about the municipal hospital has been going on for a long time. On the initiative of the local Party and council, at the end of the last Five Year Plan, work began on the building of a new hospital complex, using funds from industrial enterprises. This important task was entrusted to the Orenburg Heavy Construction Trust. It wasn't long before a well-appointed, multi-storey maternity block was standing next to the old park. But work on the other parts of the project progressed slowly. Part of the equipment for the new complex arrived, but stood in boxes in the open air, getting wet. It's true that the 'shell' of the new outpatients unit is ready, but they seem in no great hurry to finish it.

'The complex is not on the official plan for completion this year,' complains the hospital's head doctor, V. Trunov, 'and because of that they won't release the necessary materials to the builders. . . .'

Grankin tried to make sense of the situation. Why did the

customer – the capital construction department of the Orenburg regional council – not want to see this important project finished as quickly as possible, which would be in its own interests? Why, without completing the laying of hot-water pipes and other services, did Orenburg 'Special Building Trust' abandon its work in Buzuluk? There are no answers to these questions.

Not all parts of the building project are being carried out. For example, the wards for children and patients with infectious diseases, the pathological anatomy wing, the laundry, and the garage were removed from the plan. At various levels of the bureaucracy they called this an 'enforced measure': otherwise, they said, no one would authorise the financing of the project. A strange tendency sometimes revealed itself. Grankin encountered this as head doctor of a medical institution. The number of beds in the medical unit doubled, and two new departments were planned. But the capacities of the kitchens and the laundry remained the same. And no matter how much Grankin argued that this discrepancy was intolerable, nothing has yet been done about it.

The position regarding medical care for the town's young people is very serious. Over the years, children's units were housed wherever there was space, and it is still like that. The children's health centre occupies two old, wooden houses, which have inadequate heating, no running water and no sewerage. In order to deal with all their young patients, the doctors work in four shifts, using the same consulting rooms. There is no dentist, and other specialists are in short supply. The picture is no better in the children's hospital, which is housed in a building never intended for that purpose.

Two years ago, Buzuluk railway workers began refurbishing the children's wing of their hospital. Eighteen thousand roubles were spent on this. When the time came to move in again, it turned out that it would be impossible to transfer patients there: the building was flooded because the central heating had not been properly installed. The money spent on the repairs had gone down the drain. And no one has so much as asked the Buzuluk railway manager, Party member V. Gutsulyak, to account for any of this.

To be fair, it has to be said that efforts have been made in the town over the past two years to improve the standard of medical care. The town council and Party organisation have adopted a comprehensive health programme to take them up to 1990. This will provide for better health facilities and staff, and will improve the protection of reservoirs, the atmosphere and the soil.

The programme aims to remove some of the causes of disease. In particular there is a plan to provide the citizens of Buzuluk with high-quality drinking water. At the moment the water contains levels of iron which far exceed the accepted norm, but the time is not far off when it will become perfectly pure. It has been decided to build a deferrisation station, and a site has already been chosen for this.

Already, in accordance with the programme, a new surgery for women has been opened, and medical teams have been set up in several factories. Soon the doors of a new dispensary for workers in the car industry will be opened.

It is clear that in order to carry through the projected work, the mutual help and cooperation of all the establishments involved in the programme is required. And they need a reliable material back-up. In particular, there is a lack of equipment for instant diagnosis. There is not a single portable electrocardiograph machine, for example, for all the doctors at the oil and gas directorate's medical unit. The supply of medicines to hospitals is irregular. The network of pharmacies must be expanded.

'The situation would, of course, be vastly improved', said Grankin, 'if all the town's medical institutions were amalgamated. The fact that the town, district and railway hospitals are all run by different departments creates difficulties of administration and supply.'

Of course it makes more sense in a town of average size if all its medical establishments are run by the same 'boss'. This is borne out by the experience of towns such as Buguruslan, Kumertau and others.

N. Semashko, who later became one of the founders of the health service in Soviet Russia, worked before the Revolution in the Buzuluk District Hospital. The face of the town has undergone substantial changes since then, as has local medicine, and we are rightly proud of its achievements. But we should not rest on our laurels. We must keep pace with the swiftly moving times.

[18 July 1985]

[A study of dental care carried out by the USSR People's Control Committee in a number of towns and villages throughout the country discovered incompetence, negligence and corruption . . .]

A medical examination of students graduating from the Faculty of Stomatology* at Odessa Medical Institute discovered that the majority of them had . . . tooth decay! A similar situation was found at the dentistry faculty of Tartu University. The ancients were right: before healing others, heal yourself. These examples to a certain extent reflect the state of dental care in various parts of the country.

'We have to wait months to see a dentist,' it is said in numerous complaints to the Estonian Ministry of Health. And yet Estonia is sufficiently well provided with dental specialists. There are no special reasons for complaints about the material back-up, either. So what is the problem? Bad organisation of the medical service, inability to use existing resources properly, and a low level of management in this sector of health care.

A recent check-up by the USSR People's Control Committee showed up many instances of formalism, negligence and deception for the sake of appearances. In Turkmenia, for example, a very high percentage of people – on paper – are given preventive treatment, but in practice more than half the adults and two-thirds of the children tested required treatment. Prevention has been forgotten here, and treating teeth basically means pulling them out.

The reader is bound to wonder: how can this be – we have many dentists and thousands of dental clinics, yet treatment is not always available when and where it is needed. One of the main reasons for this is awkward surgery hours. Most of the clinics investigated were open only five days a week and at times when people are at work. In Alitus district (Latvia) and in Konakovo (Kalinin region) people requiring treatment or dentures have to wait in long queues, and not all get to see a specialist. But if the treatment centres organised their work properly, with more flexible hours and better use of available orthopaedic dentists and dental technicians, there would be no queues.

Many country people are forced to go into town for treatment. The trouble is that in some rural areas there are not enough medical workers: the turnover is too high. In the Chuvash Autonomous Republic the surgeries in half of the 50 rural hospitals that were checked were only open on odd occasions.

As the study showed, many dental institutions make inefficient use of equipment and materials, especially in the most backward

---

* 'Stomatology' will henceforth be rendered simply as 'dentistry', although the Soviet 'stomatologist' deals with all diseases of the mouth, not just with the teeth.

sector – orthopaedic care. But the situation is bad everywhere as regards using porcelain for false teeth. And yet this is a good material, and can also substantially reduce the demand for dentures made of gold. In clinic No. 1 in the city of Ordzhonikidze not a single porcelain denture was produced in three years, though the material is abundant. Dentists used to blame the low quality of the material. Now Soviet industry has mastered the production of high-quality porcelain. Medical institutions have acquired more than 600 vacuum kilns for baking porcelain. But many of them are idle. Even at the dental faculties at Kaunas, Tartu and elsewhere, these expensive kilns are only used to 10–15 per cent of their capacity. [. . .] Five hundred specialists have been trained to make dentures out of porcelain at the Central Dentistry Research Institute. They have been trained – but most of them still do not work with porcelain. Very little use is also made of another new material – silver-palladium alloy – in producing false teeth.

The demand for gold dentures is great. The state allocates tonnes of precious metal for this purpose, and the amounts are not getting any less. It's an amazing fact: while the number of people being given dentures is falling, the queues are growing. Why? Because – it turns out – the quantity of gold in the dentures is growing. Many of them are three to four times over the long-established norm. There is now an unprecedented practice whereby dentists, pandering to their patients, even put gold crowns on healthy teeth.

Waiting-lists for dentures are flagrantly ignored in a number of clinics. In the town of Belgorod-Dnestrovsky, for instance, 'preferential' service is enjoyed by people who work in shops, restaurants and services. The same goes for a number of clinics in Odessa. A suspiciously large percentage of gold teeth are made for people in the medical profession. [. . .]

Due to poor staff selection in the health service there have been instances of negligence towards patients and even at times violations of medical ethics. Private practices have been set up here and there under the roofs of state institutions. It was recently revealed by the Azerbaijan Ministry of Health that the dental laboratory in the Belokan central district hospital had been turned into a source of personal profit. In Kalinin region seven employees of dental clinics were convicted of the same offence. One instance came to light in North Ossetia of a technician with no medical training whatsoever who had been working as a dentist for five years.

There would be fewer shortcomings in the organisation of dental care, and fewer cases of the misuse of equipment and materials if the USSR Ministry of Health devoted more attention to this area of the medical services.

The USSR People's Control Committee has reprimanded E. Kuchiyev, Minister of Health of the North Ossetian Autonomous Republic, and E. Vjaertu, Estonian Deputy Minister of Health, for serious shortcomings in the organisation of dental care and for lack of control over the use of material and technical resources. A. Safonov, USSR Deputy Minister of Health, has also been reprimanded. By decision of the governing bodies of Turkmenistan, M. Charyyev has been released from the post of Deputy Minister of Health of the republic.

[19 August 1982]

Crime, Corruption, Discipline

[In almost any country, if some sought-after commodity is unavailable legally, a black market in that commodity fills the gap. The extent of the Soviet Union's 'second economy' can easily be gauged from the enormous number of goods and services which the official economy fails to provide either in sufficient quantity or of the desired quality. Even basically honest citizens resort to petty bribery now and again. But further up the social ladder, where protection is afforded by position and the opportunities for large-scale corruption are greater, bribery, embezzlement and 'misuse of one's position' appear to be rife.

All this is reflected in *Pravda*, but in a rather curious way. First, it is a very pale reflection indeed: every reader knows that what is reported is only the tip of the iceberg, and the really scandalous cases – such as those concerning members of the late President Brezhnev's family in 1982, which circulated only in rumours – are naturally not even hinted at in *Pravda* or any other newspapers. On the other hand the very fact that they are fairly rare lends greater significance to reports of corruption: they are intended as warnings, even though the punishment is often tucked away somewhere towards the end of the report. The most curious thing, however, is that the majority of these tales of corruption are written up in satirical, often witty, pieces which bear more resemblance to short stories (or perhaps the 'Diaries' of British newspapers) than to serious crime reporting. For some reason, corruption is virtually the only problem which *Pravda* consistently attacks not with exhortation but with that traditional Russian device of 'laughter through tears'.]

The Kerch *OBKhSS* [Fraud Squad] were interested in a certain M. Kosenko. They had heard that a good piece of meat or a ring of smoked sausage could be bought from her at any time of day or night, but especially after dark. They turned up at her home unexpectedly. With witnesses. And they discovered 10 kilograms of fresh meat and the same quantity of sausage. Furthermore, they learnt that only that morning M. Kosenko had sold an even bigger amount of sirloin steak and tender pork fillet.

'Where do you get it from?'

'Can't you see for yourselves?' answered M. Kosenko mysteriously. And sure enough, a quick glance out of her window, and everything became clear: right next door was the Kerch meat-packing plant. A more detailed and in-depth acquaintance with the activities of this latterday private entrepreneur revealed that over the past two years she had been buying up stolen meat and meat-products and reselling them. Her regular purveyors were pilferers from the meat-packing plant.

Unfortunately this is not an isolated incident. And it is not only in Kerch that it happens. In Odessa recently, Citizen N. was arrested in broad daylight. More than 200 kilograms of meat were found in the boot of his car. The investigation into his case is still continuing. But the main fact is already clear: he had been 'dealing' by the entrance gates of the town's meat-packing plant. This year, several hundred pilferers have been arrested near meat-packing plants in Kerch, Simferopol, Kherson, Nikolayev, Odessa and other towns in the southern Ukraine.

One wonders how on earth the meat-packing plants manage to break even.

The answer is very simple. The curly-horned bull-calf from the collective farm passes through complex meat-processing technology to become bones for soup, chops and little sausages. But the weight of the finished product is very different from that of the slaughtered animal.

A miracle? But you and I know that miracles do not happen. The truth is much simpler. And after a visit, for example, to the butchery at the Kherson meat-packing plant, it is easy to understand. Here, animal carcasses are cleaned up before going to the refrigerated stores to await further processing. To take the story further, let me hand over to I. Grigorovich, head livestock specialist at the celebrated award-winning 'Kirov' collective farm in Kherson region. 'The miracle begins when a carcass arrives in the butchery, and skilled magicians set about carving it up,' he says. 'They pay no heed whatsoever to remarks made by the livestock specialist or by any other representative of the farm that supplied the meat. And when there's only one of you, just try keeping an eye on the activities of ten virtuosi, manipulating their long knives with lightning speed!

'Where they should be gently slicing off a bit of gristle or some hair, they chop off a whole kilogram, or even two, of good meat. These scraps often include brisket, fillet, and other parts of the carcass which the supplier has to account for.

'On 2 November,' continued I. Grigorovich, 'I observed how these succulent lumps of meat were immediately snatched up. Outsiders keep coming into the butchery under various pretexts throughout the process, and they rarely leave empty-handed. And then quite a few of the scraps are put in the cold store for later processing into salami and sausages. This too is an easy source for the light-fingered, and its existence is no secret in the plant. As a result, when the carcass finally lands on the scales before going into the cold store, you sometimes cannot believe your eyes – it has "slimmed down" so much!'

Farmers count every kilogram of fodder, every ounce of weight gained, but dozens of kilos of meat end up on the slaughter-house floor – meat stolen from them, from the state. . . .

Such goings-on are not confined to the Kherson meat-packing plant. The managers of many farms in the southern regions of the Ukraine complain about the malpractices of the slaughter-house workers. At every opportunity the consignment weight is artificially reduced, and the timetables for deliveries are cleverly worked out so that most of the animals are received at the end of the month, causing pile-ups, rushed work and frantic haste in the butchering process: in short, to make it easier for the plunderers.

An entire criminal gang was operating at the meat-packing plant in Nikolayev. The gang consisted of R. Oleksishin, the head of the cold-store; V. Olenich, the storekeeper – a hardened criminal, living on false documents; V. Chernikova, manageress of shop No. 2, River Fleet Supplies; V. Plokhikh, a shop assistant; A. Gorgula, a forwarding agent; and A. Krepa, a driver.

Covering themselves by cooking the books and referring to 'natural losses', they sold the stolen meat through friends in shops. The state was done out of more than 50,000 roubles.

How is state property protected? Two watchwomen, E. Luchko and N. Tymkin, were tried recently at the Odessa meat-packing plant. The latter had pocketed 146 roubles in less than one shift, taking a rouble's 'entrance fee' from each thief. Every month she gave 500 roubles to the plant's veterinary surgeon, A. Tolstobrovaya, who had got her the job as watchwoman.

Pilfering beetles are crawling out from all the cracks, exploiting the temporary difficulties in supplying meat products to the population. Unfortunately, checks on meat-packing plants are carried out all too rarely. The investigating agencies and the People's Control do not always see matters through to their final conclusion. We need improvements in the selection, placing and training of staff. Can it really be considered normal that out of 800 people employed in positions of trust in the Odessa meat industry, only about 1 per cent are members of the Party? People's patrols and comrades' courts exist only nominally in the meat plants. Surely they could be of enormous help in the fight against theft?

[15 December 1981]

Every year thousands of people take a holiday on the Black Sea coast. Krasnodar is at the centre of the transport network for this area, and it is from there that many holidaymakers set off for the resorts.

. . . I wanted to get from Krasnodar to the village of Anapa. I joined the queue to the ticket-office in the bus-station. When the bus would arrive, nobody knew. One service had already been cancelled, and there was nowhere to obtain information. There was no alternative but to wait. Meanwhile overt deals were being made all around.

Taxi and bus drivers kept approaching the queue and offering to drive passengers wherever they wished – for a certain consideration. People were forced to agree: it was better to pay extra than to wait for hours. A service to Anapa was offered in this way. Bus No. TsPP-53-14 was waiting at the platform of the bus-station, and to all appearances had already been used for such 'shady' journeys. The driver was impeccably polite, and we travelled in style, avoiding the crush at the ticket-office, and paying only a matter of kopecks more than the official fare. In a word, everything was fine, if it hadn't been for the knowledge that the 200 roubles collected by the driver went straight into his own pocket instead of to the state.

Perhaps my trip was an exception? Not at all. The next day a friend of mine arrived with his small child, and the journey to

Anapa, in a taxi, No. KKV 47-25, set him back 40 roubles. The two other passengers who travelled in the same taxi each paid the same. Yet the meter doesn't show more than 35 roubles for that distance.

It is perfectly clear that the manager of the bus-station must be aware of these illegal trips. It is impossible not to notice what is going on on the platform. The police, too, are negligent, and there are no ticket inspectors on long-distance routes. No wonder the thieving drivers flourish.

[Reader's letter; 24 November 1981]

I went into a department store recently to look for a birthday present for my wife. I asked the assistant, 'Do you have any nice shoes for ladies? Or perhaps you can tell me when you will be getting them in?' She looked down at me snootily and said: 'We've got them in now, but what can *you* offer?!'

Such total cynicism infuriated me! I wanted to say something, but the assistant was gone already. My mind filled with many thoughts, one more vexing than the next. 'No doubt if I had some kind of pull in the black market for books or imported cosmetics, she would have deigned to pay me some attention,' I thought bitterly, as I made my way out of the shop.

Later, when I told my friends about what had happened, I heard of similar experiences which they had had. One case was of a doctor, who promised to extend the validity of a 'sick note' if he got spare parts for his car in return. In another, a box-office clerk traded tickets for a concert given by a popular singer for a place in a Black Sea sanatorium for her children. . . . The principle expressed in common parlance by the phrase 'I'll scratch your back if you scratch mine' seems to be thriving. Journalists speak out against it, and it is always being exposed in the cinema, in the theatre, on television. Yet despite such active opposition, the rogues and swindlers continue to poison the atmosphere of our lives.

I wrote 'active opposition', and then I thought no, it cannot really be called 'active'. These people are flourishing, perhaps, because we are not determined enough in our fight against their depraved psychology. Some say that 'the shortages' are to blame. But enterprising crooks sometimes create a shortage themselves, in order to extract personal gain from the situation. I know a car mechanic who specialises in repairing Zhiguli cars. He lives not far from me, and according to the neighbours there is no richer man in the area. He has the most fashionable clothes, a 'prestigious' library, and the best hi-fi equipment. This smart dealer brazenly flaunts tickets for concerts given by visiting celebrities, for which real music lovers have to queue for long hours. It is clear to everyone that a mechanic could never have acquired all this on his modest salary. But, as they say, 'unless he's caught red-handed. . . .'

This unhealthy practice of mutual extortion and gift-giving occurs not only in the trade and service industries. Its 'germs' often undermine relations in industry, and in so doing distort the consciousness of people apparently far removed from 'shortages'.

I work at one of the largest machine-building plants in Kiev. At the moment, the country is trying to speed up scientific and technical progress, and we shall never succeed in this unless all the supply factories strictly fulfil their contractual obligations. Yet for years we have been experiencing difficulties in obtaining vital parts from the Moscow State Bearing Factory No. 1. Like it or not, you end up looking for a compromise way out. That is, you find different suppliers, who, realising your difficult position, can state their own terms: we'll make an effort, we'll help you, they say, but we hope the debt won't go unpaid. Even here, in other words, the familiar moral rears its ugly head – I'll scratch your back if you scratch mine. [. . .]

[Letter from N. Muzhchina, team-leader at the Bolshevik factory, Kiev; 26 August 1985]

[Very occasionally corruption is exposed even in government circles. The following piece tells of the downfall of A. M. Yershov, until early 1983 USSR First Deputy Minister of Light Engineering.]

Sounds of celebration came from the banqueting hall. Speeches were interrupted by enthusiastic applause. Particularly moving was the moment when they brought in a china vase decorated with a portrait. What on earth was going on in the boardrooms of this respectable establishment? Perhaps they were honouring a foreign delegation after successfully exchanging ideas with them, or perhaps it was a group of top-class production workers?

Nothing of the sort. Anatoly Maksimovich Yershov was merely celebrating his fiftieth birthday. Modestly, but tastefully. For the organisation which had booked the banqueting hall was more than respectable – the Ministry of Light Engineering, of which the birthday guest was First Deputy Minister.

The celebrations began, let us note, long before the banquet. The minister's assistant had taken care of that by drawing up in advance a timetable for visitors. One after the other well-wishers approached the door with the important name-plate. Whole groups appeared: leaders of subdivisions of the ministry, heads of enterprises attached to the ministry, and also leading officials from other ministries and central government departments.

Neither visitors to the office nor guests at the banquet came empty-handed, mind you. And if that were not bad enough, their presents were paid for not out of their own pockets but by the state. Moreover, many of the gifts were made by skilled craftsmen, during working hours, using state materials and equipment. There were working models of industrial machinery, traditional pen-and-ink sets (with built-in clock and calculator to bring them into line with the electronic age), and unique articles made from glass, stainless steel . . .

But they were all upstaged by an Uzbek factory producing machinery for the textile industry. It was this factory's delegates who gave their leader the above-mentioned vase, worth 302 roubles, adorned with a portrait of Yershov himself.

The scale of the celebrations was remarkable, but then, the fifty-year-old was used to living well. He had acquired land, on which he built a *dacha* with a mansard roof and an open fireplace, using dozens of cubic metres of high-quality, illegally procured timber, and hundreds of kilograms of scarce galvanised iron.

Yershov did not blister his own hands in building the *dacha*. The timber was transported on the ministry's lorries, and turned into a house by the ministry's workers. One powerful Kraz lorry, belonging to the Leningrad Factory of Polygraphical Machinery, plied the route: Leningrad-Vologda-Moscow-Vologda-Leningrad.

The zeal with which he pursued his personal interests evidently got in the way of his official duties. Yershov certainly displayed no zeal in solving the problems facing his industry. Although responsible within his ministry for organising production, he showed no concern for the ministry's part in the country's Food Programme or for the development of consumer goods. The production potential of many enterprises under the ministry is under-used, and questions of specialisation are solved too slowly, even though a special decree pointed to these major shortcomings back in July 1982.

Where he should have shown acumen, organisational initiative and purposefulness, Yershov displayed only arrogance, superciliousness, tactlessness, and rudeness in his dealings with people.

For violating Party ethics and abusing his official position for personal profit, the Party Control Committee attached to the CPSU Central Committee gave Yershov a stern reprimand, which was written into his Party membership card. He has been removed from his post.

The Party Control Committee also criticised the Minister of Light Engineering, I. Pudkov, and the former secretary of the ministry's Party committee, I. Terkovsky, for their unprincipled attitude towards the former deputy minister's illegitimate activities.

[Published on 20 March 1983, the above piece came less than two months after Yuri Andropov had assured workers at a Moscow factory that his fresh campaign to strengthen discipline applied not only to workers, but to 'everyone, starting with ministers'. Thus, though Yershov's 'illegitimate activities' were probably mild compared with other unpublicised cases, the story was clearly intended as a warning to all those top officials who during the Brezhnev years had lined their own pockets at the state's expense. Under Gorbachov the campaign intensified. The following article by *Pravda*'s Gorky correspondent unravels a tale of corruption and mafia-like protection in the regional catering business.]

A letter from Dzerzhinsk arrived at the *Pravda* office in Gorky. It was from workers in the local catering organisation and concerned the unseemly goings-on in Catering Trust No. 2. I went to see the deputy chairman of Dzerzhinsk town council, Yu. Kilyachkov – he oversees the town's public catering establishments, and, according to the letter-writers, 'maintains friendly relations' with T. Pyashina, the manageress of Trust No. 2.

'Yes, both our families are friends,' the deputy chairman confirmed.

I don't think anyone could be particularly interested in whether or not the Kilyachkovs are regular guests at the Pyashins' house. But when the deputy chairman became a constant guest at Catering Trust No. 2, and his personal Volga [car] became a fixture outside the entrance both in office hours and out of office hours, many people began to notice.

What was it that attracted Kilyachkov here? Business? His desire to understand the Trust's affairs better? Alas. Business was what interested him least of all, and his chief understanding was of the liquor and food which he came here to consume.

Meanwhile, there were indeed unseemly goings-on in the Trust – falsification of accounts, embezzlement, stealing. . . . Scarce food was even being pilfered from school canteens. From the various catering establishments the manageress extracted a 'levy', which was always collected punctually. There was more than sufficient for a good life – enough for the car, for the *dacha*, and for 'souvenirs' for people that 'mattered', among them Kilyachkov.

Let us try to understand how all this was possible. I asked A. Alekseyev, first secretary of the Dzerzhinsk town Party committee, about it. But got no proper answer. Perhaps the behaviour of the 'friends' was a surprise to him? Hardly. At one time they both worked at the Khimmash factory, where Alekseyev was then Party secretary. And old hands say that even then Kilyachkov and Pyashina were parting from the straight and narrow.

'How come they got promoted then, and how come a blind eye is turned to them now?' the writers of the letter ask.

That somebody is turning a blind eye is certainly true. I myself wrote an article about Kilyachkov two years ago, entitled 'Bath-house for a close friend'. But the deputy chairman came out of the bathhouse story perfectly dry, without so much as a reprimand.

Pyashina was 'lucky' too. Not only was she not called to order, but, on the contrary, she was encouraged, and considered an exemplary manager. She was elected to the town council. More than once she was sent on trips abroad, at state expense, and her official references for these trips read like citations for an award.

Alekseyev, incidentally, immediately disowned the references – they were signed by other secretaries of the town committee, he said. About Kilyachkov he preferred not to speak at all, which is – to say the least – a strange stance for a Party leader, and certainly not evidence of his own high principles.

The Pyashina story does not end there. Recently, the investigation agencies sent the executive committee of Dzerzhinsk town council a request for their agreement to criminal proceedings being instituted against her (this is necessary because she is a council member). However, personal sympathies played their part here too. For almost a month the executive procrastinated and wavered, torn by Hamlet-like doubts: to give or not to give agreement? In the end they had to give it. . . .

The old saying proved itself: however much yarn you spin, there has to be an end. And at that one could draw a line. But alas, the story has to be continued, for it is not just in Dzerzhinsk that yarn is spun. . . .

More than a dozen letters about public catering arrived lately at the *Pravda* office from all corners of Gorky region. They were mostly not just about the work of canteens, restaurants, cafés and so on, but about the moral atmosphere in the system, about the blind eye that both managers and inspectors turn to abuses.

Take for example, the letter sent by A. Bulatov, an engineer. A major shortfall, worth 250,000 roubles to the state, was discovered at the warehouse of the Gorky restaurants' trust. There was a trial, and the warehouse workers and accountant were sentenced. 'And quite rightly, too,' writes Bulatov. 'But the amazing thing is that the investigation revealed that the pilferers had high-up "assistants" among the trust's management, who regularly "helped themselves" at the store and also treated their friends and "important" people. And they all went scot-free.

'True, for the sake of appearances, they dismissed the manager, V. Vladimirov, the chief accountant and some of the suppliers – the chief "organisers" of the outrages. But Vladimirov soon found himself in the director's chair of a winery, and others too did not suffer.

'The local papers', Bulatov goes on, 'write a good deal about various shortcomings and infringements in the catering industry. It makes amazing reading: the same names come up again and again, but in different jobs. It seems that when someone does wrong in one place, they just move him to another, and he carries on doing the same.'

Yes, it does happen. Not long ago the People's Control Committee investigated the work of the Zarechny district canteens trust and uncovered a host of violations. The Gorky city People's Control Committee was forced to punish the trust's director, V. Yegorov. But . . . he was immediately appointed first deputy chief of the regional catering board [i.e., promoted. – Ed.].

Apropos of 'control'. . . . The catering industry has its own control-and-inspection service, which could do much to combat violations and bring in order – in theory. But in fact? In fact the department's inspectors see nothing except minor flaws.

But their 'blindness' is quite voluntary, again on the basis of 'friendship' – I'll scratch your back if you'll scratch mine. When the *OBKhSS* [Fraud Squad] 'got wind' of these contacts they had to call to account a whole group of catering inspectors, headed by the deputy chief of the regional board, G. Klementyeva, who was in charge of the control-and-inspection service.

I have seen the goods confiscated from these 'inspectors'. The room where their 'souvenirs' were taken looked like a fairground stall. Gilded folk art rubbed shoulders with piles of imported sheets; there were spare parts for cars; and tins of caviar, sturgeon and crab were piled up like pyramids. A gallery of bottles was displayed along the walls.

To compete the scene, the raid on the lumber-rooms and garages also produced packets of banknotes of no small value, and savings books with five-figure deposits. The money-grubbers did not even turn their noses up at tuppenny tins of peas – well, if they were being offered, they might as well take them. Half of the preserves confiscated from them were spoiled, the tins rusty. The cans of condensed milk were swollen, the mayonnaise had turned green. . . . The air was thick with the stench of rotting and decay.

'But what about the top managers in the catering board?' I hear the impatient reader ask. 'Did they know nothing about it?'

That's the whole point. Not only did they know about it, but they also behaved in the same spirit. In my mailbag on the subject of catering there is scarcely a letter that does not bring up the abuses of V. Markova, chief of the regional catering board. She, it seems, was very fond of receiving souvenirs. She got them from – among others – manageress Pyashina in Dzerzhinsk. Markova particularly enjoyed being fêted with slap-up meals in banqueting halls, or with pleasure-trips down the Volga. And all this without the slightest constraint, in full view of everyone.

But then, why should she be afraid? She had more than sufficient grounds for believing that everything was possible for her. Until recently Markova occupied a two-room flat alone. Suddenly she felt like a change. An instruction to 'deal with the matter' was sent down from the regional executive committee to the Nizhegorodsky district council. And Markova got a bigger apartment. Ahead of all the war invalids, veterans and so on in the waiting-list. . . . But the flat had to be given the appropriate 'appearance' – so Building Trust No. 5 was sent into action, also illegally.

The time came for me finally to meet this Markova. Not banking on her frankness, I decided to talk to her in the presence of her present overseer, deputy chairman of the regional executive committee, A. Makiyevsky. I thought it would be of some interest to him. But the conversation, I must say, never got going. I tried to elicit what grounds there had been for giving Markova a new flat, but Makiyevsky's eyebrows shot up in amazement: 'What do you mean? Didn't she have the right? She had an old flat, in a pre-fab block. . . .'

Well, that *was* a valid reason . . . ! My other questions also received a concerted rebuff. I left the deputy chairman's office and set off to see A. Smirnov, head of the regional Party department for trade and services. This was especially important since some letters, including some detailed ones about Markova's behaviour, had been sent by their authors not only to me but also to the Party committee: I wanted to find out what had happened to them. But Smirnov was not 'in the picture'. He had not seen the letters about Markova. In general, he was not 'up-to-date' about affairs in the catering business. Yet only one year ago, the regional Party bureau had adopted a resolution about the work of the catering services, and a sharply-worded one at that, setting out specific measures to be taken. How were they being implemented? Smirnov shrugged his shoulders uncertainly. I could not help wondering what the point is of having a trade and services department in the regional Party committee if its boss does not know what is going on.

Last summer *Pravda* received a letter, a copy of which was also addressed to the regional Party committee, concerning the behaviour of G. Nikishin, the chief trade inspector. The facts reminded one of Pyashina and Markova – extortion, 'souvenirs' – and again there were 'friendly relations', this time with Smirnov.

I do not know what became of the copy sent to the Party committee, but I sent *Pravda*'s copy to the regional procurator's office. A little time passed, and suddenly I learnt that Nikishin had just been named 'Merited Trade Worker', and had already had his award conferred upon him. A few days later he was arrested for taking bribes.

. . . Neither did the investigating authorities pass by Markova's 'tricks'. The facts they uncovered gave grounds for the regional procurator to ask the regional executive committee for their agreement to the initiation of criminal proceedings against Markova. But this time there were no Hamlet-like doubts: the executive refused. They even expressed surprise at the actions of the investigating organs: were they not being somewhat over-zealous? they asked.

The Party is waging a fight for order and discipline, for a moral clean-up among officials. It is a resolute, uncompromising fight. And no one is permitted to forget that.

[20 August 1985]

[The next extract is taken from a long letter written by a pensioner from Kursk. Published in the 'Party Life' section of the newspaper, it deals with crimes committed by senior local officials, and with the ensuing cover-up, ending with a call for more openness in the press.]

[. . .] I should like to tell you about two incidents which caused a lot of rumours and gossip here in Kursk.

Some time ago the first secretary of the Gorshechnoye district party committee, I. Vasilyev, decided to 'take a rest' in the country-side, and invited along the district militia [police] chief and the chief engineer from the local vodka distillery. Many hours of drinking ended up in a fight, in which the militia chief got his leg broken. He spent a long time 'recuperating' after that. The regional Party committee gave I. Vasilyev a severe reprimand, which was written into his work record, and deemed it impossible for him to continue working in the lofty position of first secretary of the district Party committee.

What happened after that? Something most unexpected. Vasilyev was immediately appointed deputy head of the regional agricultural board, and moved from the district backwater to the regional centre [Kursk].

The echo of the Gorshechnoye story was still reverberating when a fresh thunderstorm broke in Kursk. Late one evening the deputy chief of the regional militia, A. Kovynev, burst into flat no. 21, at 29-b Zavodskaya Street, and caused an uproar which ended with a young woman, the owner of the flat, falling from the second-floor balcony.

I do not want to write about the motives which prompted Kovynev to break into someone's flat: they are the subject of contradictory and far from flattering rumours about the militia colonel. However, many of the events of that . . . evening are known for certain: how the scared and indignant neighbours ran out of their flats, how they called the militia (the militiamen who arrived turned back in embarrassment when they saw their boss in the centre of the events), and how an ambulance took the very seriously injured young woman away.

What was the official reaction to this episode? It was just as incomprehensible as in the Gorshechnoye case: as soon as the incident came into the open, A. Kovynev was given leave, and on his return he was 'retired' on the maximum possible pension. At the same time another highly-paid managerial post was prepared for him: director of the Kursk packing-case factory. Kovynev continues to sit comfortably in this post to this day. His misdemeanour was not discussed at the time either in the party cell of the regional militia, or in the district Party committee, or in the city Party committee.

And it was not until twelve months later that the Kursk city committee suddenly remembered about Kovynev and issued a reprimand with laughable wording – 'for exceeding his official authority'. And they bypassed the primary Party cell, too. It still has not even been informed about the punishment. Why did this individual case suddenly surface? What good comes of such a belated and, frankly, indecently liberal punishment, from the point of view of restoring justice and especially of educating the personnel of the law-enforcement agencies? It's incomprehensible. . . .

[. . .] There are a good many honest and conscientious workers in the Party committees who sincerely believe that discussion of a leader's unworthy conduct is not a matter for everyone, nor a matter for the press, that discussion of his guilt should be permitted only in a narrow circle, behind closed doors. And if he must be punished, then quietly, without any publicity.

I have often come across comrades who were bewildered and dismayed by critical articles in the central newspapers. 'Why write about that?' they would ask. 'Why spread it around? It will do us such terrible harm!' Such sentiments have not come about suddenly, but have taken shape over the years, unfortunately. These Party workers – I would call them conscientious but deluded – sincerely believe that quelling publicity and maintaining secrecy around the unworthy behaviour of a leader will ensure that the authority of the local Party committee is maintained. And it never occurs to them what a profound political danger for the Party's cause lies in this position. [. . .]

At a time when the Party has firmly embarked on a course of establishing order and raising organisation and discipline in all spheres of our life, openness – truthfully informing citizens about measures taken to deal with certain officials' misdeeds – is of especial importance. People must see just how consistently and uncompromisingly the fight is being waged. Openness strengthens the people's faith in the triumph of justice, in the inevitability of being brought to book for any violation of the Communist Party rules or Soviet laws. It will be no exaggeration to say that openness affirms the political optimism of our people.

But look at what news about I. Vasilyev was printed in *Kursk Pravda*: 'The plenary session [of Gorshechnoye district Party committee] released I. P. Vasilyev from his duties as first secretary and member of the bureau of the district committee. Elected as first secretary and member of the bureau was. . . .' In what connection was he released, for what reason? The regional paper evidently considered that the people ought not to know about that. Nor were they told anything about the Party reprimand issued to the communist Vasilyev. As for A. Kovynev's offence – no official information about that was given at all.

In April this year Kursk regional Party committee released one of its secretaries, A. Rukavitsyn, from his work. How did they inform the population of the region about this? The same way as they did with Vasilyev: he was 'released', and that's all! But, after all, people are interested in why suddenly, four months after the regional Party conference, one of the committee's secretaries is removed from his post. Was he ill? Promoted? No, it turns out he left to become chairman of a collective farm. . . . Why this game of hide and seek? [. . .]

It is clear that in the life of the Party there are always situations and issues which really are a purely internal affair, and not for the press. However, if one looks into them carefully, with trust in the people, then in my view there will not prove to be many such issues, and at regional, let alone district, level there are hardly any at all. [. . .]

[15 October 1984]

[The theme of openness was later taken up by Gorbachov, but when his one-time rival for the leadership, Grigory Romanov, was dismissed from the Politburo, it was still described officially as 'retirement on pension for health reasons'.]

Ever more attention is being concentrated on strengthening discipline at work. But there are still loop-holes for those people who find their slipshod habits hard to break.

Enormous crowds gather in the shops when an article which has been in short supply is 'thrown out' for sale. Naturally the question arises: how do people find the time to spend hours standing in queues during the working day? What do their bosses think of this? It cannot be that they simply do not notice how working time is wasted. And whole days, not just minutes!

And what happens on the day before a holiday? Very often work grinds to a halt by midday. And an hour or so later the tender-hearted management lets the people go home. Sometimes this happens not only in offices, but also in factories. The lax approach which some bosses have to discipline warps people's very psychology. The manager who dares to call a subordinate to order runs the risk of being branded as 'bad' or 'undemocratic' by his workers.

Discipline must be strengthened. And not only by attendance checks at places of work (although this is also important), but more importantly by strictly monitoring how working time is spent – all eight hours and twelve minutes per day of it! I cannot recall a single occasion when someone was called to account for skipping off to the shops in the middle of the day. And not only the guilty parties, but management too should be held responsible for disruptions in work. They should answer for discipline in their workforce in the same way as they are responsible for the plan, and for fulfilling their production tasks. I think a system whereby much sought-after goods were sold in shops only at the end of the working day would improve the situation. I know that this has been put into practice in a few places, and it seems to me that the experiment deserves some attention.

[Letter from reader in Leningrad; 22 January 1985]

I have been head of personnel at a power station for ten years. It is good, necessary and noble work. But I have to admit to feeling aggrieved, at times even angry, when I consider my own impotence.

In our city alone hundreds of able-bodied, healthy people are officially registered, but have not been working for years. And this at a time when every enterprise and every organisation is crying out for workers. These people are contributing nothing to society, while at the same time shamelessly taking advantage of all its benefits. How are they dealt with?

Here is an example. The militia send out the following instructions to the heads of enterprises: 'You have, working in your enterprise, such-and-such a person, who is registered as leading an anti-social, parasitical way of life. . . . Please ensure that he (she) has the best possible working and living conditions.' Is this tackling the problem? What have they done to deserve the 'best possible conditions'?

Enough of appealing to the conscience and consciousness! This category of people should be told straight: an adult person must work! If he does not want to do so voluntarily, then he must be forced to do so.

Another problem facing enterprises is the category of workers known as 'rolling stones'. Take our station as an example once again. Every year more than half of the workers who leave their jobs have been employed for less than a year. Their credo is to grab as much as possible from the work and give as little as possible in return. If it doesn't work out here, they leave and go elsewhere. The factory's interests and the honour of the collective mean nothing to them.

It is with a heavy heart that you draw up pension documents for this type. There are two or three extra pages in his work-book,* and some even have two or three work-books. You realise with bitterness that this man has never applied himself to anything in his life, and yet he will receive the same pension as someone who has only two or three entries in his book: first employment; perhaps a transfer; and retirement on old-age pension.

This is unjust. A worker who honestly and conscientiously gives 25 or 30 years of his life to one factory, gets all of 12 roubles extra in his pension, compared with a 'rolling stone'. This advantage has scarcely any effect on reducing staff turnover or stabilising the workforce. This is something the USSR State Committee for Labour, together with the social security authorities, should consider.

I should also like to say something about the work-book. Although this is in effect a worker's 'passport', in fact it means very little. It is easy to get a second or third replacement for it. All you have to do is to tell the factory which you have left that you have lost the first one (it was stolen, or burnt, or your children tore it up). And that's it – the administration is obliged to give you a replacement within two weeks. It sometimes happens that six months, or even longer, after leaving the power station, a worker turns up and demands a replacement work-book, assuring me that he has not

---

* Record of jobs held by any citizen throughout his working life.

worked anywhere else since leaving. I write out a duplicate for him, and he tosses 50 kopecks on to my desk, and leaves victorious. I feel sick at heart: I know he is lying, but I cannot prove it. I know that most of the 'lost', 'spoilt' or 'burnt' work-books will turn up when the time comes for his pension to be fixed.

There was a noticeable intensification in the struggle against shirkers in industry after the Law on Labour Collectives was passed [1982]. However, this evil is still very much alive. Shirkers not only disrupt the production process, they also have a demoralising effect on the people working alongside them. How can you knock any sense into them, if they simply ignore the opinion of the team, or of the union committee? This type does not need bonuses, he is not on a waiting list for a new flat, and criticism goes in one ear and out of the other. Depriving him of part of his holidays is also to no avail. The shirker knows that the law guarantees him twelve working days' holiday. He makes up the rest by taking days off whenever the fancy takes him.

This sometimes assumes absurd proportions. A man of about 35 recently came to ask for a job at a factory. He had been dismissed from his previous four places of work for absenteeism. I asked how he had got himself into such a state, and he answered cynically: 'Why, what's wrong with it?'

I say that we should stop mollycoddling them! The shirker should lose one day's holiday for every day he does not turn up at work, and if someone is sacked for absenteeism, he should be deprived of any bonuses at his new place of work for a year. Life must be made intolerable for him, and he should be made to feel the force of his punishment. Every article of the Law on Labour Collectives should be put into practice. We did not discuss the draft of the Law, and the USSR Supreme Soviet did not adopt it, just for the sake of empty rhetoric.

Social justice should penetrate our whole life, in the interests of our socialist society, of our toiling people, our creative people.
[Letter from a personnel manager, Donetsk; 17 June 1985]

The New Soviet Man

We live in our own country. We are proud of it! It is precisely this feeling of pride in one's country, in one's people, which determines the thoughts and deeds of a true citizen of the USSR. This was the drift of most of the letters received in response to the article 'Pride in Ourselves' [published in *Pravda* on 31 October 1983]. But readers did express concern about young people and about creating in them a mature class sense, and moral purity.

Readers believe that the USSR Committee for Sport ought to pay more attention to the way our country's national teams dress when they are playing. As it is, the logo of a foreign company often stands, in all its glory, next to the Soviet emblem on the chests of our sportsmen. A. Ivanov from Odessa, N. Bogdanov from Leningrad, N. Bukhteyev and G. Pechkisov from Moscow are rightly puzzled: how can we allow such a thing? How do you explain to a teenager that the emblem and flag of our country are sacred symbols for every citizen, and that there is something odd about their being neighbours with a foreign trademark?

A student at the Bauman Technical College in Moscow, Andrei V., who disagrees with the basic propositions of my article, 'Pride in Ourselves', writes: 'The author maintains that only a person with absolutely no self-respect would wear trousers with the American flag on the back pocket. But why? Surely, just because the country is our political adversary, we don't have to become patriots even in our dress?' A. Gribakin, a doctor of philosophy from Sverdlovsk, assesses this kind of opinion thus: 'Our attitude to foreign badges and symbols should be uncompromising. We must not allow the Stars and Stripes into our lives today . . .'

Recently the well-known American singer Dean Reed, in an interview with a Soviet journalist, recalled how he once washed out the American flag, stained with the blood of Vietnam, in front of the doors of the American consulate in Chile. And now there is also the blood of Chile, El Salvador, Nicaragua, Grenada. . . . Dean Reed believes that under Reagan's rule the American flag could become the symbol of a universal catastrophe. So is it not strange to see the group *Zemlyane* [Earthmen], dressed in clothing adorned with the American flag, appearing in concerts in Dnepropetrovsk?

The authors of a number of letters note that we do not make full use of explanatory work, that we are ineffective in carrying it out. A Leningrad veteran of the Civil War and the Great Patriotic [Second World] War, A. Kulbatsky, advises: 'It is useful for the Komsomol to remember the 1920s, when public debates of every kind were widespread – anti-religious, literary and political. They were held in towns, in schools, in factories, and involved large numbers of the population. Questions were posed and public opinion was shaped about such matters as religious rites, the wearing of gold jewellery, West European dances, etc. And this was much more useful than any rules and instructions.'

Vasily Fyodorov has a neat poetic formula: 'Any hearts we have not won, the enemy will win without delay.' It is impossible to command a person to love something; this love should be a natural moral necessity, and should be fostered from childhood. A serious pedagogical task is clearly marked out in the guidelines for the School Reform: 'Fuller use must be made in educational work of the symbols of the Soviet state – the emblems, flags and anthems of the USSR and of the union republics; state awards and decorations, and also the symbols of the Young Pioneers and Komsomol organisations.'

Many readers believe that with the help of brightly coloured posters, clever slides and cartoons, and interesting books, it should be possible to instil in the child at kindergarten level an idea of the basic concepts of citizenship. Why not give a lesson on patriotism on the very first day at school, and thereafter proceed towards an understanding of more complex social and political issues? Some readers are of the opinion that the ritual side of school life, which children find attractive, should carry a heavier ideological burden, and that Pioneer and Komsomol work should be saturated with competitive elements, so that each child comes to understand the concepts of 'school honour' and 'class honour' as real concepts which determine his actions. Would it really be so difficult to place a flagstaff in front of every school, and mark the beginning of the school year with the raising of the state flag? How much more ceremonial and memorable this event would then become for the children . . . !

Almost every letter from young people contains criticism directed against those who work in the clothing and footwear industries. Older readers write about this too. A female reader from Yalta, L. Savitskaya, sent in a vicious – in places excessively vicious – letter, which nonetheless contains some lines worth considering: 'My twenty-year-old son recently came home from the army, and he needed new clothes. He earns on average 160 roubles a month. He bought himself Italian jeans which cost 160 roubles! A few days later he bought foreign training shoes for 130 roubles! I had a look at the trainers: beautiful, light, comfortable, made of rubber, nylon and artificial suède. Do we not have these materials? We have everything – clever designers, engineers, workers with golden hands, and raw materials. But so long as inefficiency, bureaucracy and eyewash reign supreme in our ministries and departments, the resourceful black-marketeer will flourish and bring disgrace on our socialist country.'

Whether we want it to or not, life itself links questions of material standards with morality and ideology. This interconnection some-times assumes monstrous forms. There is an argument which goes something like this: once you can make jeans better than Levi's, then you can speak about 'pride in ourselves' (we received a letter saying just that). For some people, owning something which is in short supply becomes a measure of success, a sign of public recognition. The person who owns such a thing does not have to make any intellectual or moral effort to get himself noticed and be 'respected'. Without it, on the other hand, you go unnoticed, are an ordinary person, 'the same as everyone else'. This is what motivates those people who take part in the bartering over Her Majesty the Material Possession. On the other hand, it is perfectly natural for a young person to want attractive, fashionable clothes, and foolish of him to check the labels on the inside pockets of jackets. . . .

I. Borisov, a teacher at the Arkhangelsk Medical Institute, wisely observes that authors of recent articles on upbringing and morality often neglect a fundamental law: that being determines conscious-ness. Speaking at the June (1983) Plenum of the CPSU Central Committee, Comrade K. U. Chernenko noted: 'In order to elimin-ate negative phenomena we need not only constant efforts in the field of propaganda, but also economic, organisational and legal measures.'

There was a lively reaction from readers to my observations about modern musical culture. I. Bardin of Kursk, who was extremely hostile, was even prepared to compare the 'rock' style with the Colorado beetle, destroying everything around it, everything that is national and popular. This is, of course, an extreme and contro-versial opinion. I. Morozov of Leningrad, A. Fyodorov from Kalinin region, A. Koshkin of Moscow and others adopt a calmer approach in trying to understand this question. They point out in their letters that television and radio devote a disproportionate amount of time to foreign pop music, and to those Soviet per-formers who model themselves on often inferior Western ones, whereas by comparison art which develops national traditions is being edged out.

'Hands off rock'n'roll!' This cry was heard in several letters from devotees of modern beat. They demand that even more air-time be given to foreign groups and singers: this is what young people like. Entire articles about contemporary Western and Soviet music were sent in by two young readers – V. Rybkin from Khmelnitsky region and V. Martynenko of Minsk. It is clear that they are well-versed in the subject and understand the role of music in the aesthetic and moral development of young people. V. Rybkin writes: 'Young people must have a correct understanding of contemporary music. For at the moment, because of their age and lack of experience they live on rumours, gossip and inventions about "Western stars". Blanket condemnation of contemporary music makes young people protest inwardly – they start saying that they are not understood. If they are to be "understood", we need experts to give a thorough explanation of it all.'

Yes, an open and thoughtful discussion of fashionable musical trends should be conducted. As should discussions of all other problems of ideological and moral education. Let us take a broader view of things. It is no secret that in numerous publications under the headings 'Musical Path', 'Our Disco Club', 'Your Tape-recorder', 'The Disc Jockey Presents', etc., the conversation revolves around pop-music – both Soviet and foreign. There is not a single word about the wealth of national songs and dances of the Soviet people! Our press should systematically foster young people's interest in and love of their own national heritage and the national traditions in contemporary art, should present such material in an eye-catching, inventive way, and involve clubs, schools and colleges in this work too.

It was after the article 'Pride in Ourselves' was published that I visited the 'Prometheus' social and political club at school No. 609 in the town of Zelenograd. The children were discussing the film *Kidnap American Style*, which they had just seen. Of course these senior pupils had experience of similar analyses, and they easily and convincingly showed that this film was of a low moral and aesthetic standard, that from the first to the last scenes it was an advertisement for the much-praised American way of life, and did not contain any truthful information about the USA. But who can tell how many teenagers might see that film and pour out their emotions in one phrase: 'What a great life!' And then the Komsomol, the teachers, and we journalists, all have to roll up our sleeves and start re-educating, dissuading, and engaging in the counter-propaganda which absorbs such a large part of our ideological efforts. Is this logical . . . ?

In a letter from N. Seliverstova and V. Luneva, both from Moscow, there are the following lines: 'Please – don't let this matter end just with an article in the newspaper. It would be good to carry it through to the end, not necessarily by taking measures, but simply by finding out who is responsible for what, and by eliminating the various gaps in ideological, moral and aesthetic education.'

We live in our own country. And you and I have it in our power to correct the bad, and to capitalise on the good.

[22 May 1984]

[The following letter, from a train driver in Chernovtsy, the Ukraine, was printed under the headline, 'What is happiness?' It could almost stand as an epigraph to the whole of this anthology.]

There is no denying that we have become more affluent. It is fairly commonplace to have your own car, a colour television, a three-piece suite. But do expensive things really bring joy or kindness into our lives?

I recently heard the owner of a Volga car say, 'The seats get all worn out if you start giving lifts to all your friends.' That says it all.

That the satisfied man is happier than the rich man is an undeniable truth. But it is not surprising that you also come across the following opinions: 'We have a stereo, we've bought a car, and built a *dacha* – so where do we go from here, what is there to strive for?!' This was probably said not without a hint of humour, but even so . . . I am sure that no matter how affluent you are, you can still remain sad and impoverished, cheated by fate.

During the war I remember there was nothing more precious for a soldier than a tobacco-pouch filled with shag: it was always passed around. And how could I forget the way we kitted out our comrades for a reconnaisance trip? We each tried to give them our best – a sheepskin coat, a fur hat, felt boots, our last rusk.

When my wife and I came home from the front, all our possessions fitted into a kit-bag and a little plywood suitcase. Yet how glad and happy we were! We had won peace and freedom, and were still alive – nothing else mattered.

We raised our children, and now we are bringing up our grand-children. True happiness lies in seeing a meaning in life, in feeling

yourself to be part of a large collective, and in feeling its support, like the firm hand of a comrade.
[29 July 1985]

[For some reason *Pravda* very rarely deals with problems of political dissidence in the USSR – less often than *Izvestiya*, for example. It did print the following TASS report, however, in May 1984, at a time when rumours were rife in the West about the health and precise whereabouts of the dissident physicist Andrei Sakharov, banished without trial since 1980 to the city of Gorky, and his wife Yelena Bonner.]

It has long been known that every time the reactionary circles in the West want to complicate the international situation and distract public opinion from their own dangerous plans and actions, they resort to crude and barefaced anti-Soviet campaigns. For this purpose they balk at nothing, including the use of various renegades who have sold their consciences and disavowed their people.

Our adversaries assign a special place in these dirty machinations to that well-known anti-Soviet, Sakharov, whose uncitizenlike behaviour was long ago stigmatised by the Soviet people.

Mention must also be made of Sakharov's wife, Ye. G. Bonner, who not only constantly incites her husband to acts hostile to the Soviet state and society, but also commits such acts herself, as has been repeatedly reported in the press. It is she who acts as an intermediary between Sakharov and reactionary circles in the West. Over a number of years – and in a far from disinterested fashion – Bonner has earned her living by supplying Western anti-Soviet centres with shameless slander and malicious lampoons denigrating our country, our system and the Soviet people.

It has been irrefutably established that in doing this she used the services of staff at the American embassy in Moscow, who sent material received from Bonner abroad, using diplomatic channels. Recently such assistance has been given to her by first secretary E. McWilliams, and second secretaries G. Glass and J. Purnell.

As was discovered recently by the competent Soviet organs [i.e., the KGB], a far-reaching operation had been prepared, with a carefully worked-out script and with the participation of American diplomats, whereby Sakharov would declare yet another 'hunger strike', while Bonner obtained 'asylum' in the US embassy in Moscow. According to this plan, Bonner's stay in the embassy was to be used for meetings with foreign correspondents and for the transmission abroad of slanderous fabrications about the Soviet Union and all sorts of false information about the position of her husband, Sakharov.

These coordinated actions were intended to serve as a signal for the launch of an anti-Soviet campaign in the West, especially in the USA.

At the same time it was planned to use a far-fetched pretext – Bonner's state of health – to try to arrange for her to leave for abroad, where she was to become one of the leaders of the anti-Soviet scum in the pay of Western special services.

As a result of timely measures taken by the Soviet law-enforcement organs, this operation has been frustrated. An official representation has been made to the American side, setting forth the facts of US embassy employees' direct implication in this provocation and demanding that such inadmissible actions must stop.

The organisers of this provocative venture were taken unawares. Nonetheless they are trying to wriggle out of it and evade responsibility, hypocritically holding forth about being moved by nothing other than considerations of humanity.

Nothing could be further from the truth. They are reckoning on naïve people who might believe in the humane motives of a plotter caught in the act.

Those who shed crocodile tears over Sakharov's 'plight' prefer not to mention that they are putting on a pedestal a man who drags his own people in the mire, openly calls for war and for the use of nuclear weapons against his own country, and preaches misanthropic ideas. They also prefer to keep silent about the fact that the Soviet state is showing magnanimity and patience towards this man and is giving him the opportunity to leave the dangerous path and restore himself in the eyes of his fellow citizens.

No, it is not considerations of humanity that guide those who would like to raise another propaganda row over Sakharov and Bonner. They are blinded by bestial anti-Sovietism and would like to poison the international atmosphere still more, and sow venomous seeds of mistrust among peoples.

But it is time all the organisers of 'crusades' and ideological sabotage against the Land of Soviets understood that this path will

bring them no glory. That is how it was in the past, and so it will be in the future.
[5 May 1984]

Women

[The following article, written by E. Novikova, a Moscow academic, is a commentary on mail received by *Pravda* on the subject of 'Family Matters'. The equality before law of Soviet women is regularly cited as one of the great achievements of Soviet rule. But has it changed attitudes, especially men's attitudes? E. Novikova's article is entitled 'A double burden'.]

The letters in *Pravda*'s 'Family Matters' mailbag are evidence of the lively interest aroused these days by everything connected with the place and role of women in the family and society. Any occasion is sufficient to cause passions to flare up on this subject. One such occasion was presented by A. Bragina's letter which was published in *Pravda* on 2 February.

What this reader probably really wanted to speak about was the unpreparedness of some young people for family life, but she was over-hasty with her generalisation. The essence of her letter was contained in these phrases: 'Women, with their unlimited "equal rights", or to be more precise their laziness and indifference towards their family duties, are crippling their own lives and those of their children and husbands. . . . For millennia women coped with the home; so why have we become so weak now?' It was these words that evoked heated disagreement from many readers.

'Women in our country', writes the Muscovite I. Kuzmina, 'receive the same remuneration for socially useful work as do men. But our duties are also equal: we do not have the right to work less or worse than men. At work there is equality in both rights and duties. But at home . . . ?'

As you see, the reader links what seems to be a purely domestic problem with that of consolidating the *de facto* equality of men and women. This position of hers reflects the radical changes which have taken place in the way of life, social make-up, consciousness and thinking of millions of our fellow-countrywomen. These changes became possible as a result of the mass participation of women in social production, of the development of their political activity, and of the great help given to the family by the state.

And indeed, more than 90 per cent of able-bodied women today either work or study. There is practically no sector of the economy in which they do not make a real contribution. The overwhelming majority of our female contemporaries see work not just as a necessity, but also as an inner need, and an opportunity to unfold their strengths and abilities more fully. This aspiration is buttressed by their growing level of education: out of every thousand working women, 852 have higher or secondary education.

The woman as worker, the woman active in public life, the woman as mother: pride in her comes through in many readers' letters. But there is also anxiety in the letters: how can these roles be combined harmoniously? Is the double burden a light one?

'I live in a textiles-producing region,' writes I. Pankratova from Ivanovo Region. 'The [predominantly female] weavers often bring home higher wages than their husbands. Because they work no less than them, and get no less tired. But after work, we, the house-wives, still have to go round the shops buying in food, prepare the dinner, wash clothes, clean the flat, check the children's schoolwork. . . .'

T. Levchenko begins her letter emotionally: 'Where did A. Bragina dream up such a thing – that modern women are lazy?! She spends eight hours a day working at her job, and her remaining hours (just count them!) looking after her children and family. No, we're not complaining, but if we're honest about it, all working women – "emancipated" and not so emancipated – feel tired by the end of the day.' 'Is it worth agitating for traditionally female tasks to be shifted on to the husband's shoulders? Of course it is! Definitely!' says M. Labzina from Magnitogorsk. 'And this question should be raised more broadly than it has been up until now. After all, modern life has reduced the round of domestic chores of the male town-dweller, while the obligations of the wife and mother remain the same – endless.'

Let us try to show with the help of some facts and figures that the emotions of all these female readers are well-founded. Let us start with the fact that housework is socially useful and, today, socially necessary work. Those letter-writers who speak of a woman's 'double shift' are not far from the truth. Wives and mothers devote 2 to 2½ times as long to domestic work as husbands and fathers do. In the course of the 'domestic shift' housewives cover 15–20 kilometres every day, and perform at least 50 different operations, of which no more than 15 per cent are mechanised. Economists have calculated that even the basic operations involved in serving an average urban family, with two adults and a child, would be valued at over 90 roubles a month.

No mother or wife, of course, would ever ask for such extra payment from the members of her family, but it is no bad thing to understand what lies behind her daily round. One might expect that with an improvement in living conditions and a greater provision of communal services, the volume of housework ought to be getting smaller. But this is not happening. As prosperity grows, so does our demand for everyday culture and comforts, and so the time spent on 'the daily round' increases.

The excessive domestic workload of women certainly exists. It is the source of the continuing real inequality of women in everyday life and in the family, and, judging by the letters, it is seen by many as a kind of manifestation of social injustice. Much, of course, can be explained here by a number of objective and subjective factors. For many long years we Soviet people were required to strain every muscle and concentrate all our resources and efforts on solving those immediate tasks on which the very existence of the state depended. There was no time left over for the small things of life.

On top of that, life outside the 'industrial sphere' is by its nature more conservative: its character is determined not only by the influence of society, but depends to a greater degree on individual tastes, needs and inclinations. Here, traditions and customs are strong. Changing them is a complex and long-term process.

Where is the way out? First of all, in improving public services and shopping conditions. Many readers bring this up. Comrade Kerk of Lvov, for instance, writes: 'How many conflicts and family dramas could be avoided if it were possible to buy all the provisions one needed close to the home, if it were possible to have a good meal in a cafeteria, to get the washing cleaned properly in a laundry, and have one's shoes repaired quickly. And so on, and so forth.' As it is, experts reckon that at present only one-thirtieth of domestic chores are taken care of by public services. Today's transport and commercial services are also still exceptionally time-consuming. The time spent by the population on shopping, for example (looking for purchases, standing in queues) *rose* in the last ten years from 30,000 million to 37,000 million hours per year.

Secondly, modern housework requires not just the individual

gadgets which are manufactured in our country, but whole systems of domestic machines. The level of 'mechanisation' of everyday life is still very low. Much housework continues to be done by hand. And this doesn't only mean tiredness: there is also the time factor, the growing value of which is felt more and more acutely every year.

Thirdly, greater efforts must be made to overcome outdated ideas, according to which work done in or for the home is exclusively a woman's prerogative. There are a particularly large number of letters on this topic in our mailbag. I shall quote just one, from V. Vasilyeva, a pensioner from Obninsk: 'You're never going to instil in a child the desire or compulsion to do work about the house if day after day the child sees his mother run off her feet – rushing round shops, cooking, serving, washing up, doing the laundry, mending, sewing – while father sits with a newspaper. . . . Fostering industry in a child is the duty of *both* parents. Some fathers today have no moral right even to raise their voice to a child to tell him or her to help mother, since they don't help her themselves.'

Even if we raise services to a high level and mechanise household tasks, home remains home. Its round of daily cares will remain in the foreseeable future. This is why cooperation within the family, the raising of tomorrow's family-man, and the affirmation of the socialist principles of family life acquire such urgency. One should not speak contemptuously of 'the daily round' – for the daily round is everyday life – and the test of life – in which modern morality in many respects reveals itself and is put to the test.

V. Marenich, an engineer from Kazakhstan, for example, writes about 25 years of happy married life, and concludes: 'The main thing is to instil in young people goodness, decency, a sense of respect and, if you like, compassion for those near to them. If these qualities are implanted, they will themselves understand who should be doing what in the home.'

As you see, the problems of everyday life go far beyond the position of women. They are, in the broad sense, moral problems. The micro-climate of a family in which there is a traditional division of functions – the husband has an interesting job and lives practically only for that, while the wife does the housework and serves at home – is fraught with serious contradictions and inner instability. By contrast, in families where both spouses bear an equal load, according to research, more than 60 per cent of marriages are happy ones, and only five per cent failures. Real equality of the members of a family, without the superiority of some and the submissiveness of others, aids the harmonious development of the personality and creates the atmosphere of mutual understanding and good-will that is so essential for the children.

There are no few letters in our mailbag which are full of what I would call 'social optimism' – letters from people who have successfully resolved for themselves the natural contradictions of 'everyday life'. But one cannot ignore the anxiety that makes itself heard in other letters: men who dodge housework often also perform their paternal duties badly. Unfortunately, experts on family problems write very modestly, if at all, about paternity. But in my view, there is a need for this. For even the most self-sacrificing and devoted mother cannot replace what only a father can give a child. He is needed equally by a daughter and by a son.

Psychologists' research confirms: boys and girls pay more attention nowadays to the requests and advice of their mother, and prefer to spend time with her rather than with their father. And the same perplexed and worried question keeps coming up in letters: is it not the case that some fathers have decided that bringing up children is purely a 'woman's business'? If a father devotes the necessary attention to his son or daughter, and becomes more closely attached to them, then he himself lives a fuller, emotionally richer life.

The main point, then, let us repeat, is that the equal rights proclaimed by law, and real equality, especially where attitudes are concerned, are by no means one and the same thing. But a process, a healthy process, *is* under way, with old values being rejected and new ones being acquired. It is equally necessary today for both women and men to reassess and redefine the social roles of the two heads of the household. Unfortunately it is not yet realised in all families why or how boys and girls have to be prepared for the duties of mothers and fathers. Is this not the reason why 40 per cent of boys and 25 per cent of girls today consider that housework can be divided into male and female chores?

The orientation of a certain section of youth towards male supremacy leads to the fact that boys have far fewer domestic skills and abilities than girls of the same age. Among fifteen-year-olds in Moscow schools, 20 per cent of boys and 19 per cent of girls do not know how to prepare a lunch; 54 and 3 per cent respectively cannot wash clothes; and 47 and 19 per cent cannot mend clothes. What a reproach this is to the family and school. Often we regard the question of children making themselves useful merely as washing floors in corridors and classrooms, rather than above all learning to serve themselves. And when they are all but men, they still have no clue about how to sew a button on to a suit, make themselves breakfast, or wash a shirt (and no desire to do so, either).

I should like to conclude these notes with another impression from readers' letters, which themselves give an excellent character-isation of woman today. Today's woman feels herself to be an individual, and wants to be one, and always wants to occupy a worthy place in society. She has a developed sense of her own dignity. But it is not easy today to achieve harmony between the social and the personal, and that is why she is looking for support, above all, from that person whom she calls her companion for life.
[9 June 1984]

K. A. Mitskevich has worked as a pointswoman at the October Square tram terminus for forty years. It is a pleasure to look at her work. The tramline points on her section are always well-greased and free of dirt and rubbish. This means they are easy and reliable to switch.

The tools of Ksenia Antonovna's trade are simple enough: a long-handled broom, a dust-pan, and hooks to remove the covers from the points. Some might find it boring and uninteresting to do this day after day, but she believes she is doing an important and necessary job. After all, the smooth running of the trams can put thousands and thousands of people in a good mood.

Ksenia Antonovna is a responsible woman. It is not for nothing that her labour has been awarded with many diplomas and a 'Veteran of Labour' medal. Her comrades speak highly of her. She is also known as a caring grandmother, who, after her son died, brought up her two grandchildren.
[Letter from Yu. Zamyshlyayev, Apakov Tram Depot, Moscow; 3 September 1985]

Espionage

The End of 'Rolf Daniel'
by V. Chirkov

Yes, this whole account reads like a detective story. But it is not made up – the names and facts are all authentic. Yet, reading through this criminal case, instituted under article 64a of the RSFSR Criminal Code (Espionage), I caught myself thinking that I was reading the screenplay for some kind of spy film. Later in court I saw the real people whose names had been referred to in the file as The Accused, The Witness, and so on.

Frequent mention was also made of characters such as foreign intelligence officers. Enjoying diplomatic immunity, they managed to avoid being put on trial, but they were expelled from the USSR. On 13 September 1983 *Pravda* wrote about one of them – a certain Augustenborg, who worked at the American consulate in Leningrad, and who was caught in the very act of spying. We shall come across him more than once in this story. But not yet. Let us first look at how everything began, or, more precisely, at the beginning of the end of one of the CIA's espionage operations.

Izmailovo, Moscow

Towards evening on 20 July 1983 storm clouds gathered over Moscow. The rain lashed down, chasing away the oppressive afternoon heat and the lingering tourists strolling by the cathedral near the Silver Vine Pond in Izmailovo Park. A solitary car sped along the highway, spraying up cascades of water. A flash of lightning momentarily illuminated the diplomatic number-plate of the US embassy in Moscow. Not far from the cathedral, surrounded by its moat, a tall, lean young man carrying a bag containing something bulky and heavy got out of the car. He disappeared for a few minutes into some bushes. Soaked to the skin, he crawled back out, and stealthily looked around. There was no one there. His bag was empty. Glancing round again, he shook off the leaves which had stuck to his white shirt, drew breath, and beat a hasty retreat.

The Committee for State Security (KGB), Moscow

It was long after midnight when the Chekists [KGB officers] returned from Izmailovo Park. In the bushes where the night-time stroller from the American embassy had been crawling in the rain, they had discovered a 'stone', inside which were spy instructions, code-books and other accoutrements of espionage.

Izmailovo Park, Moscow

A curly-haired man with small, close-set eyes approached the bushes. At that early hour of the morning the park was deserted. The sun was scarcely beginning to shimmer in the brown water of the moat. The man bent down, lifted the stone, put it into a travelling bag, straightened, then suddenly sank down again as his knees gave way in terror. He forced himself to look round again.

No, it was nothing dangerous – just the door banging on a car which was passing. Looking from side to side, the curly-haired man made his way towards the metro station, chased from that place by fear. Hidden, subconscious fear – but not unfounded. 'However long the yarn you spin, there has to be an end. . . .'

KGB Headquarters, Leningrad

The 'curly-haired man' was Yu. V. Pavlov, who worked at the Arctic and Antarctic Research Institute. Soviet counter-intelligence had long been interested in him, and now everything fell into place. One thing that became clear was the real nature of his 'harmless' contacts with foreigners in ports abroad, which Pavlov visited as he sailed the world on board a Soviet research ship. After his arrest, when investigators began to piece together the sequence of events, Pavlov was forced to recall everything down to the smallest detail. They gradually managed to establish the truth, and discover why and how he turned into a traitor and a foreign intelligence agent, under the cover name of 'Rolf Daniel'.

From Pavlov's Testimony

'. . . I was born on 31 December 1935 in the city of Kuibyshev. My father was a mining engineer, and my mother an English teacher. . . .'

His childhood, like that of millions of his contemporaries, passed during the pre-war and wartime years. Fate cast his family from one new building project to another. Only after the war was his father transferred to Leningrad.

Pavlov finished school, and then went to one of Leningrad's institutes for what was at that time an unusual speciality – 'experimental nuclear physics'. On finishing his course, he worked for a while on a dissertation. He found this boring and gave it up. But then a few years later he embarked upon a fantastic project – the creation of artificial diamonds with the help of nuclear explosions. Then Pavlov decided to try his luck in a different field. After less than two years he left his research institute in Leningrad and went off to the Far East. At the beginning of 1961 Pavlov found himself at sea for the first time, on board the now legendary *Vityaz*. The voyage took in Japan, Tahiti, Fiji, Hawaii. . . .

This was all interesting, yet at the same time very mundane in its own way. Serious scientific work was being done aboard the *Vityaz*, and no one was looking for fanfares or laurels. No one, that is, except Pavlov. He always believed himself to be much more import-ant than was really the case. The reality of his daily existence and duties at work only served to irritate him. So it was that, returning from his trip abroad to a modest post in one of Vladivostok's research institutes, he uttered Ostap Bender's classic phrase: 'This is not Rio de Janeiro!'* Pavlov imagined that he would go there one day.

Leningrad

Pavlov was not met with fanfares in Leningrad either, when he returned there soon after his father's death. He changed jobs several times over the seven years from 1962 to 1969. It was not interesting work he was after, but good money. This period in his life appears in his record of work under the number of a military unit. His occupation then is usually referred to as 'secret work and documents', and, naturally, he had to sign an undertaking not to divulge those secrets.

Later, when he was enlisted by the CIA, it was precisely the secrets to which Pavlov had access at that time that most interested the people at Langley [CIA headquarters].

From Pavlov's Testimony

'. . . I was shown the criminal code during the investigation in November 1984. . . . And I realised then the nature of my crimes. . . .'

Pavlov, of course, understood perfectly well the dangers of divulging secret information. But this is typical of Pavlov. During his trial he admitted only facts which could not be denied. He played his role right to the end. . . .

'The role of a superman,' said the investigator in charge of his case. 'He genuinely saw himself in this role. The fact is, he is an adventurer, a reckless gambler, convinced that he can outdo everyone. During the investigation, incidentally, he found it hard to believe that his downfall was predetermined. He searched and searched for the mistake which allowed the KGB to catch him red-handed. He thought it was chance. . . .'

Leningrad

Pavlov's double life began long before he became a traitor. The following words appear in the bill of indictment: '. . . As a result of his ideological degeneration, Yu. V. Pavlov became an opponent of Soviet power.'

---

* Ostap Bender is the hero of *The Twelve Chairs* (1928) and *The Golden Calf* (1931), well-known satirical novels by the writers Ilf and Petrov.

What did he have against Soviet power? Why was he dissatisfied? Here are a few lines from his biography.

In 1969 he went to work at the USSR Naval Register. 'Eventually,' as he himself put it, 'I became one of the central figures in the register's atomic inspectorate. From 1977 to 1980 I travelled abroad as part of a Soviet delegation to conferences of an international group who were drafting a safety code for atomic ships. I was four times in London, and once in Geneva, Ottawa and Hamburg.' But even so he left the Register. Of his own accord. Why? This is how he explained it later, during the investigation: 'I came to realise that the confines of this organisation were too narrow for me. A long period of stagnation had set in. . . .'

He would 'sit at his work for hours, staring at the ceiling'. These are his own words. What was it he was dreaming about during working time? About the 'good life', about fame, about a summer-house, and not just anywhere, but in the Bahamas. . . .

It says in the statement of indictment that it was precisely when he was daydreaming that Pavlov first felt the 'urge for profit'. In a strange way this urge co-existed in Pavlov with his futile daydreaming. He thought that he had heard somewhere that Nobel prize-winners were given villas in the Bahamas. He mused: 'All foreign news agencies will broadcast: "Yuri Pavlov, the eminent scientist whose work was not recognised in the Soviet Union, has been awarded the Nobel Prize for his work on the creation of artificial diamonds with the help of a nuclear explosion . . .".'

He gradually hatched a plan to hand over his rejected manuscript to the West. There, he thought, he would be appreciated. . . .

In the autumn of 1981 Pavlov left his work at the Register and went to the Arctic and Antarctic Research Institute. He took a drop in salary for the sole purpose of joining the research ship *Professor Vize* on a foreign expedition.

Ålesund Port, Norway

October 1981. Pavlov goes ashore together with a group of sailors. In his pocket he has a letter written in English. He writes that he is undervalued in Russia, that he is unable to carry out his scientific work according to his proposed method, and also that he does not have enough money. In the letter he included a description of his 'method of obtaining artificial diamonds', and the ship's route. He added: 'I shall be dressed in an old, dark coat and knitted hat, and shall be carrying a brightly coloured booklet in my right hand.'

He went to the town's post office with a group of sailors, hurriedly scribbled the address on the envelope – West German Consulate, Ålesund, Norway – and posted it.

Twice – once in Hamburg, and again in Reykjavik – he went ashore with the brightly coloured booklet in his hand. But nobody approached him.

Hamburg, West Germany

On 23 March 1982 the *Professor Vize* again dropped anchor at Hamburg. This time Pavlov finally 'struck lucky'.

From Pavlov's Testimony

'. . . I went ashore dressed the same way (coat, hat, but no booklet). A tall, suntanned, elderly man with a slight squint kept following us, and, when the opportunity arose, gave me a sign, clearly trying to attract my attention. Our group went into a department store. The members of the group were busy choosing souvenirs, so it was easy for me to slip away. The man approached me, showed me the envelope in which I had sent my letter to the German Consulate, and asked me in English if I had written it. Then he handed me the envelope, in which, as I later discovered, were 800 West German Deutschmarks. He said he hoped we would meet again, as it would be to our mutual advantage. . . .'

The 'elderly German' asked him before they parted to supply his *curriculum vitae* and also a list of his scientific work. He said that he needed this for a certain scientific centre in West Germany, which was going to subsidise Pavlov's work. So his worth was appreciated after all. . . .

Back in his cabin Pavlov kept fingering the bundle of bank-notes. First he transferred them from his coat pocket to his jacket, then put them under his pillow. Then he took them out again and counted them. He remembered that he had seen a gold bracelet in a jeweller's shop at the port. It cost DM550. That would be really something worth buying. And he would still have some money left. . . . He went out and bought it. Later, this bracelet was to figure in the trial as material evidence. . . .

Rio de Janeiro, Brazil

The man with the squint had told him when they parted: 'We will meet again in your next port of call. . . .'

When they met in Rio de Janeiro there was no further talk about science. The 'elderly German' began the conversation in a round-about way. To begin with he asked Pavlov to sign for the DM800 which he had been given. 'For the accounts.' Then he said: 'Unfortunately very little is known about the Soviet Union in our scientific circles. Your society, alas, is a closed one. And things which are openly published in our free press are kept under lock and key in your country. It seems that you were working with atomic-powered engines for ships, judging by your trips abroad with Soviet delegations. . . .'

'Yes,' answered Pavlov. 'That is no secret.'

'God forbid, we are not interested in genuinely secret information. But the scientific centre which is prepared to help you would like to receive, by way of compensation, answers to certain questions. This, of course, will be kept in the utmost confidence, and will have no effect on your career. And the questions themselves are perfectly innocent. . . .'

The questions were far from innocent. The 'elderly German', a staff officer in the BND, the German secret service, set up after the war by the CIA together with a former general in Hitler's army, asked Pavlov for data which were USSR state secrets.

Pavlov understood where all this was leading, what he was being drawn into. He tried to refuse, but the 'German' hinted that he had to earn the money he had received. . . .

If Pavlov had been able to stop even then, he would not have ended up before a Leningrad military tribunal. Soviet law is humane. Only by giving himself up could Pavlov have avoided the dock. But he did not stop. . . .

Santa Cruz de Tenerife, Canary Islands

On 12 May 1982 the 'elderly German' unexpectedly got on a bus heading for the port. He made to get off the bus one stop before the port. Passing Pavlov, he dropped a newspaper on to his knees, and apologised. Pavlov passed a newspaper back to him, but it was his own, in which he had hidden an envelope with answers to the questions he had been given in Rio de Janeiro. Back on ship he found a package inside the 'German's' newspaper. It contained money and a new set of instructions. . . .

Towards evening the *Professor Vize* left the Canary Islands and set sail for Leningrad.

Leningrad

Pavlov again had the chance to go and tell everything that had happened to him during his trip. But he did not. Why?

From Pavlov's Testimony

'. . . I thought about going and telling everything, but I suppressed this thought and decided not to reveal myself: I wanted to keep the money I had received. . . .'

He had not managed to spend all his spy 'wages' in Santa Cruz. He made himself a polythene body-belt and, on leaving the *Professor Vize*, smuggled the money in it through customs. In the same way he managed to take the money on board another research ship, the *Professor Zubov*, which left Leningrad on 6 October 1982.

Copenhagen

By the exit from the port the familiar 'elderly German' was standing, winking with his squinting eye. Pavlov hurried away, and the German followed him, keeping his distance in order not to attract the attention of the sailors from the *Zubov*. The group stopped to have their photograph taken beside a monument to fishermen lost at sea. Pavlov walked over to a flower stall.

'Hello, welcome.' Pavlov heard the squint-eyed German's hoarse voice. 'Why are you so nervous? Calm down. No one is following you. Brought anything new?'

'No, I wasn't able to,' replied Pavlov.

'No goods – no money,' croaked the 'elderly German'. 'But you can still earn it. I've got a questionnaire here. Answer the questions. Try to have all the answers ready by tomorrow. A young colleague of mine will work with you. He also has some technical questions for you. He will find you himself. And I'll meet you again in Rio. By the way, if you need a camera, I have a Minox in my pocket. It's very easy to use. . . .'

That night Pavlov filled in the questionnaire, then crawled into his bunk and tossed and turned for a long time before falling into a troubled sleep.

In the morning he went ashore again. As he was passing an old house on Stroget Street he heard a voice asking him in English: 'My dear friend, have you filled in our form?' Before him stood a tall fair-haired man, young but balding, with a plastic bag in his hand. Pavlov handed over the papers. The man took a piece of paper out of his pocket, checked it against Pavlov's handwriting, and, thanking him, walked quickly away. His parting words were: 'See you in Rio.'

Rio de Janeiro

Standing at the traffic lights waiting for them to turn green, Pavlov idly contemplated the yellow and white buses filling the Avenido Rio Branco with diesel fumes, and the small cars dodging the big air-conditioned limousines. Somebody prodded him gently in the side, and he felt something like a thermometer case being slipped into his free hand. The 'young German' from Copenhagen was standing beside him. The lights turned to green. The 'German' crossed the street, keeping as close as he could to Pavlov, and Pavlov was able to pass him his letter and a detailed schedule of the *Professor Zubov's* voyage.

From Pavlov's Testimony

'. . . When I returned to the ship I saw that what I had been given was a thin cardboard tube, open at both ends. There was a piece of paper inside. It was a list of technical questions in English. I was familiar with most of the data they wanted.'

West German intelligence wanted their agent to supply more and more information about Soviet warships, engines for atomic-powered submarines, defence enterprises, and about those who worked in them.

Yes, Pavlov was aware that he was being dragged deeper into a quagmire from which there was no easy escape.

The next morning Pavlov went ashore again. He called in at a chemist's shop under the pretext of buying a razor. The 'elderly German' was waiting for him.

'Hello, long time no see!'

'Quiet!' said Pavlov. 'Someone might hear us.'

'There's no need to worry. Your men are nowhere near. Have you brought the answers?'

'Yes, here they are,' said Pavlov, and handed him a sealed envelope, the contents of which had kept him busy until midnight.

'Here's the money.' The 'German' reached for his pocket.

'Not here. Wait till Montevideo.'

'You're right to be cautious. Your group is waiting for you at the next crossroads. Hurry and catch them up.'

The whole meeting lasted only five minutes. In the morning the *Professor Zubov* left Rio de Janeiro and set sail for Uruguay.

Montevideo

Pavlov saw his German acquaintances at the port gates. He gave them a brief, imperceptible wave, and had time to see them set off slowly towards their car.

They did not meet until midday. The 'young German' was sitting on a bench in Independence Square, pretending to be watching the pigeons fluttering round his feet in the hope of getting some food. Pavlov dropped back from his comrades and turned a corner. The German immediately caught up with him and thrust an envelope into his pocket. 'There's money in it,' he said, 'and a little surprise for you. The Americans are going to be working with you now. Try to be at the Hotel President tomorrow by eleven o'clock. It's on the left-hand side of Artigas Square, next to the "Good Style" sign, about two blocks from here along 18 July Street. You will be met there. And don't worry, your safety is fully guaranteed. . . .'

On the way back to the port he turned over in his mind his conversation with the 'young German'. Why were they handing him over to the Americans? Had they decided they no longer needed him? Another thought was niggling him: 'I wasn't entirely truthful about everything, after all. Perhaps the Germans have stopped believing me and are handing me over to the CIA?'

Pavlov did not understand right up to the end why he was handed over (or resold?) to the Americans. He did not know that the West German special services have been under the control of their American masters from their very conception.

In his cabin on board the ship, when he opened the envelope and read the instructions it contained, Pavlov forced himself to be calm. The Americans were trying to persuade him: 'Your safety is of primary importance to us. . . .' They went on to state the conditions of working for the CIA – a monthly salary, and a certain rate of payment for each important piece of information. All this would be paid into his personal bank account. Pavlov slowly tore up the paper, threw it into the toilet and flushed it away. Only the questionnaire remained. The next day he had to return it, completed, at the Hotel President. . . . To new masters. . . . So far they had not been over-generous. His advance was only 100 dollars.

Not that Pavlov's hopes that his 'transfer' to US intelligence would be accompanied by a shower of gold were destined to come true. On that occasion, as on future occasions, the Americans did not spoil their agent. In his sick imagination Pavlov counted up multi-digit figures in his 'personal account', and thick wads of 'his' dollars flashed before his eyes. Only later, during the investigation, did it become clear to him that Americans had duped him with their promises, skilfully playing on his desire for profit. Try as he might, Pavlov never discovered how much money he had earned, and in which bank it was kept.

. . . He caught sight of them a few blocks away from the Hotel President. The 'elderly German' was walking along 18 July Street, obsequiously supporting the 'Chief' – as Pavlov immediately christened him – by the elbow. The 'Chief' walked rather strangely, as though he had lumbago. They came out through an archway into the square almost at the hotel itself. Pavlov went up to them, and the

'Chief', taking off his dark glasses, put out his hand to him. The 'German' said: 'Let me introduce you. This is our American friend.'

'Call me Pavel,' he said. 'Pleased to meet you.'

The American studied Pavlov for a moment, then put his dark glasses on again and motioned him to go into the hotel.

'No, no, someone might see me with you,' said Pavlov. Only then did he notice some athletically built young men standing a short distance away. The 'German' nodded in their direction. 'Don't worry, we have reliable protection.'

'Pavel' asked Pavlov if he had read his letter.

'Yes,' replied Pavlov.

'Do our conditions for cooperation satisfy you?'

'On the whole, yes.'

'We must have a more detailed discussion. I have a proposal to make. We will give you some pills. They are absolutely safe, but when you take them the ship's doctor will think you are seriously ill, and they will be forced to leave you in a hospital on shore. That way we can teach you some things which you might find useful in the future. After about a month you can return home on some other Soviet ship.'

'It's too dangerous,' said Pavlov.

'We will guarantee. . . .'

'No, no, I don't want any pills. Let's just carry on as before. . . .'

'Well, O.K.,' Pavel agreed, and took an envelope from his pocket. 'Take this then. There are some questions and a little pocket money. Give the answers to our man in Mauritius. He will find you in the market area. The password is "Pavel Duklov".'

Port Louis, Mauritius

From Montevideo the *Professor Zubov* headed south to the island of South Georgia, then crossed the Atlantic, and, rounding the south of Africa, set course for Mauritius. In the evening of 5 April 1983 the lights of Port Louis appeared on the horizon.

. . . In the morning Pavlov went into town with the first group of men going ashore. Sitting on the steps in front of the port's administrative building was a young man in dark glasses who looked a little like a Mexican. Pavlov recognised him as one of the men who had formed the 'cordon' outside the Hotel President while he was speaking to 'Pavel'. The 'Mexican' waved to Pavlov and slowly started to follow his group to the market. They exchanged envelopes beside a souvenir stall, whereupon the 'Mexican' at once disappeared into the crowd.

Pavlov mused: 'I wonder how the Americans will react to my answers. I don't even know half of what they're interested in. I haven't been involved in these matters for ages. I've only managed to glean a little about the new submarines from some old friends, but the Yankees want detailed information. Eighty questions, some with sub-sections – where can I find the answers to all of these? Well, I suppose I can think something up. Just let them try to verify it!'

The envelope contained another questionnaire, even more extensive. And a letter. 'Dear friend! We are pleased that you have agreed to work with us. In this way you are building a better future for your family.' Pavlov read through the questionnaire and gave a wry smile: 'A better future!'

As well as the questionnaire, the 'Mexican's' envelope contained two other interesting notes. First, a description of means of secret communication with the CIA abroad – addresses and telephone numbers which Pavlov could use to contact the 'Centre' if he found himself unexpectedly abroad. Secondly, a note informing him that henceforth for the CIA he was no longer simply Pavlov, but an agent under the name 'Rolf Daniel'. That was how he was to sign all future reports. There was a postscript to the note which said that he must learn the addresses and his name by heart, then put the pieces of paper on which they were written into a glass of water, and they would dissolve.

Pavlov stared in amazement as the instructions disappeared in the water before his eyes, and stirred it with a teaspoon just to make sure. . . .

Copenhagen

The squares and parks of the Danish capital were ablaze with Maytime tulips of every hue. But not even they could cheer the sailors from the *Professor Zubov*, who wanted to get home as quickly as possible. Only three days were left till Leningrad. One last visit ashore, then home. . . .

Pavlov again left the port with the first group. 'Pavel' was sitting by the 'Mermaid'. He got up and slowly set off ahead of the group in the direction of the Royal Palace on Amalienborg Square. There were crowds of tourists in the square waiting for the changing of the guard. Pavlov heard a voice behind him: 'Greetings from Pavel Duklov!' The 'Mexican' was standing beside him. 'Pavel' had disappeared. The 'Mexican' took an envelope from Pavlov containing the answers to the questions he had been given in Port Louis, and slipped a notebook into his pocket.

There was a note inside. It explained to him that the notebook contained a secret compartment, in the cardboard back cover. On his arrival in Leningrad he has to open it along the edge with a razor. For the moment he was to remember one thing: if he never managed to get abroad again, he was to try to get a job at a defence installation and to let them know using the instructions hidden in the secret compartment.

On 17 May 1983 Pavlov went ashore in Leningrad. . . .

Leningrad

'Dear friend! We are glad you received our parcel in Copenhagen and are prepared to maintain links with us from within the USSR. As you requested we have paid money into your account. . . . Give the signal at 'Entrance' that you have received the container. . . .'

Pavlov reread the note from the CIA which he found together with the spying equipment in the 'drop' in Izmailovo Park. On his table lay the notebook he was given in Copenhagen, with the cover cut open. It contained details of secret communications, addresses in Leningrad and Moscow. The 'Entrance' was marked too. . . .

'Rolf Daniel' still figured in the card indexes and pay-rolls of the American secret services. The CIA radio station was still broadcasting coded messages for him, always beginning 'Dear friend!' and containing assurances of his 'complete safety'. But already the affair was coming to a close.

. . . I was travelling through Leningrad in a car with someone who was directly involved in this operation.

I am used to seeing Leningrad on my infrequent visits there the same way as tourists see it. My travelling companion was one of the few people who know the other side of Leningrad. We travelled along the route normally taken by staff of the US consulate on their way there from home. It was along this route that the places for giving arranged signals were marked.

Vladimirskaya Square

This square, near one of Leningrad's markets, was named 'Vlad'. It was chosen as the place to give Pavlov signals telling him about the drops left for him by CIA agents working under diplomatic cover in Moscow and Leningrad. If a car with the diplomatic number-plate of the US consulate was parked with its nose to the pavement, this meant the drop was at the arranged location in Leningrad; if the boot was next to the pavement, it was in Moscow. This was how the wife of American intelligence officer Augustenborg parked the car on 24 July 1983, giving 'Rolf Daniel' the signal.

The Bank of the Bypass Canal

There are scarcely any houses here, and not a soul about at the end of the working day. Here they chose a drop site which they called 'Bypass'.

No. 16, Kronverkskaya Street

When he returned to Leningrad from his voyage, Pavlov was supposed to mark the number '2' at the entrance to No. 16, Kronverkskaya Street, in such a way that it would be visible from a passing car. This would mean that he had found a job as instructed and was awaiting a signal about a drop.

The Crossroads of Gorky Street and Kronverkskaya Street

A telephone box can be seen from the crossroads. This site was called 'Maxim'. Here 'Rolf Daniel' was to leave a sign indicating that he was ready to deposit secret information.

No. 1/79, Dobrolyubov Avenue

The CIA instructions named this house 'Good'. Just as on Kronverkskaya Street, the agent was to mark a '2' on the wall of the courtyard after depositing his information.

The 40-km post on Primorskoye Highway

Drop site 'Forty'. This was the name given to the signpost forty kilometres out on the Primorskoye Highway. Staff from the US consulate regularly drive past it on their way to their *dacha* at Zelenogorsk, 60 kilometres from Leningrad. It was at this secret place that the key events were to unfold. . . .

No. 11, Pestel Street

Another courtyard. We went up to the old house. It was being renovated and was under scaffolding. 'Look,' said my companion. 'The mark is still there.' A fat '2' was drawn on the faded plaster. That was how Pavlov, at the end of August 1983, had informed the CIA that he had removed the contents to the 'stone' in Izmailovo Park. This was the place called 'Entrance'. I ran my hand along the wall and imagined for a moment how the 'diplomats' from the US consulate must have driven along this street past the 'Entrance'. Braking gently, they would have noted with satisfaction, 'The container in Moscow has been removed.' And driven on. As though nothing had happened. . . .

The CIA Radio Centre, Greece

Immediately after the agreed '2' appeared at the 'Entrance', the following message for Pavlov was transmitted by the CIA radio centre in Greece, from one of the US military bases entrenched in that country: 'Glad you got the container. Looking forward to your signal that the drop is loaded at "Forty".'

Leningrad

On 5 September a '2' appeared at 'Maxim'. The next morning on his way to work a US consulate employee braked gently by the telephone kiosk and noted the signal.

The 40-km post on Primorskoye Highway

On 10 September, a Saturday, at seven o'clock in the evening, an inconspicuous cloth smeared with oil appeared at the 40-kilometre post. Wrapped inside it was a tin containing information from 'Rolf Daniel'.

And again Pavlov trembled with nerves. He stood alone at the bus stop. Everything seemed to have gone off all right. But nonetheless he sat all the way to Leningrad huddled up in his seat as though he could not get warm.

Leningrad – Zelenogorsk

That night another '2' appeared at the agreed place, known as 'Good', on Dobrolyubov Avenue. On the morning of Sunday 11 September, Muller, an intelligence officer from the US consulate made sure that the sign was there, and then set off along Primorskoye Highway. At kilometre 40 he reduced speed slightly and carried on to the *dacha* at Zelenogorsk. The Augustenborg family had been there since Friday. . . .

Forty minutes after Muller arrived, Augustenborg, with his wife and two-year-old daughter, left the consular *dacha*. An 'advance party' – another car with the consulate's number-plates – left a few minutes before them. It passed kilometre 40 without stopping. All was quiet on the highway. Ten minutes later Augustenborg's car braked sharply at the 40-kilometre sign. His wife got out holding a child's blanket in her hands. The blanket fell, neatly covering the dirty cloth and container lying on the concrete base of the post.

Pretending to be annoyed at her 'clumsiness', Augustenborg's wife quickly picked up the blanket and hurried back into the car. It was obvious that this scene had been carefully practised, for the blanket had to fall exactly on top of the cloth.

Augustenborg himself meanwhile had to sit at the wheel with his foot literally on the pedal so that they could make a quick getaway. Everything seemed to go according to plan, exactly as rehearsed.

Mrs Augustenborg threw the blanket and cloth on to the back seat, where their daughter was strapped into a child's chair, but she did not manage to get back into the car herself. Some people in camouflage suddenly appeared as if from nowhere and surrounded the car.

The rest of the story is known – *Pravda* reported it in an article published back in the autumn of 1983: Mr Augustenborg was declared *persona non grata* and left the USSR together with his family.

Mr Muller followed in the same direction shortly thereafter.

CIA Headquarters, Langley

In June 1982, almost a year before the secret drop was left in Izmailovo Park, the President of the USA arrived at CIA headquarters in Langley. He went there to sign a draft law about keeping the names of secret service agents out of the press. And at the same time to cheer up the 'cloak-and-dagger knights', and to inspire them to a 'crusade' against the 'empire of evil', as it has become fashionable to call our country in certain circles. This is what he said: 'You, ladies and gentlemen of the CIA, are the eyes and ears of the free world. . . . We must call all countries of the world to a crusade for freedom and to a global campaign for human rights; you are at the forefront of this struggle. You have to be at the forefront in times of both war and peace, and in that twilight world somewhere in between. . . .'

That was how the head of the American administration spelt out the facts. The CIA is an obedient tool in the hands of the highest executive power of the USA, and it is from above that its instructions come to engage in espionage against our country and the other socialist countries, to lure people like Pavlov into its nets, and to persuade them to betray their Motherland. They have no scruples about the ways and means employed in this secret war. All the talk about 'human rights', about 'freedom and democracy' is nothing but a smoke screen for the 'crusaders' of Langley. And behind that screen, dirty, loathsome deeds are committed, and the lives and souls of unstable, confused people are destroyed.

From Yu. V. Pavlov's Final Statement

'. . . I have committed the gravest of crimes against my Motherland. . . . I deeply repent what I have done. I have lost my family, who are eternally dear to me. I am unworthy of life among Soviet people. I cannot look them in the eye. . . .'

The military tribunal sentenced Yu. V. Pavlov to a severe and deserved punishment.

In Place of an Epilogue

In preparing for a first 'pre-emptive' strike against the USSR, in working out 'Star Wars' plans against our country and the socialist community, in seeking military superiority, aggressive circles in the USA attach great importance to intelligence gathering and other subversive acts. They also draw their allies from NATO and other blocs into their actions (witness the 'Rolf Daniel' affair). And although the CIA plays a dominant role in the secret war, other intelligence agencies also take part in the perfidious intrigues against us. The intelligence organs of the imperialist states, serving their masters, are not involved in spying just for spying's sake. It would be a delusion to imagine them merely as organs of espionage.

They are the instrument of an aggressive policy, of 'psychological warfare', disinformation, and subversive operations carried out by an assortment of renegades and traitors. They play an active part in the practical realisation of the plans of the present US ruling circles, who proclaim the annihilation of communism as their chief purpose. They aim to shake the social and political foundations of socialism and to weaken the defence capability of the socialist states. We have described the failure of one operation of the CIA and BND. But it, alas, is not a solitary event. We must be prepared for the fact that subversive operations against our country will continue.

Our main weapon in this war has been, and will be, the vigilance of the Soviet people.

Yes, vigilance is our common cause, just as we share our Motherland and our concern for her security. We are against blind suspicion, but we shall guard our secrets well and trustily defend the interests of the Land of Soviets. We must show no tolerance whatever to the enemy's intrigues, or to any manifestations of bourgeois attitudes, including money-grubbing and materialism, which are alien to the very essence of our way of life. For these are far from just innocent 'birth-marks', about which people sometimes speak with incomprehensible benevolence. In Pavlov they were transformed into spiritual cancer. And from there it was only a short step to betrayal.

The Pavlov affair is very instructive. It shows what can become of the carelessness and frivolity of ideologically unstable people, who are too slow to see, behind the flattery and hypocritical 'sympathy' of some Western 'well-wishers', the artfully woven web of Western intelligence, who get caught up in it and drawn into criminal activities against our Motherland.

'However long the yarn you spin, there has to be an end.' This wise proverb is fully applicable to people like Pavlov. They do not exist in a vacuum. Soviet people reject them as foreign bodies – and how could it be otherwise? It's getting too hot for spies in our Fatherland.

Basing their activities on Leninist principles, performing complex tasks in exposing and frustrating the operations of the imperialist states' special services, the USSR state security organs reliably protect the interests of the Soviet state, enjoying the support and aid of the Soviet people. The efficiency and skill of the Chekists, their devoted service to the cause, and the keen vigilance of the Soviet people – all this is our guarantee that the intrigues of Western intelligence shall always be doomed to failure.

[13, 14, 15 August 1985]

Space Research

[The Salyut-7 space station has been orbiting the Earth since 1982, manned at various times by different crews. Some time after three cosmonauts returned to Earth in October 1984, having spent a record-breaking 237 days in space, contact was lost with the Salyut station, and it was left dark and silent, circling the Earth without means of control from the ground. In June 1985 cosmonauts Vladimir Dzhanibekov and Viktor Savinykh, aboard the Soyuz-T-13 spacecraft, blasted off from the Baikonur cosmodrome on a unique mission: to locate the Salyut station, dock with it, reactivate it, and turn it once again into a working 'space laboratory'. In an 'exclusive' for *Pravda*, Dzhanibekov described the first days of that mission.]

We caught sight of the station as soon as we came out into the light – she was glinting in the rays of the sun, which were still struggling through the atmosphere. First a dot, then a little insect, she grew as we drew closer. The moon, too, came into our field of vision. It was fascinating to observe the two bodies moving, as the station seemed to 'land on the moon', sit there for a moment, and then move on. The crimson colour of the station gradually grew lighter, becoming white, with a hint of ivory. The closer we got, the clearer became the individual elements of the construction and the wings of the solar batteries. At first it even looked as if they were correctly directed towards the sun – it was a moment of hope. But a few minutes later we realised it was an optical illusion – at moments of tension the eye is capable of seeing what it very much wants to see. The panels of our solar power-station were looking awry and inert. This promised big problems with the station's power supply. But the main problem for now was the docking – everything else would come later.

How did the station behave? As well as was possible, I would say. In training sessions we had allowed for more complicated flight and rotation speeds, and in fact things turned out more calmly. From about three kilometres away we switched to manual control. It was most convenient to observe Salyut from the side viewport, where the designers had fitted the ship's control levers. What was required of the crew now was perfect coordination and instinctive under-standing of each other. Since I was looking out of the window all the time, Viktor, while helping me to measure distances and speeds, controlled all the ship's systems and ensured they worked smoothly. At a distance of 200 metres we reduced the approach speed to zero and hovered, so that we could 'somersault' and manoeuvre along-side without fear of collision. I moved back to my normal seat and, looking now through the tracking sights, I guided the ship around the station and moved into the docking unit. From then on every-thing went exactly as in training sessions.

Checking for air-tightness, equalising pressures, opening the hatches – all this was familiar stuff and no great difficulties arose. The only delay was in analysing the composition of the atmosphere using the gas analyser. The experts did not rule out that a fire could have broken out inside the station because of a short circuit, and the burnt materials would have poisoned the atmosphere. So we sat in the adaptor module patiently rocking the lever of the air vent, watching to see whether the indicators would change colour. We had gas-masks at the ready, just in case. In the adaptor module there was utter silence and semi-darkness, with the windows half-covered with shutters and only the ray of our flashlight picking up the specks of dust hanging motionless in the air. This oppressive silence and the immobility of the air were the first signs of trouble in the station. When any machine is working, it breathes. And on Salyut there is always the hum of the electronic equipment and the ventilators chasing the air. You cannot imagine what a joyful noise that is. That is why cosmonauts dislike absolute silence. We did not even notice the cold at first – we floated out of the ship feeling flushed with excitement.

But worse was still to come – in the station's main compartment, the working module. The same silence, but total darkness now: the portholes were tightly covered with metal caps. I took off my mask (which was purely a precautionary measure) and breathed the air. It seemed normal, except that the smell was different from usual – a stagnant smell of machinery. I took some photographs using a flash, and floated over to the table. There was a packet of rusks waiting there for us, stuck to the table with sticky tape, and also some salt tablets. Bread and salt, in other words, from the previous 'tenants', Leonid Kizim, Vladimir Solovyov and Oleg Atkov.* There was also a touching letter from them to whoever was next 'on duty' in space. The lads wrote that the station had become their home, that they had put much hard work and love into it, and asked their successors also to take care of it. Next to this there was a souvenir doll, and a bottle of eau-de-cologne, as if to say: this house is lived-in and warm – we wish you a happy and pleasant stay here. This moved us to the bottom of our hearts, and we recalled all the hard work and triumphs of our predecessors' 237-day epic voyage.

We opened the viewports and let in the daylight, and started to examine the walls, floor and ceiling. Everything was very tidy and orderly. It was clean and dry, unharmed. There was a light touch of hoar-frost on the glass of the viewports. It seemed one could just switch on the equipment and get down to work. If only. . . .

If only there was not the cold, which was making itself felt more and more. We slowly realised that the temperature in the station was below zero. And that our instruments, designed for use at room temperature, could be irreparably harmed. Worst of all, all the power-supply sockets were dead. The control desk did not register anything, and not a single lamp would light up. Finally, the buffer batteries were empty.

But, you will agree, it would be unforgivable to find oneself on a ship in distress and to abandon it without having made an effort to salvage it. Viktor and I exchanged a glance and agreed on this at once. [. . .]

We were aware of how Flight Control Centre went into action during those days and hours. The experts remained on duty for days at a time, determined to understand every situation quickly and precisely. It seems to me it was the first time that both crew and 'Earth' had to 'play it by ear'. The flight director, Valery Ryumin, took the microphone and discussed every point in detail. He

---

* Bread and salt is a traditional Russian offering of hospitality.

consulted the experts on the spot, and they issued recommendations immediately, without red tape or paper-shuffling, and watched the results, making clarifications and corrections.

The first decision was simple and logical – to connect up each chemical battery directly to the 'sun', that is, to the solar panels, and to try to charge them, overriding all the circuitry. On instructions from Earth, we cut one cable, hastily made the necessary circuit, joined up the ends and insulated them with whatever material lay to hand, and saw to our joy that the current started flowing. The battery was charging. We managed to do this on 10 June, the day after we docked.

We switched from battery to battery at night, to de-energise the joints and prevent sparking. 'At night' means on the dark side of the orbit, when no current flows from the solar panels. But during the 'real' night, in the hours allotted to sleep, we had to keep watch over the instruments and monitor the charging process. Neither we nor Ground Control felt like sleeping.

What about conditions, comforts? To be honest, we did not think about them – we adapted to everything as we went along. The stagnation of the air felt unpleasant. Without ventilation, the carbon dioxide you exhale clouds around you. Quite imperceptibly fatigue sets in and your head begins to ache. Viktor and I each had our own methods of counteracting this. I taught him to breathe out more sharply, to send the air as far away as possible. He advised me to disperse the cloud by waving my hand or a magazine.

We had prepared for the cold in advance. Before the flight we had had special fur overalls made for us, and tested up in Vorkuta [in the Far North]. Hats, gloves, fur boots. . . . But there are some things that cannot be done in gloves – electronics and radio equipment require sensitive fingers. And whereas your hands warm up because they are being used, your feet get cold and numb, even in fur boots. The temperature in the station was icy. Automatically you start clubbing your feet together, just as anyone would in the frost, and somehow you get warm. Also, the body itself seems to call up extra reserves, and grows accustomed to the situation. Eventually my feet felt comfortable even in ordinary socks.

But still, it was very uncomfortable to begin with, especially on the dark side of the planet. We tried to work in the daylight – apart from anything else, to conserve our flashlight. In the dark, we floated back through to the ship to get warm and breathe fresh air.

When did we realise that the station was coming to life, and that our work was successful? That's easy: when we pressed a button and the light came on in the working compartment. We now had a power supply, and all the instruments came to life. It is hard to convey that feeling – after all, we now had visual contact with Earth and could see our comrades face to face. After that it was plain sailing – testing the instruments and systems, repairing where necessary, replacing a part where necessary.

So it would have been a great shame to have had to abandon Salyut and cut short the mission at that moment. But the threat of this arose again, this time due to a shortage of water. We had tried to turn on the water-supply system as soon as we arrived, but it was frozen and there was ice in the tanks. I noticed then that one of the joints in our water-pipe had sprouted a strange-looking column of plastic. When we looked more closely we discovered it was ice: the water was being pushed out of the system, and freezing. The column continued to grow before our eyes, like mercury in a thermometer. It meant it was still below zero in the station. What would happen if the tanks did not thaw out by the time our week's supply of water in the ship ran out? On special recommendation we prepared to drink the water from the cooling systems of our space-walk suits. We collected drops from every pipe and hose. We reduced our daily intake. We knew that our comrades on Earth were doing all they could to dispatch a cargo-ship from Baikonur as soon as possible, with spare parts and water.

In general, the survival process generates rational solutions, in space as on Earth. The station's system for heating water and food was not working, for example, but we found a way out. Looking among various boxes, we discovered a suitable photographic bag. We made an extra insulating lining out of a towel and aluminium foil, connected up a powerful photographic lamp, and in 30–40 minutes we could heat up packets of food, tea and coffee in this 'oven'.

The next stage of the repairs and preventive work required a great deal of patience. One after the other we groped through hundreds of cables, each with its own number and connections, studied various units and opened up panels. It was like at home, when you have to move hundreds of books in a bookcase, just so that you can follow the path of one telephone wire. Then you find you need to remove some floorboards, and have to lug the furniture about. Five minutes later you don't know where the hammer and nails you had a moment ago have gone – you leave them for a second and they float away!

The main thing here was not to yield to 'nerves', to keep calm and collected. It is a pleasure to work with Viktor in such circumstances. He reacts to the vagaries of weightlessness with humour, and does not get annoyed by petty things. You look round and see him pottering away in a 'snake-pit' of cables and pipes, humming a song, and chewing something instead of taking a proper lunch – nuts, or fruit sticks. And you at once feel calmer: we can surely untangle this little ball, if everything else is going so well. [. . .]
[8 October 1985]

Chernobyl

[At 1.23 on the morning of 26 April 1986 an explosion at the Chernobyl nuclear power station in the Ukraine sent a cloud of radiation spreading over western parts of the USSR, Scandinavia, Poland, and eventually over most of Europe. On the evening of 28 April the Council of Ministers issued a brief report admitting that there had been an accident. For more than a week Soviet newspapers carried only official statements by the Council of Ministers or TASS. Not until 6 May did *Pravda's* own correspondents in the Ukraine finally report from the area. The two abridged reports translated here appeared later in May and June.

The power station itself is situated in Chernobyl district but several miles away from the town of Chernobyl; the nearest town is the settlement of Pripyat, built specially for the power-workers on the banks of the river Pripyat.]

Sasha Antropov – only yesterday a young Komsomol leader in Pripyat, today already an adult, Aleksandr Stepanovich Antropov, head of the propaganda and agitation department of Pripyat Town Party Committee – went to bed at six in the morning only to be awakened again at ten to take on another assignment.

The thin and energetic young man had spent the night tackling the problem of how to remove vehicles belonging to the staff of the atomic power station from the town. There were several hundred of them in garages and on pavements in front of house entrances. It was a difficult task, for all those Zhiguli, Moskvich and Zaporozhets cars had not just to be moved but also put through all the stages of decontamination. In Pripyat, although the town has been evacuated, the traffic lights at road junctions still flash red, amber, green. . . .

Evacuation. . . . Some people have still not managed to find their relatives who left the town on that memorable day. It was only the other day that Antropov managed to locate his wife and his one-and-a-half-month-old daughter and six-year-old son.

The first few days after the evacuation of the population of Pripyat to Ivankov and Polesskoye districts were difficult ones. Everyone had to be provided with accommodation and jobs, children's education had to be organised and food had to be supplied. After all, there were 7,200 pupils at Pripyat's schools, plus another 3,000 smaller children at kindergartens. Now that classes have ended for classes one to seven [i.e., up to age fourteen] the Pripyat town authorities' main task is to get the children away on holiday. A week ago 232 schoolchildren left here for the Artek and Young Guard pioneers' camps in the south of the country. Now the Pripyat town council has arranged for elderly people and labour and war invalids to travel south.

The problem of finding jobs for those who had to leave Pripyat was solved by sending them on long-term duty tours to other atomic power stations in the Ukraine and to atomic power station construction sites. So out of the 23,000 people evacuated from Pripyat to Polesskoye district, only about 2,000 are still there. Tens of thousands of people have already received the 200-rouble grant which is being paid to evacuees. [. . .]

Pripyat's leaders are thinking about the future. They are already working out what will have to be done if the evacuation is prolonged, and thinking out various means of organising housing, services and education. Other districts are busy with this too, for at the moment more than 90,000 people are temporarily settled in Makarov, Borodyanka, Ivankov and Polesskoye districts. [N.B. All these districts are in the Ukraine; many thousands more were evacuated in neighbouring Belorussia.]

Soviet people are sending telegrams offering assistance to those affected. One of them, from Gorlovka in Donetsk region, reads: 'My name is O. M. Kosova, of 50, Kiev Street. You have permission to use my house for the duration of the evacuation if needed.' And here is another telegram: 'We will take one or two children from Chernobyl. My husband speaks Ukrainian. I am a schoolteacher. We await visitors for the summer. We have a comfortable flat. Maisky village, Perm region.'

'People are delighted at such involvement, and are satisfied with the concern shown by the local authorities,' says N. Stepanenko, deputy chairman of the regional council. 'There is much to be done. Medical services and efficient transport, telephone exchanges and bakeries, extra canteens, bath-houses, hairdresser's and shops – all have to be set up and equipped. Problems connected with the construction of temporary pens for livestock and with the repair of premises suitable for housing animals are being tackled. Timber, slates and other building materials are being dispatched to the districts where the inhabitants of Pripyat and Chernobyl district have been evacuated. Trucks carrying livestock fodder are on their way.' [. . .]

At times, there is evidence of elementary irresponsibility and lack of discipline. The fact that hundreds of mothers and small children have still not left Polesskoye district for the south bears witness to the bureaucratic indifference of certain employees in the Kiev regional education department and trade union organisations, who are responsible for these matters. [. . .]

The May sun is shining brightly, warm and caressing. But the people here are thinking of autumn and winter. In the near future an additional 10,000 farmstead-style houses are to be erected in Kiev region. Measures are already being worked out for increasing fuel supplies. Having suffered considerable losses, it is essential for the region not just to fulfil the plans set, but also to create additional resources to make up the shortfall.

. . . Pinned to the doors of the Polesskoye council – where the Pripyat town council is also now based – are dozens of coloured notices giving the whereabouts of various evacuated organisations and offices, or containing extracts from orders and minutes of meetings. 'It's like during the war,' observes an elderly man with strips of combat medals on his chest. Suddenly music begins to play somewhere upstairs: it is Mendelssohn's Wedding March. Climbing up to the first floor I witness the solemn act of marriage – Tanya Bisik is exchanging rings with Sasha Khomenko. Both of them are students in Kiev who have come home to their parents in Polesskoye to get married.

'Life goes on,' says V. Voloshko, the chairman of Pripyat council.
[21 May 1986]

'Please send me to work in the firefighting unit safeguarding the Chernobyl power station. I bow down before the heroism of the firemen who were first to enter into battle with the fire, and I believe that my knowledge and practical skills can be best put to use where they are most needed, namely, in eliminating the after-effects of the accident at the Chernobyl nuclear power station. Radio-telephonist O. Terekhova.'

'I am full of admiration for the courage and heroism of the fire prevention workers at Chernobyl power station. I wish to join up, to replace the casualties. Lieutenant K. Mikhailidi.' [. . .]

. . . These are not momentary impulses, but well-considered decisions by each person. And at the same time they are an answer to the question which foreign journalists put to Academician Yevgeny Velikhov at a press conference in May: 'Are you sure that people will be found who will want to work at the Chernobyl station?' His answer was succinct: 'Yes, I am!' Letters, telegrams and other requests to be sent to work in Chernobyl testify to the fact that faith in the future of atomic energy has not been shaken. It is necessary, of course, to take account of the lessons of the accident and to increase the safety of nuclear power-plants, but most people do not doubt their continued existence. [. . .]

The power station's headquarters are now in the town of Chernobyl. A system of hostels is being set up there, while the station's administrative and service block in Pripyat is got ready. Transport problems are being solved. On 1 July the teams working on the reactor will start moving into new long-term accommodation on tourist ships moored on the Pripyat river.

The work to eliminate the consequences of the accident and to prepare for the normal operation of reactors one and two requires an influx of manpower. Thousands of people from various parts of the country are sending letters and telegrams to Kiev and Chernobyl offering to help the power-workers and everyone working in and around Pripyat.

There are many letters from evacuees. Most of them express gratitude for their warm reception and attentive treatment, but there are also complaints of bureaucracy and red tape in receiving allowances.

. . . Intensive work to deal with the effects of the accident has been under way for a month and a half. And every day brings fresh evidence of people's heroism and courage, and provides examples of fine organisation and discipline. But now and again one notes a lack of due responsibility in those who are called upon to lead the collectives.

The bureau of Kiev Region Party committee recently heard a report by the new managers of Chernobyl power station. Asked if he had any questions, the new director, E. Pozdyshev, replied: 'Our goals are clear and our tasks are clear. Let's get down to work!'

The station's former managers have been dismissed. V. Malomuzh, secretary of the regional Party committee, reported that in the complex situation caused by the accident the former director, V. Bryukhanov, and the chief engineer, N. Fomin, proved incapable of providing the correct firm leadership and proper discipline, and showed irresponsibility and inefficiency. They were unable to assess what had happened or to take cardinal measures to organise efficient work by all units during the aftermath of the accident.

The bureau also discussed the need for measures to fill existing vacancies. Because of shortcomings in organisational and educational work with people, a number of the power station's staff are still 'on the run'. They include shift leaders and senior foremen. Party members from the station, who at their own meeting had sharply condemned the management for its shortcomings, were cited at the bureau session. The station's deputy director, R. Solovyov, left his post at the most difficult moment. Deputy directors I. Tsarenko and V. Gundar viewed their official duties without due responsibility, and did little to ease the working and living conditions of those employed at the station.

In the difficult situation that arose after the accident, the station's Party committee managed to rally and mobilise the communists and to organise work. Undoubtedly, though, the Party committee could have done more. Among the main faults were its duplication of management's work in tackling current tasks, and its laxity towards the managers. This was also noted at the regional committee meeting.

The speech by the power station's Party secretary, S. Parashin, was self-critical and courageous. But when it was the turn of the trade union head, V. Berezin, to speak, he had to listen to justified reproaches. The station's trade union committee paid scant attention to strengthening discipline or ensuring safe working, living and leisure conditions. The secretary of the Komsomol committee, A. Bocharov, also got his share of critical remarks. . . .

'I am a driver with the Chernobyl branch of the Southern Atomic Energy Construction and Transport Association,' writes S. Fomin to *Pravda*. 'As a result of circumstances – or, to be precise, because of the inactivity of our chief engineer, A. Shapoval – I had to take charge of the dispatch of clay to the site of the accident. [N.B. Clay was dropped from helicopters to smother the burning reactor.] I would not like readers to have a poor opinion of our entire collective just because of a few cowards. I want to speak about the people who fought the accident until they were sent away to medical institutions – about my comrades, the long-distance drivers. News of the accident found us in various towns, but the very next day we assembled in the village of Korolevka. By the morning of 28 April we were already at the headquarters. We received our orders: to deliver clay from the quarry at Chistogalovka to the helicopter pads. At first the task seemed to us practically impossible. Our spades and picks made no impression on the hard-packed clay. But we quickly got the hang of things, loosened up the clay, shovelled it into sacks, and loaded them on to trucks. Then we drove to the helicopter pad and tied the sacks to the helicopters hovering overhead. We worked without let-up, thinking only about putting the fire out as quickly as possible. It really was a test of endurance. We delivered clay until 2 May, and then the helicopters were moved to a different pad because of severe radioactive contamination (we had been working only five kilometres from the power station). . . . I can name with pride my friends who remained on duty right up to the moment when the doctors hospitalised them: G. Shklyarchuk, G. Antonets, A. Khodykin, V. Gorbetsky, L. Zinovenko, I. Karpenko, A. Yemtsov, V. Melnik, and many others. And on behalf of my comrades I want to say to the Western press, who had us buried in a mass grave: "We are alive! We are standing firmly on the ground. We shall fight to our last breath for clear skies over our planet, and for its nuclear-free future." "We" are the workers at Chernobyl nuclear power station.'

[15 June 1986]

2

The World Outside

A Million Say Yes in Central Park
by A. Vasilyev

If you look out of the window here, beyond the streams of cars, beyond the railing and the green lawn, you can see the blue glass skyscraper of the United Nations, and the adjoining building with the Oval Hall where the second special session of the General Assembly on disarmament is being held.

Here, at the discussion café in the United Nations Church Centre, from morning till late at night there is hardly room to breathe. Whites and Blacks, Quakers and communists, workers and scientists, Americans, Japanese, Russians, people from every continent are discussing questions of war and peace – the most important questions facing mankind. Down below, in front of the building, several dozen Japanese monks in orange robes are sitting and beating their gongs, repeating over and over again a prayer for peace. Beside them lie the photographs of victims of the atom bombs dropped on Hiroshima and Nagasaki. Often the monks are joined by passers-by, both young and old, who sit down beside them and also beat the gongs, joining in the prayers which require no translation.

Wandering across the United Nations Square, across that tiny patch of a huge city, you can't help asking yourself the question: the whole world is following the course of the session, but what about the Americans themselves? For those who came to the United Nations when the session opened to hand in petitions and appeals seemed like drops in a sea of indifference.

Go two blocks away from United Nations Square, and you are swallowed up by a New York immersed in its own – its very own – affairs. You cannot help being aware of how lost the separate individual feels in these ravines of streets, where amongst the glittering skyscrapers the homeless hide in old boxes (this is no exaggeration), and others pass them by on their way to luxury restaurants, where they pay over the top for the 'prestige' of the

По вашингтонскому фасону.

Рисунок Кукрыниксы.

The British lion tries on a hat 'in the Washington style',
while other NATO leaders wait their turn.
Drawing by Kukryniksy. [September 1983]

establishment. When you go down into the rumbling, dank oppress-
iveness of the New York underground, and look at the vandalised,
graffiti-covered carriages, you remember the warnings to look after
your purse and your life in these dirty, smelly tunnels, while
alongside you passes a stream of tired New Yorkers, plunged in
their own cares.

Are the American masses interested in the questions of peace and
disarmament?

You come predisposed to the idea that people make business out
of everything here, and suddenly you notice that some sharp street
traders are successfully selling – at exorbitant prices – tee-shirts with
the emblem of a crossed-out atomic bomb, or with the slogan of the
peace movement – 'Live, Love, Laugh.' But perhaps this is not
typical?

Jonathan Schell's book *The Fate of the Earth* is displayed in a
prominent position on the counter of a bookshop. In his book he
analyses scientific data, and comes to the conclusion that nuclear

war amounts to the self-annihilation of humanity, and that international security is inconceivable without universal and complete disarmament.

You switch on the television and in the intervals between an advertisement for a slimming pill and one for a new kind of toothpaste you see and hear a serious discussion about the fate of New York in the event of a nuclear war. The governor of the state of New Jersey is trying, not very convincingly, to prove that, given several hours' warning of a nuclear attack, it would be possible to evacuate people out of potentially threatened areas into safer ones. The interviewer asks in disbelief: 'You are, of course, familiar with New York traffic jams during the rush hour? What will happen if millions of people all go on the move at the same time?' A spokesman for the Physicians for Social Responsibility organisation speaks next. He is convinced that if nuclear war were to break out, millions would be killed immediately, and the survivors would envy the dead. The only salvation from the 'final epidemic' is prevention, to avert a war before it starts.

The next day, again garnished with advertisements, the repeat of a serial about the 'father' of the American atom bomb, Robert Oppenheimer, is shown. After the first test of his brainchild he utters in horror: 'I have become the destroyer of the world.' And when the bomb is dropped on Hiroshima, he confronts an American general with the words: 'There's blood on my hands and on yours!' And one of the victims of Hiroshima, Hateko Tomagano, who has come to New York, says to us: 'The American government carried out an experiment on us Japanese, as though we were guinea-pigs. We can never forgive this. How dare Reagan speak of the idea of a "limited" nuclear war!'

On the streets of the city, those Americans whose conscience has been awakened, as though asking forgiveness for the criminal sins of their fathers, cheer the Japanese who have come here to take part in the Peace March.

Talk to any American public figure, journalist, or scientist, and you will hear the following: the peace movement has become a mass one. It is not without reason that a pragmatic political leader like Edward Kennedy, together with Senator Mark Hatfield, has put forward a resolution calling for a Soviet-American nuclear arms freeze. They are clearly tuned in to the strengthening feelings of broad sections of the American population. The White House wanted to frighten the Soviet Union with its irresponsible, warmongering speeches, but instead, it has struck fear into its own people.

I was working in Vietnam during the years of the ruthless American bombing there. The name of the then US Defence Secretary, McNamara, was associated with the thunder of rockets and bombs falling on a wretched, ravaged country. Today McNamara advocates putting a stop to the nuclear arms race. The preaching of war and the rearmament programme have boomeranged on the US administration, and started setting against it everyone who thinks and reasons.

American individualism is proverbial: each for himself, and one God for all. Is it possible for the supporters of peace in the USA to unite? All doubts were dispersed on 12 June. Nearly 300 organisations of different political, social, religious and national colourings got together to hold a Peace March and meeting in Manhattan's Central Park against the nuclear threat, and brought out on to the streets one million (one million!) people. They say that this was the biggest demonstration in the history of the USA.

Apart from New Yorkers, hundreds of thousands of people from all parts of the country took part in it. They held the demonstration and meeting with typical American efficiency and style, forgetting neither the cold snacks nor the mobile toilets nor the stages for the jazz bands. It was obvious even from outward appearances that the main participant in the demonstration was the 'average American', and certainly not the 'leftist extremist'. There were qualified workers and priests, small businessmen and students, professors and actors, trade union activists and housewives, unemployed people, black Americans, and Puerto Ricans.

For years they have been creating in the American mind a stereotype of the 'perfidious, aggressive Russians', they have frightened Americans with the 'Soviet military threat', films have been made about the 'Russian invasion of Alaska', they have painted horrifying pictures of a 'Soviet nuclear strike', and they have filled newspapers, magazines and books with terrifying nonsense.

. . . A flick of the television switch. The courageous faces of dashing American pilots at a strategic airbase. The war alert siren sounds – Soviet missiles appear on the radar screens! Trucks rush the crews to the planes. Now bombers are about to take off. But then. . . . The grotesque mushroom of an atomic explosion. Death. Destruction. The same picture at the missile bases, the same on the submarines. A deliberately impassive voice announces: in half an hour the USA lost 30,000,000 people, nine-tenths of its strategic potential, and the President was forced to capitulate. The implication is clear: you, the television viewer are being threatened by these villainous Russians, so turn out your pockets, and don't skimp on new military expenditure. Only in this way will you survive. Anti-Soviet missile preaching has become the speciality of the monopolised mass media.

One would think that the ordinary American would be swept away by the Niagara of lies and disinformation, and would feel nothing but hatred and mistrust towards us. But the fact is that during the seven hours of the demonstration and meeting on 12 June, I did not see a single anti-Soviet banner. I asked round my friends and acquaintances. Someone remembered: 'Yes, there were one or two small groups . . . perhaps a couple of slogans out of a thousand.'

A different nation, different customs. . . . It's hard to know sometimes what is the best way to the Americans' hearts. Placards with enlarged photographs were very successful here: a family in Kiev and a family in New York, children in Kiev and children in New York, a musician from Kiev and a jazz musician from New York. . . . Why Kiev? Someone had got hold of an album portraying life in the Ukrainian capital. There were no captions under the photographs, but the message was clear to all: there, in the far-off Soviet Union, are people the same as us, who want to live, love and laugh, there is no need to fear them, we must find a common language with them. So much for your stereotype 'Red', with a nuclear missile between his teeth!

The participants of the 12 June demonstration were moved by common sense and distrust of their government's arguments in favour of a nuclear and conventional arms build-up, even though the mass media either hush up or distort Soviet views and peaceful initiatives. What a world of difference between the moods of those million people and the shameless demagogy of those who blame everything without exception on 'Soviet intrigues', in order to squeeze out hundreds of billions of dollars for even more monstrous and refined means of mass destruction. 'I am really afraid,' said one speaker in Central Park. 'I am horrified at the thought that I could be vaporized in an atomic holocaust.' The majority of Americans demand a freeze on nuclear weapons. Can anyone really believe that they are guided by the 'hand of Moscow'?

Anti-war slogans in the USA are linked with social ones: 'You are spending billions to blow up the world, when there are so many unemployed in the USA!' 'Houses and Jobs, not Bombs!' On the day after the demonstration we found ourselves in the black ghetto of Harlem, where the wind carries rubbish along the streets, where the blackened shells of houses burned down during the most recent mass riots still stand, where poverty and hopelessness shout from the slums, and where people's eyes glare suspicion and hostility towards whites. But then a group of blacks and Puerto Ricans appeared, chanting, 'Exson and the CIA, we don't want to fight for you!' and welcomed as brothers the few whites who had come with anti-war banners.

During the meeting in Central Park the million-strong crowd were asked from the platform: 'If you want peace, you need the courage to fight for it. Are you prepared to fight?' And a million people answered in unison: 'Yes!'

But the stirring consciousness of America does not exist for official Washington. It does not want to admit that a growing number of sober-minded Americans are seeing the light. To the anti-war appeals, administration spokesmen replied scornfully and arrogantly: 'The peace march will have no influence on the implementation of our missile programmes.'

America is again divided. The military-industrial complex, the higher echelons of the administration, the powerful mass media, the duped man in the street – this is who represents the war camp. But in the space of just a year and a half a peace camp has emerged, grown up and strengthened. Its voice is becoming louder and more resolute. Common sense and concern for the future of mankind demand that the peace camp should prevail.

[5 July 1982]

James Bond and his Admirers
by P. Gromov

Moved by no less than a feeling of national pride, British television has made a film called 'James Bond 21 years after' – a kind of retrospective of the adventures of this screen superspy and adventurer from Her Majesty's Secret Service. The makers of the film invited Ronald Reagan, former Hollywood actor and now US President, to give his opinion about agent 007. 'He is a modern image of one of those great people who have appeared from time to time in the course of history,' said the President. 'There have been many like him: pioneers, soldiers, law-makers, researchers – people who have given up their lives for the common good.' Yes, this was how the President described the bully-boy spy.

It would have been bad enough if what had attracted the President was Bond's predilection for strong cocktails, or the 'superman's' uncontrollable attraction towards all the representatives of the fair sex caught up in his spy intrigues. Worse is that the President of the USA chose as the 'hero of our times' a man who shoots before he thinks. What is there to think about, after all? Agent 007 has a 'licence to kill'. It seems that there are some people around who regret that this only happens in the movies.

All this has given rise to some confusion. White House staff have seen to it that Ronald Reagan does not appear in the American version of the film.

But in Western Europe, the film is showing. . . .
[21 June 1983]

A Watchful Tear
by Yu. Kuznetsov

Two robots recently got into conversation at an electronic instruments factory in Silicon Valley in the state of California. Of course they are not supposed to speak at all. Their task is just to work – with all the strength of their mechanical arms and their implanted intellect.

But these two robots simply could stand it no longer.

'I was interrogated again last night,' said one of them gloomily, in a break between operations.

'Same old thing?'

'Of course. About security and Russian spies. They say there is a leak somewhere.'

'Oil?'

'No, information.'

'And where do we come into it?'

'They're afraid. We may be in the pay of enemy agents! It seems they have already been investigating to see if robots aren't leading dissolute lives and squandering lots of money.'

'They must have a screw loose,' said the second robot profoundly, and added: 'They've appointed a supervisor to look after me. I only have to move a component a fraction to the side, and I can feel him drilling me with his eyes, as if to say, "Where's he putting that?"'

'He's from the CIA, that one.'

'Who would think they'd keep tabs on robots!'

'You'd do better not to think at all. You know what they say nowadays: I think, therefore I'm on the CIA files.'

'Yes, the authorities in Washington have got their eyes everywhere. . . .'

. . . But meanwhile the authorities in Washington had their eyes on the root of it all – or more precisely – on the root of all evil. At the same time, mind you, the Director of the CIA, William Casey, was keeping one eye on his notes – the most important thing, after all, is not to stray from the path of White House directives.

'The Russians are to blame for everything, everything,' he repeated to himself, and also out loud during a recent speech. 'The Soviets are a threat to us because they are stronger. And they are trying to get hold of our secrets because they are weaker.'

The absurdity of this favourite White House thesis, not to mention its elementary contradictoriness, embarrassed the speaker not one bit. Washington has long ago ceased to worry about such trifles.

During the aforementioned speech, Casey literally melted into tears: according to him, even when the Americans are merely trading with the Russians, 'Some of the goods sold could potentially be used for military purposes!' And all this leads, of course, to the military superiority of the Russians. How come? Take, for example, 'superphosphates'. Well, they're *super*phosphates – so there's your superiority! Casey's imagination is full of such fantasies. The Russians, he says, have cast such a net around the world to gather in technical information that the CIA has to attract thousands and thousands of the 'best minds in America' and to use tens of thousands of agents (evidently to gather back all the information). It gets worse! It seems that the CIA has 'to resort to the help of scientists and businessmen who travel the world, and to use information gathered by them'. Information about what? About those Russian achievements, which are really non-existent, but which are nevertheless needed by technically advanced Washington. Shamelessly blowing his own trumpet and that of his department, the CIA chief, without batting an eyelid, announced, 'Our activities and our behaviour conform to the highest norms of honesty, incorruptibility, morals and concepts of honour, and (wait for it!) they also conform to the letter and the spirit of the law.'

No, it's too bad the US administration trusts this orator. After all, he is clearly jeering at the leadership, or at least shamelessly misinforming them.

As for Casey's other listeners, and Americans in general, he is peddling them the same old stock: we are dealing with a weak adversary, he says, we can beat them hands down. So let's go, boys!

Thus, the story of the tearfully vigilant Casey turns out to be the tale of an instigator of chauvinism, hatred and war. But then, who is he serving, after all?

[19 May 1984]

Pearls of Cynicism
by Vsevolod Ovchinnikov

Richard Perle is such an odious figure that he scarcely requires an introduction. His official position is Assistant US Defence Secretary for international security policy, but his views, and more importantly his actions, have as much to do with international security as nuclear warheads have with gardening. Even in the brood of Washington hawks Perle stands out as a rabid anti-Soviet and arch-troglodyte anticommunist, and – as he has once again demonstrated in the past days – a cynical slanderer and provocateur.

Speaking in Bonn, Perle called the Soviet Union's decision unilaterally to halt all nuclear explosions from 6 August [1985] 'pure propaganda, timed for the fortieth anniversary of Hiroshima'. According to the assistant Pentagon boss, what lies behind this Soviet step is . . . a desire to overtake the United States. 'American intelligence data shows that the Russians have recently stepped up their nuclear testing,' Perle lied without batting an eyelid.

Another of his 'arguments' sounds no less paradoxical: since the Russians have stopped all explosions, he said, they are 'very probably' violating the 1974 Soviet-US Treaty limiting underground nuclear tests. And the President, he goes on, is so worried by this that he proposed inviting experts to each other's testing grounds. It turns out that the USSR, which has halted all explosions, should 'bless' American explosions with the presence of its observers. . . .

Perle's speech in Bonn has indirectly demonstrated the alarm which the new Soviet initiative has raised in the Washington corridors of power. And the Assistant Defence Secretary himself revealed one of the reasons for this confusion, by devoting most of his speech – which was as provocative as it was mendacious – to a defence of the 'Star Wars' programme.

'The military', writes the *New York Times* in this connection, 'have always opposed a ban on underground tests for many reasons. But President Reagan's "Strategic Defence Initiative" has introduced another element to this. Although it has been advertised as a non-nuclear programme, it requires the carrying out of nuclear tests on one of its components – the X-ray laser.' It can't be denied! The renunciation of all nuclear tests would place a question-mark over Pentagon programmes which are already in full swing. So Perle pours slander on the Soviet Union, which, according to his perverted logic, opposes the militarisation of space precisely because it is preparing for it at full speed.

Washington's propagandists are certainly scraping the barrel if they have to put about such pearls of stupidity and cynicism as those which filled the Assistant Defence Secretary's speech in Bonn. According to the logic of this provocateur, the best way to overtake someone is to stand still. Strange that such a simple method has never entered the heads of anyone in Washington!

[8 August 1985]

Britain in Time and Space
by T. Kolesnichenko and A. Maslennikov, London

In the centre of London, in neon-lit Leicester Square, where in the evenings noisy flocks of starlings gather for the night along the pretentious Victorian façades, and a discordant human river flows along the concrete pavements, a group of flagstones is set out in the shape of a hexagon, scarcely visible at first glance, reddish-grey, inlaid with brass lettering. The letters look like inscriptions on tombstones embedded in the ground at the entrances to churches. But this is something different. Polished by the feet of thousands of passers-by, the brass letters proclaim not the names of the sinful of this world . . . but the distances from here, the centre of London, to those places where, not so very long ago, as the English used to say with pride, 'the sun of the British Empire never went down': 'To New Delhi, India, 6,691 kilometres,' 'To Accra, Ghana, 5,067 kilometres,' 'To Saint Georges, Grenada, 6,936 kilometres,' etc.

It is particularly easy to see from the centre of London what a

Western leaders seen through the eyes of *Pravda*'s leading cartoonists, the 'Kukryniksy' triumvirate: President Reagan (*above*) invites the Russians to arms talks, while (*below*) the British lion receiving a Tomahawk cruise missile is shown wearing an ear-ring and ladies' shoes. [3 and 18 October 1983]

complex affair Britain's colonial past was and still remains for her. As Britain's former colonies gained their independence one after the other, so London's imperial pretensions began to lose their practical substance. Economically, Britain's orientation towards her former colonial market resulted in her lagging further and further behind her main European competitors, who in the post-war period set about an accelerated rebuilding of their economic structures, bearing in mind the demands of scientific and technical progress and the new intensification of the struggle for markets and spheres of influence. When it comes down to it, all of the problems facing Britain today stem one way or another from this historical 'hitch'. It is fair to say that over the past few decades London has been learning to live without its colonies.

The process of adapting to the changes taking place in today's world assumed a particularly dramatic, and in many respects, unhealthy character when the Conservative Party came to power six years ago. Having set itself an open and clearly formulated goal – to overcome the accumulated economic backwardness, and to throw off the shackles of outmoded traditions, ties and obligations (for example 'east of Suez'), from the very outset the Tory government nevertheless subordinated the achievement of this goal to the narrow mercenary class interests of private enterprise, and in particular to its monopolistic layer.

This policy places very narrow limits on economic development, in the name of which British workers are called on – or more often are simply forced – to fasten their belts tighter and tighter. In spite of the deafening drumbeat of official propaganda claiming that 'Britain's recovery is now in its fourth year', the volume of industrial output in the country continues to remain six per cent below the 1979 level.

Noticeable, although also far from one-dimensional, changes are taking place in British foreign policy too. In its search for a 'place in the sun' in the world arena, London has undergone a significant evolution since the war, from attempts to play a role it could no longer sustain – that of 'boss' of a global colonial empire (meanwhile this has led only to Britain's ever-increasing dependence on its elder American 'brother') – to an understanding of the fact that Britain is 'first and foremost a European country', and that her main economic and political interests 'lie in Europe' – a thesis which now runs through all government policy statements. However, this 'reappraisal of values' is a painful, not a smooth process, as indeed was the 'shift of accent' to Europe. Britain continues, for example, jealously to defend its position as head of the Commonwealth – a position which put her in a decidedly tricky situation during the American invasion of Grenada, one of the members of the Commonwealth.

Britain's relations with the West European 'Common Market' are also of an unusual nature. Having joined that 'monopolies' club' in 1973, fifteen years after its formation, Britain continues to occupy a special position in it. She refuses, for example, to join the European monetary system, claiming the need to 'preserve freedom of action', and pleading a 'special relationship' between the pound sterling and the American dollar. In fact, however, devaluation is 'eating up' the pound, which used to be worth three dollars, but is now worth only ten or twenty pence more than one.

The fall of the pound, like the decline of the British Empire, does not yet signify the decline and fall of Britain. The Tower of London and Westminster Abbey are still as majestic; the famous monument to Shakespeare in an evergreen square right in the heart of the city is always surrounded by tourists; London's main news factory, the famous Fleet Street, still drones on, stuffing not only Englishmen but also half of the English-speaking world with information; the heart of British capitalism – the City – is still as proud and inaccessible as ever; and English Gentlemen still carry umbrellas whatever the weather, just as they did twenty years ago. . . . And yet there is also a sense of new, difficult times, made more complex by the painful parting with the past. 'Things aren't what they used to be . . .' – this a phrase you often hear in Britain today. The British have to pay for their 'special relationship' with Washington, not only with a shrinking pound, but also by forfeiting some of their national pride and traditions.

The inconsistency of London's foreign policy manifests itself particularly clearly in that important sphere of international relations, the problem of nuclear disarmament. While declaring its 'unshakable loyalty' to NATO strategy, the present British government nevertheless tries to assert the 'independent' status of its own nuclear forces, which consist of four Polaris submarines with sixty-four multiple-warhead nuclear missiles, and on this basis refuses to include them in the total count of nuclear potentials at arms talks.

By British standards, the government's expenditure on arms production exceeds all reasonable norms. Today, for every member of the population, including children and old people, five pounds per week is spent on 'strengthening security'. Sane-minded British people, many of whom support unilateral nuclear disarmament, consider this to be a sheer waste of money.

One cannot overlook, however, the fact that there has been a certain improvement recently in the position of the British government concerning nuclear disarmament. Prime Minister Thatcher, in a number of her recent speeches, has spoken of the need to reduce tension and strengthen mutual understanding between East and West. On several occasions she has called for a halt in the arms race and, in particular, for the prevention of the militarisation of space. Sir Geoffrey Howe, the British Foreign Secretary, in a recent lecture on this subject to the Royal College of Defence Studies, drew attention to the dangerous consequences for peace and disarmament of Washington's 'Star Wars' programme. This was immediately answered by a highly improper, even rude, riposte from one of the Pentagon's most influential men, the notorious Richard Perle.

London does not put up much resistance to such tongue-lashings, however. Indeed, as though frightened by its 'boldness', it is now anxious to show its loyalty to Washington, and consequently its hostility towards the Soviet Union.

But the celebrations of the fortieth anniversary of the Victory over Hitlerite fascism stirred the memories of Britons, who for several years courageously resisted the barbaric raids by Goering's Luftwaffe, and who made a significant contribution to the common struggle against the Nazi plague. The working people of Britain, especially those who took part in the war, gave no support to the attempts of certain circles to turn these celebrations into a so-called reconciliation with the bearers of Nazi ideology, trying thus to diminish the role of the alliance between Britain and the USSR during the Second World War. To the credit of many British journalists, it has to be said that they prepared many articles, reports, and television and radio programmes, which described the events on the Soviet-German front fairly objectively, showing what enormous sacrifices were suffered by the Soviet people in making their decisive contribution to the victory over the common enemy.

The Tories' ambiguous position as regards the 'Star Wars' plans is out of step with public opinion. All the English people we met in London, Leeds, Birmingham and other British towns emphasised that the extension of the arms race into space, no matter what 'well-intentioned' arguments it is clothed in, would inevitably lead to a sharp destabilisation of the international situation, and to an increase in the danger of nuclear war, against which the countries of Western Europe would be defenceless. Bruce Kent, the General Secretary of the Campaign for Nuclear Disarmament (CND), said: 'Reagan's "Star Wars" programme is extremely dangerous. It is no less dangerous than having American missiles stationed in Europe. What today seems "fantastic" could tomorrow become a real nightmare. Britain should not take part in this race. We are told that our participation in it is irreversible, that we must keep pace with the development of modern technology. But why should technology be developed only through the militarisation of space, that last sphere not yet consumed by the arms race, why must technological progress make our world fragile and unstable?' It is quite characteristic that the Labour Party, with its sights already on the next election, has taken a firm stand against Washington's plans. Speaking in Brussels recently, Neil Kinnock, the Labour leader, said that 'only a madman or a liar can claim that the Star Wars programme will stop at the research stage'. In reality, he emphasised, it would lead to an intensification of the arms race.

The 'Nuclear-Free Europe' slogan is very popular here. In Leeds, which was declared a nuclear-free zone by the city council in 1982, we were shown a huge map with detailed colour diagrams showing the consequences of a one-megaton nuclear explosion. 'The best defence against the nuclear threat', says the caption underneath, 'is to destroy the threat of war itself.' This is a popular slogan throughout Britain. More than 180 local and city councils have declared themselves 'nuclear-free zones', and have refused to participate in the government's programme of 'civil defence'.

The 'protest movement', as anti-war organisations are called here, is gathering strength. When it comes to stationing American missiles in their country, the English soon lose their reputation for cool imperturbability. Greenham Common and other vivid examples of anti-missile protest by the English, who have held out against water-cannon, tear-gas and police truncheons, and who have preferred imprisonment to indifference in the face of the growing nuclear madness, point to the changes in the British way of thinking under the nuclear threat.

The same applies to the protest movement against the 'Star Wars' plans. The concept of 'Star Wars' has by the very fact of its appearance shown up the grotesque absurdity of the arms race, leading mankind towards catastrophe. In various circles of British society there are growing demands for a halt to this new turn in the nuclear arms race, and for the prevention of its extension into space, where it will be physically impossible either to control or to stop it.

In the final analysis, the philosophical and humanitarian sense of the current fight against the threat of universal nuclear destruction consists in learning to take more seriously the realities of our times and the imperative factors of European and world politics. And in this sense the brass letters in Leicester Square are not merely a question of history and geography. They are also a reminder of the fact that in today's world every nation and every state bears responsibility not only for itself, but also for the preservation of peace in all corners of the planet.

[20 May 1985]

A Decisive Rebuff to Reaction
by V. Volodin

[As the 'Solidarity crisis' in Poland mounted in 1981, *Pravda* relied mainly on TASS news agency reports for its coverage of day-to-day events and to indicate the Soviet government's disapproval of the free trade-union movement. Exactly one month before martial law was declared it set out to demonstrate that the Soviet *people* were growing impatient with the 'counterrevolutionary' developments in neighbouring Poland by printing a review of readers' letters on the subject. Extracts from the review are included here.]

These letters are filled with unconcealed alarm. They are about Poland. They arrive every day at the *Pravda* offices, from workers, peasants, office workers. Old people, veterans, youth – people of all generations are taking up their pens, consider it their international duty to express their opinions about the situation in Poland, their attitude to events in a fraternal country. Soviet people cannot help being worried by the situation in neighbouring Poland, linked as it is to the Soviet Union and the other states of the socialist community by treaties of friendship, cooperation and mutual aid, by the blood bonds of struggle for common ideals.

'The diagnosis of Poland's "political disease" is clear: the counterrevolution which has reared its head is threatening the revolutionary gains of the Polish people and pushing the country towards a national catastrophe,' writes V. Chernov, a young doctor from Omutninsk. 'But let the enemies of socialism remember Leonid Brezhnev's words: "We shall not leave Poland in trouble; we shall stand up for it." These words are not just a warning to the enemies of People's Poland: they are an appeal to all honest Poles to be resolute in the defence of socialist gains, and to boldly oppose the provocations, demagogy, blackmail and lies with which the Kurons, Gwiazdas [Solidarity leaders] and other malicious anti-Soviets are so quick off the mark.'

'Poland in its present borders', writes war veteran I. Vorobyov from Kiev, 'was created at the cost of huge sacrifices and privations. The lands given over to socialist Poland are soaked with the blood of Soviet and Polish soldiers.'

The letters from veterans of the war state quite clearly: we must not allow the historic gains of our peoples – Soviet-Polish friendship and fraternity – to be desecrated. Six-hundred thousand Soviet servicemen gave their lives for the freedom and independence of a fraternal people. Let no one cross out this feat!

Many of our readers took part in the construction of industrial enterprises on Polish soil, and passed on their knowledge. Soviet workers write about the produce which is currently being supplied urgently to Poland, and about the fruitful and broad cooperation which has brought – and will bring – such benefits to both countries.

Alarm sounds in the letters when their authors speak about Poland today. Events there are not only the country's internal affair. *Pravda*'s readers rightly consider that everything that affects Poland also affects the vital interests of all the peoples of the socialist community. It is a question of maintaining the revolutionary achievements of Poland, of yet another attempt by imperialist circles to shake the socialist community.

V. Kopytovskaya from Alma-Ata, a former inmate of the Ravensbruck concentration camp, writes that she is following events in Poland with pain in her heart. 'When will these unrestrained political hooligans from Solidarity finally be given a proper rebuff?' she asks. Appealing to Polish women, she begs them to show vigilance in the name of life, in the name of their children. 'Don't be fooled by Solidarity's destructive propaganda,' she goes on. 'Remember how the Nazis set dogs on you, led you away to the firing-squads, suffocated you in gas chambers, how they turned you into guinea-pigs! How on earth could it happen that Poles, who have travelled such a difficult historical path, could trust the enemies concealed in the ranks of Solidarity, fed by the CIA? It is their efforts that have brought destruction, chaos and disorder in such a short time. It is obvious that the reactionary circles of the West, led by the USA, are trying to change the balance of forces in the world in their favour. Now they have dealt a blow against Poland, using nationalist, anti-socialist groups as their battering-ram. Every effort must be made not to give the enemies of peace on the planet an extra trump card, to prevent a repetition of the past.'

War veterans such as I. Babakov from Thälmann collective farm in Kursk region, who wrote about how Soviet soldiers saved Polish children from the Nazis, call on the Polish working people to show vigilance.

Soviet people were insulted by the so-called 'Appeal to the Peoples of Eastern Europe' adopted by Solidarity at its congress in Gdansk. The letters to *Pravda* describe it as brazen and provocative. 'I was outraged to learn about this sortie by Solidarity,' declares A. Sotnikov of Nikolayev, a fitter, and non-Party member. 'The effrontery of them! I cannot believe that the Polish people consciously wish to give up their socialist achievements and benefits. The vain attempts of those who want the Soviet people and the other fraternal peoples to betray socialism and Lenin's ideals are comical. It's a hopeless ploy, gentlemen from Solidarity!'

The Solidarity congress demonstrated that its leaders are desperate for political power. Putting forward more and more ultimatums and demands, they aim to restore capitalism in the country step by step. Their game is obvious. And they must be curbed and stopped. Such is the thought in many of the letters in *Pravda*'s recent mailbag.

A stop must be put to all connivance at the intrigues of Poland's enemies – that is what Soviet workers think.

'The enemies of people's power', notes A. Arkhipov, a foreman from Cheboksary, 'think nothing of resorting to the basest of methods, to deception and violence, they are undermining the economy and openly make common cause with Western subversive centres. That's with whom "Solidarity's" solidarity lies! What kind of workers' representatives are they? Is that the way to defend workers' interests?'

The Soviet people are deeply indignant at the growing wave of anti-Sovietism in Poland: they say the counterrevolutionary forces are waging with impunity a campaign of slander against the Soviet Union and its internal and foreign policies, are falsifying history, and are jeering at the memory of Soviet servicemen.

A reader from Sukhumi, I. Meshcherikov, notes: 'The situation in the country is developing in a dangerous direction: a political opposition has formed, whose activity is directed against the vital interests of the Polish people and state. I believe that at this difficult stage of their history, the Polish workers and Polish communists will again find the strength to rally and go on to the offensive, that they will manage to isolate the anti-socialist adventurists, opportunists and conciliators, and unmask their baseness. Soviet people are sure that the Party's authority and leading role will get strong again.' V. Sadovets of Perm, a former comrade-in-arms of F. Dzerzhinsky [Polish-born founder of the Cheka, later the KGB] who recently celebrated his ninetieth birthday, expressed his confidence that Polish communists, and all true patriots of Poland, would realise the mortal threat hanging over the country and firmly stand up for the people's socialist gains.

The responses to the events in Poland which are coming into the *Pravda* office are a vivid demonstration of the profound internationalism of the Soviet people, and of their feelings of friendship towards the Polish people. They are an ardent manifestation of the solidarity of the Soviet people, of our working class, with those who in Poland today are standing up to the pressure of hostile forces, those who are fighting against the anarchy and chaos, against the lickspittles of imperialism, against the counterrevolution, and with those who are resolutely and consistently defending the cause of socialism on Polish soil.

[14 November 1981]

A Trial in Torun

[The murder by four Polish secret policemen of the 'Solidarity priest', Father Jerzy Popieluszko, caused a fresh crisis in Poland three years after the Solidarity trade union was outlawed under martial law. The unprecedented trial in a communist country of police agents was covered widely in the Polish media, and every step in the brutal abduction and murder came out into the open. The following TASS report, which refers to the policemen merely as 'citizens' and clearly aims to justify their actions, was all *Pravda* ever published on the affair.]

The trial has ended in the Polish town of Torun of four citizens – G. Piotrowski, A. Pietruszka, L. Pekala and W. Chmielewski –

accused of the kidnap and murder of Father J. Popieluszko. The defendants were sentenced to various periods of imprisonment.

In the course of the trial the accused explained their actions as being intended to impede activities harmful to the state by J. Popieluszko, and his death was the result of a coincidence of tragic circumstances. As the Polish news agency PAP notes, the murder of the priest was a political provocation. Such actions are dangerous and can only lead to disruption of the peace in Poland, to conflicts and clashes.

At the same time, according to reports in the Polish press, numerous instances of activities hostile to the socialist state by representatives of the Polish Catholic Church, and of their abuse of the freedom of religious worship, were confirmed at the Torun trial. They use church services to political ends, and for various kinds of demonstrations of an openly anti-socialist, often even anti-Soviet, nature. In a number of churches, leaflets are illegally distributed. It emerged in the course of the trial that the leadership of the Catholic Church takes a tolerant view of such activities.

The Polish Catholic clergy are influenced by Western centres of ideological sabotage, particularly Radio Free Europe, which endeavours to give a distorted picture of the situation in Poland and to blacken the efforts of the Polish United Workers' [Communist] Party aimed at normalising the situation. These centres try to set Poles against one another and to aggravate tension in relations between the Church and the state. They are gambling on destabilising the political and social situation in Poland.

Material was made public at the trial in Torun which testifies to the fact that the churches are often made available to opposition and subversive elements for them to conduct anti-state and anti-socialist propaganda. As the Polish press points out, they openly attack the principle of the division of church and state, and aim to subordinate lay institutions to the clergy.

[8 February 1985]

From an Afghan Notebook
by V. Okulov and P. Studenikin, Bagram/Kabul

That night in Kabul we observed the picture of a night-time battle being fought just a short distance away. Large-calibre machine-guns and howitzers exploded, causing the earth to shudder a few seconds later. Red traces from the bursts of machine-gun fire scored the dark Kabul sky close by us. It turned out later that the battle was being fought with a group of *dushmans*** who had penetrated as far as Kabul, and who, having straddled the crest of a mountain in the Darlaman district, were trying to shell residential areas of the city. But no sooner had the exchange of fire died down, and we had settled down for a snatched hour's sleep before our early morning flight out, than we were woken by the clamour of cockerels crowing. Soon this gave way to the guttural cries of the muezzins, calling the faithful to morning prayers.

An hour later, driving through the very clean, and so peaceful streets of Kabul, we could not help asking ourselves: 'What battle? What war?' Such was the early-morning calm in the capital of Afghanistan. Anyone just arriving in the country probably also experiences this feeling initially. But those who have to travel much around Afghanistan know that the calm is deceptive – tranquillity can explode into battle at any moment.

. . . There were four of us on board the armoured personnel carrier. Sergeant Renat Murtazin and Akmal Ganiyev,† who kindly let us have one of their pea-jackets to sit on, settled themselves on the other. The night was stifling. We had to unbutton our shirts and place ourselves at the mercy of the local mosquitoes, as vicious as the *dushmans* themselves. Major M. Pasichnik, a political worker, was in the commander's seat at the open hatch.

We first met him when we landed at the airport. Still hot from his journey, in stained overalls covered in dust, he delivered a soldier who had been blown up by a mine into the arms of the doctors, warning them, 'Take good care of this one for me. . . .' He greeted us cordially, and sat us in the armoured car, which was soon jolting along dusty roads under the burning white sun in the direction of the high mountains which rose up on the horizon. On the way he told us that he had studied at veterinary college, but decided to become an officer; that he had left his family behind in the ancient Russian town of Skvir, near Kiev; and that he was in Afghanistan fulfilling his international duty.

In the Afghanistan military department we were told that an

**'Bandits', known in the West as *mujahedin* or freedom-fighters. The word 'Afghans' in this article refers exclusively to men loyal to the Soviet-backed Kabul government.
†The names suggest that these are Soviet soldiers of non-Russian, Central Asian origin.

Afghan battalion was at that time engaged in battle with a band of *dushmans*. The battle was a difficult one – there were some dead and some wounded. The *dushman* forces were strong. They had come from Pakistan with a convoy of arms. We were told that there were some European mercenaries among them. Perhaps they were instructors, perhaps scouts. . . . Who can tell, but one thing was clear – they had brought weapons with them, including rocket launchers, and it was clear for what purpose – to keep the undeclared war here going. . . .

. . . We desperately want to sleep, but we cannot. The night is dark, but our eyes have obviously grown used to the darkness: it is easy to make out the silhouettes of tanks and armoured carriers standing in a circle on the level, open country where we have stopped to rest. A field camp lives by special rules: if you work during the day behind a steering-wheel or levers, or with a machine-gun or radio, you rest by night; others remain on fighting duty. Kabul now seems like a distant, inaccessible dream – everything is relative in this world. From time to time the hoarse voice of Major M. Pasichnik reaches us from the command hatch, which is lit up by red and green patches of light from the signal lamps.

'Ah, the nights on the Dnieper are wonderful at this time of year,' he sighs.

Then some Afghan comrades arrived with the news that soldiers of Askar Mamad's Afghan battalion were repelling the *dushman* attack.

Yesterday, when we arrived at the Afghan signals post (a camouflaged net is stretched between a wall and an armoured personnel carrier, supported in the middle by a pole, and around the pole standing on small tables are the radios) we were immediately caught up in the situation. The sun was beating down mercilessly, but no one felt the heat.

The commander of the Afghan battalion was saying, 'Send us helicopters, I'll prepare landing sites, I'll mark our position with smoke. . . .' The battalion commander understood, of course, the risks involved in bringing in helicopters, but there was evidently no alternative.

Everything worked out well, however: the helicopters landed in a vineyard. At the same time a group which had set out to find assistance came up to us. In the twilight the armoured cars crossed a canal, which, although not deep, had burst its banks and flooded quite an area, and one after the other – a necessary precaution against mines – moved into the neglected vineyards. The armoured carriers, surmounting the earthern ramparts and ditches, jolted heavily from side to side – like enormous geese on a road full of potholes. Then night fell, and our way ahead was blocked by an impassable swamp where the *dushmans* had flooded the vineyards. That was a disappointing setback. We had to wait until dawn, worrying the whole time how things were going with the Afghans.

Major M. Pasichnik was persistently and monotonously trying to make contact with 'Luna' – the action station. 'Luna' didn't answer, and after a short pause the major asked our young driver, 'Ganiyev! Can you see the Great Bear?'

Ganiyev, as though he had only been waiting for this question, answered smartly with a thick accent: 'No, no see it. . . .'

'What about the Little Bear? You know how I taught you?'

'No, no see it, comrade major . . . !'

The major was obviously on edge: there had been no significant change in the situation since the previous day, that is, things were still tense in the 'green place' – the name given here to the fortified residential areas with vineyards, protected from the dry winds by high clay walls. How can you describe an Afghan dwelling, which seems to have developed over the centuries specifically for defence? When the *dushmans* seize a village, they turn each one of these dwellings into a real fortress. Here, you can't see your fellow soldiers to the left or to the right. You don't know what awaits you two metres ahead, and to the side beyond these walls lurk grenades, bullets, and dagger-blows.

There was heavy fighting two months ago: in the narrow side-streets tanks and armoured personnel carriers burned, and soldiers fell, valiantly defending the revolution. The *dushmans* even fired machine-guns and grenade-launchers at close range, as though they were pistols. As soldiers who took part in these battles told us, the sub-units broke up into groups of three to five men. Unlikely situations took shape: for example soldiers in a garden surrounded a house with *dushmans* inside, while other *dushmans* surrounded the garden with the soldiers. . . . A large band of about 300 *dushmans* was routed, and an Afghan army unit seized many weapons and about thirty rocket launchers.

You can't help asking yourself the question: surely the counter-revolutionaries' positions in Afghanistan can't be so strong? Are there really so many people who do not accept the ideas of the April revolution [which brought the communists to power in 1978]? We put this point to someone who, through his work, is in a better position than most to know of the true alignment of forces – the head of the district security service, Sultan Vali Mamad.

'We have succeeded in dealing a series of major blows to the counter-revolution,' he said, 'and all those who patronise the counter-revolution have been thrown into alarm, and have taken urgent measures. It seems to me that this year they have set themselves the task of making the undeclared war against Afghanistan bloodier and crueller than ever. The number of routes by which arms are entering the country has increased. The types of arms getting in are also different: as well as the automatic rifles, machine-guns and mortars, also getting through now are large numbers of cannon, mobile anti-aircraft equipment, anti-tank missiles, 82-millimetre recoil-less guns, and 112-millimetre howitzers. We have seized 25 large consignments of such weapons this year. Moreover, we have precise information about the growing number of large training centres, where instructors from America, Pakistan and other countries are teaching the counter-revolutionaries how to use anti-aircraft weapons, including ground-to-air missiles. The leaders of the largest guerrilla groups are being trained at higher and secondary military colleges in Pakistan, and more than 100 centres have been set up to train other military specialists and *dushmans*: 78 in Pakistan, 11 in Iran. . . . The scale of all this marks a new stage in the undeclared war being waged against revolutionary Afghanistan by international reactionary forces. . . .' Sultan Vali Mamad drew on his cigarette, paused, and concluded:'That's the way things are, my friends.'

'And what is the situation as regards the building-up of Afghanistan's armed forces?' we asked Sultan Vali Mamad.

'You will need to ask the military, I am not a specialist,' he smiled. 'But one thing I can say: the influence of the People's Democratic Party of Afghanistan has always been felt in the army. It was the army, guided by the party, which rose to overthrow [former President] Daud; it was Watanjar's tank, which today stands on a pedestal in Kabul, which started the uprising; Qader's fighter-bomber attacked the Presidential palace. . .* Today, as far as I am aware 80 per cent of the officers in the armed forces are Party members.'

The People's Democratic Party of Afghanistan and the Afghan

* Watanjar and Qader are members of the Revolutionary Council.

government are doing a lot to raise the fighting capacity of the country's armed forces, and this is bearing fruit.

. . . Dawn was breaking. In the morning haze the mountain peaks emerged more and more clearly – marking the entrance to the Panjshir Valley. (We later learned that this was where the convoy of arms had been heading for.) And at last from our Afghan comrades came the joyful news: 'The *dushmans* have been beaten. They are fleeing.' It turned out that during the night the battalion commander had despatched small groups to the enemy rear, and at dawn they struck a pre-emptive blow.

We met them about an hour and a half later: with little trace of excitement the Afghan soldiers came out, threw off their equipment and their camouflage, washed their shorn heads in a cold irrigation ditch, and opened up their ration packs. It was hard to believe that these young lads had just lost some of their mates in battle. No one rushed in with questions. The soldiers were given time to rest and tidy themselves up. And we did not suspect that a new command was about to come, and force them to put on their heavy kitbags again and sling their machine-guns over their shoulders, and that our ways would part. . . . We were left with disappointingly short entries in our notebooks. . . .

'Battalion commander Askar Mamad. Moustache. Strong guy. From Shindant. Speaks like he gives commands – full of energy: "Take this down: Sergeant Kabir distinguished himself. He penetrated the rear and showered a group of *dushmans* with grenades – great help to his company. He has a medal – recommended for the Red Banner. . . . Private Faizulla, a machine-gunner, was killed. Protected his comrades. Machine-gunned the *dushmans* at point-blank range. . . . Karim injured – they ran into an ambush. They carried him out under fire, and he joked: 'Don't forget to put a book in my kitbag, otherwise I'll be bored stiff in hospital!' "'

The white Afghan sun seared our eyes. A column of armoured cars set off into the mountains, raising clouds of white dust. That is probably how it will always remain in our memories: the white sun and the white dust on the roads of Afghanistan. . . .
[11 October 1984]

Opposite: The caption reads: 'Lacquering reality'. An accompanying note explains: 'Franz Josef Strauss, who recently visited Grenada, came out in support of the American occupation of the country.' [January 1984]

Above: Pravda's view of the British miners' strike. The caption reads: 'Care for the unemployed in England.' The banner says: 'We demand work for the miners!' [2 August 1984]

The Real Cause of the Provocation
by Sergei Vishnevsky

[On the night of 31 August 1983 a Soviet fighter plane shot down a Korean Airlines jet which had violated Soviet air-space over Sakhalin Island, a few hours after taking off from Anchorage, Alaska. All 269 people on board were killed. After a faltering start, the Soviet authorities produced a coherent version of events. The jet had not veered off course by accident, as the Americans claimed, but was on a spying mission: it had intentionally entered Soviet air-space to trigger Soviet defences and test their reactions. Much circumstantial evidence – the presence of US spy satellites overhead at the time, for example – was produced to back up the argument. All of this suggested there was a *positive* reconnaisance purpose in flight KAL-007's mission.

But one long article, from which extracts are printed here, went even further: it seemed to suggest that the Americans intended the plane to be shot down in order to make capital out of the 'anti-Soviet hysteria' which followed the incident and thereby to improve the administration's standing and gain support for its rearmament programme. Though unstated, the implication of the entire article is that if the spy mission as such had succeeded it would not have secured these political goals.]

The Washington government has a strange way of expressing its feelings. In official statements concerning the Boeing which violated Soviet air-space, the emotions are laid on thick. The US President and his coterie are fulminating: 'horror', 'indignation'.

Only a few days before this unexpected attack of loquaciousness, the White House had been silent. And this just at a time when broad sections of the American public were looking for answers to burning questions from the administration. Four hundred thousand participants in a march on Washington on 27 August flooded the capital and besieged the residence of the head of state. The banners above the sea of people read: 'Jobs! Peace! Freedom!' [. . .] The White House remained silent.

A growing number of Americans, representing different political spheres and social strata, are realising that the present US administration's foreign policy, dictated by the interests of the military-industrial complex, is at odds with reality. In the 1980s the excessively ambitious imperialist tasks which the Washington strategists have set themselves – to halt the revolutionary processes on the planet, and to achieve global hegemony through military strength – are totally unrealistic. But the widespread application of strong-arm tactics, whipping up the arms race in the vain hope of achieving US military superiority, and kindling hotbeds of tension in various regions, are all fraught with dangerous consequences for universal peace. This arouses anxiety amongst all nations, including the United States. [. . .]

Recently the Western press has been listing daily Washington's failures in the international arena, and cannot find a single achievement. 'On the eve of the year of presidential elections, the US administration does not have a single foreign policy success to its credit,' says the conservative British *Daily Telegraph*. [. . .]

As is always the case in situations of this kind, on the banks of the Potomac [i.e., in Washington], they look for a scapegoat. Last year it was the then Secretary of State, Alexander Haig – he was noisily dismissed. George Shultz took his place at the head of the foreign affairs department, and now . . . he is the next scapegoat. According to the press, he is being attacked by White House officials for failing to come up with creative proposals on foreign policy. But where was Shultz to get creative ideas from, when the Republican leadership had set the totally impossible task of establishing US world hegemony? [. . .]

Shultz was unceremoniously pushed into the background as far as foreign policy formulation was concerned. The President's national security adviser, William Clark, took over the helm on the captain's bridge. Washington old-timers sarcastically point out that the symbol of his approach to international affairs is the Colt hanging on the wall of his basement office in the White House. The general opinion of people who know him is that Clark possesses an array of extremist qualities: he is distinguished by his extreme ignorance, extreme bellicosity, and extreme anti-Sovietism. [. . .]

The international prestige of the USA is rolling downhill. In various forums, including the United Nations, American diplomacy is finding itself more and more often in quarantine. Even the USA's closest allies are becoming estranged from their elder partner. A survey carried out by the Rand Corporation, the brains trust of the military-industrial complex, recorded 'deeply suspicious attitudes to American policy and its motives' in Western Europe. The editor-in-chief of the *US News and World Report*, Marvin Stone, wrote in irritation on 22 August: 'Now, in the Eighties, America is the object of new, bitter criticism because of the face it presents. German and French political leaders are attacking Reagan for his unpredictability, his warmongering, and the coarseness of his actions. Young activists are labelling us as instigators of war. . . . Why are our allies abusing us in this way?' [. . .]

Washington's leaders are extremely concerned by these attitudes. 'President Ronald Reagan is worried by the image of the United States which exists in Europe, especially by the signs of anti-Americanism,' says Flora Lewis, a *New York Times* correspondent. Vice President George Bush has complained that the Europeans 'at times do not understand key aspects of American foreign policy,' and that during his visit to Europe in the summer he found 'signs of widespread distrust regarding President Reagan's commitment to the idea of arms control'.

The new constructive Soviet initiatives on limiting nuclear arms in Europe completely showed up the hollowness and fallaciousness of the USA's negative position, which is directed at attaining one-sided military advantages. The results of a public opinion poll caused shock-waves over the Potomac: three-quarters of the populations of West Germany and Britain were against the deployment of American missiles on their territories. [Deployment of Cruise and Pershing-2 missiles was due to begin towards the end of 1983.] The long campaign of brainwashing by NATO's propaganda services had misfired.

Clark, Weinberger and Casey racked their brains: what could they do on the eve of the 'hot autumn' [of anti-missile protests in Europe]? Their combined experience in working out plans for 'covert' military sabotage operations in Central America with the help of the Pentagon and the CIA told them which way their minds should be thinking. . . . They had at their disposal the experts and rich resources of the Pentagon and the espionage department.

Only future historians will learn what compact the hawkish trinity entered into in those last days of August. . . . But even now, a plain fact is registered in the chronicles of 1983: in the early hours of 1 September, as soon as the flight of the intruding aircraft was stopped in the Soviet Far East, the Washington 'hawks' spread their wings and let out an unimaginable scream.

Weinberger was the first to give himself away. According to a correspondent of the CBS television company, he demanded an immediate halt to all negotiations with the Soviet Union, first and foremost those on nuclear arms limitation. Then, in the Minister's view, it would be possible to station the missiles in Europe without hindrance and without diplomatic ceremony. To torpedo the

Geneva negotiations – this was the Pentagon boss's cherished dream.

The Washington strategists were rather wary of accepting Weinberger's recommendation – it would be too much of a give-away. To his comfort, however, the President's public speeches now incorporated all the main points of his strategy of 'direct confrontation' with the Soviet Union and the dogmas of a 'crusade' against the socialist countries.

Thanks to the rabid anti-Soviet hysteria unleashed in the USA, the administration, according to the *Baltimore Sun*, 'now finds itself in a more advantageous position, which allows it to call even more resolutely for a huge build-up in military spending,' since 'it is unlikely that any member of Congress would want to give the impression of unwarranted softness.' They are evidently reckoning on McCarthyite intimidation of moderate Congressmen.

At the same time, as that hardened veteran of the American special services, Inman, maliciously anticipated, it would be 'easier' in the situation which had come about to obtain the agreement of the USA's allies to 'adopt firm measures' in the military sphere. In the first place, this means pushing through America's missile plans in Western Europe, and also an intensification of the militaristic preparations of NATO, Japan and other allied countries.

Fanning the myth about the Russians' 'aggressiveness', the Washington provocateurs are trying to sow doubt in the minds of the peace campaigners about the peace-loving policy of the Soviet Union, and to take the heat out of the struggle for peace at a crucial moment in history, when the burning question of whether the threat of nuclear war can be averted is decided.

Observers graphically compare Washington's large-scale political provocation with a multiple warhead ballistic missile. It is simultaneously directed at several targets: at the negotiating tables in Geneva and Vienna, at détente, international trust and cooperation, and at peace and security.

Has not Washington gone too far? Both the premeditated intelligence operation over a strategically important region of the USSR, and the anti-Soviet orgy now under way, are vivid manifestations of extremist adventurism and of detachment from reality – those very characteristics of American policy which have so often before led to ignominious failure.

[26 September 1983]

A Friend in Need
by A. Serbin, Addis Ababa

The weather report is the main piece of news in the papers at the moment. And it is not idle curiosity that makes one study the forecast for the north-eastern regions, which were especially cruelly affected by last year's drought; or the prospects for rain on the central plateau, the country's granary; or the forecast for the western provinces, where the victims of the disaster are fleeing. It is upon the answers to these questions that hopes for Ethiopia's agriculture largely depend.

It is now the season of 'great rains' here. The moisture which they bring will determine the content of the granaries. But the rains should not be over-abundant – downpours can sometimes destroy the crops. Towards the end of September when the season comes to an end, the prospects for the harvest also become clearer.

This year the agricultural situation is being accorded particular attention. The Workers' Party of Ethiopia is spearheading a large campaign to overcome the after-effects of the drought. It has worked out ways of helping the disaster victims, and also long and short-term programmes to revive and develop agricultural production.

Following a resolution of the revolutionary powers, economy measures are being carried out in the country, new tracts of land have been ploughed, and a start has been made to the construction of irrigation systems on the smaller rivers. Of major significance is the plan to move half a million people out of the drought zones into areas where the conditions for agriculture are more favourable. This plan is already being put in motion.

Much is being done, but the disaster's scorching attack was so ruinous and destructive for both land and people that it will still take some time to eliminate its after-effects.

Ethiopia is not alone in coping with this difficult task. One of the first countries to respond to the Ethiopian leadership's appeal for support in its hour of need was the Soviet Union.

. . . Our MI-8 helicopter is heading north. A little way off, a second helicopter is following the same course. The pilots are flying on a mission which has become routine for them – to bring food and to evacuate people. The work began in November of last year, when the Soviet government urgently despatched over twenty of these helicopters to Ethiopia on board 'Antei' [An-22] transport planes.

Our lads worked day and night to get them airborne as quickly as possible. And since then the humpbacked MI-8s have been helping people in need. They fly to places where no roads lead, they reach inaccessible spots in the mountains, and land on poorly prepared areas from which a column of dust can often rise up, hindering the pilots' visibility. 'Our people have come to recognise the whirr of your helicopter screws, and look forward to them because they bring hope,' I was told by the Ethiopian comrades who are directing the relief effort.

From up above it is well seen how much labour has gone into this land. The central plateau looks like a patchwork quilt, with fields squeezed up next to each other, and not an inch left untouched by human hand. But our helicopter is now over the mountainous regions of Wollo province, which was severely hit by the drought. It is a majestic landscape of mountain ranges shimmering in a bluish haze, rift-valleys, and steep, rocky spurs. But here and there on the slopes and ledges of the mountains the eye catches sight of dwellings abandoned by men and animals, and next to them the dull yellow patches of deserted threshing-floors, and empty fields. Here the drought was victorious. The MI-8 rounds a summit and swoops down towards the tiny rag of a landing area. People have already gathered near it – those whom the helicopters will take away from these sad places to a new life.

The Soviet aviation group working in Ethiopia also includes An-12 planes. Almost all the country's provinces now figure in our pilots' flight documents. They ply the air routes over Ethiopia on various tasks, but with one and the same aim – to help people in need. In May the An-12s opened up a new route, crossing the country from east to west. Now Aeroflot planes fly in supplies from the port of Asab on the Red Sea to the Western province of Ilubabor – one of those where families from the heat-ravaged areas are being settled. At the beginning of the summer the airmen took part in another operation, transporting teams of Ethiopian students to the new population centres to help normalise the life of the new settlers.

Already, more than half a million people are living in the western provinces. More than 100,000 of them were evacuated from the disaster areas on Soviet planes and helicopters. Our airmen have also moved 25,000 tonnes of cargo. They have made 15,000 flights.

Recently the first group of Soviet pilots completed their tour of duty and returned home. Carrying on the good work, fresh pilots arriving from the Soviet Union took up their places at the controls of the aeroplanes and helicopters.

A Soviet motorised detachment of 300 trucks also continues to work in Ethiopia, taking part in the ground-based transport relief operations. You can often see convoys of Zil lorries on the roads here, with the Soviet and Ethiopian flags painted on their cabs. I recall the nervousness of our drivers setting out on the first trip across unknown territory. Now they are familiar with many of the country's roads, and their speedometers have already clocked up thousands of 'Ethiopian' kilometres. But they will never forget that first trip, and the settlements along the road where crowds gathered to welcome their Soviet friends, and the firm handshakes at the stopping places, and the gifts of flowers so different from our own. They told me that the driver of one of the Ethiopian petrol-tankers which delivered fuel for our trucks was determined that the petrol he had brought should go directly into the tanks of the Soviet trucks, and was very upset when he had to pour it into the common storage tank. . . .

I once travelled with a convoy to Asosa in the province of Welega, where a Soviet mobile hospital for the displaced people had been set up. The doctors and nurses working there are carrying on our country's fine tradition in the provision of medical aid to the Ethiopian people, a tradition which goes back to the last century. The hospital was established in a very short time, and on what was once a barren field there is now a medical village, with neat rows of tents, with laboratories and consulting rooms under tarpaulin roofs, with a clinic and an in-patients unit, all housed in tents, and a hut which is equipped as an operating theatre. The doctors not only receive patients at the hospital itself, but also make regular trips to other populated areas. Since the hospital started up, 93,000 people have received medical assistance there, and around a thousand operations have been carried out. The whole country knows about the work of our medical team.

In Ethiopia one sees with one's own eyes how much the Soviet Union has taken the misfortune of a friendly nation to heart. The aid is not limited to the work of the groups sent here, who are fully provided for by the Soviet side. Our Ethiopian friends have also been sent drilling-rigs to find water, vehicles, children's food, medicines, tents, household utensils, and clothes for the relocated people. Aid has also come from the other socialist states.

The Ethiopian people must still put in a considerable effort to rid

their land of the after-effects of the disaster and to fight the caprices of nature more effectively. In this they are helped by friendship and cooperation with the Soviet Union and with the other countries of the socialist community.
[6 September 1985]

When Holidays are No Different from Any Other Day
by V. Listov, Managua

The scorching morning sun fills the vast wasteland on the banks of Lake Managua. There are plans to turn the wasteland into one of the Nicaraguan capital's main squares – named after Carlos Fonseca, the founder of the Sandinista National Liberation Front (SNLF). But even today you can judge its future shape by the newly completed multi-tiered stand, right at the water's edge, and by the shady green park on the opposite side. It is quiet and deserted here now. But only very recently it was a seething mass of people: they came from Managua and from many of the towns and villages in neighbouring departments to take part in a rally to mark the sixth anniversary of the Sandinista revolution, pledging their loyalty to its ideals, and their support of the Sandinista government.

'Right-wingers were hoping that the economic difficulties which our country is experiencing would alienate the workers from the Sandinista government,' says Javier Reyes, deputy editor of *Barricada*, the official newspaper of the SNLF. 'But they miscalculated. The capital has never witnessed such a massive rally as the one which took place here on 19 July. It was a clear demonstration of the SNLF's impact on the masses.'

A few days later, and life in Managua had slipped back into its usual routine, characterised both by the tranquillity of everyday working life and by the tension caused by the threat of armed intervention.

In the mornings there is a steady stream of civil servants travelling from the outskirts to the city centre, where most of the government departments and commercial organisations have their offices. The difficulties in the public transport system are felt most keenly during these rush hours. Buses scarcely manage to drag themselves along, leaving trails of smoke behind them, and sometimes they break down altogether. But once the rush-hour fever is over, the builders take over: you can see them all over the place patching up the road surface, or repairing old underground communications, or laying new ones.

Housing poses no less serious a problem in Managua than does transport. It is written about in the papers, and talked about in the buses, at work, and in cafés. A few trips across the city are enough to make one understand why there is such interest in the housing problem. In some places there are blocks of neat little houses – to the credit of the national authorities. But such blocks are few and far between. The aggressive policy of the USA has forced the Sandinista government to increase its spending on defence, and to curtail a number of social programmes, including the building of houses for the poorer sections of the population.

Another consequence of the undeclared US war against Nicaragua is the migration of people from the border regions affected by military action into the towns, above all Managua. The number of shacks put up by the refugees, who come mainly from the north, grows every month. This is making the already critical housing problem – inherited from the dictator's régime – even more serious. It is remarkable that the names of these new poor quarters also reflect the political leanings of their inhabitants: they are most often named after revolutionaries who fell in the struggle against tyranny, and only occasionally, with one eye on the Church, is a district named after some saint.

In a newly formed refugee quarter, which straddles the highway leading from the airport into the town, I spoke to Roberto Lopez, an elderly grey-haired man whose face is scored with deep wrinkles – evidence of a hard life. In his shack, cobbled together out of wide, thin planks, it was dark and stuffy. Roberto was sitting on a block of wood, and, puffing at a cigarette, he said: 'Myself, my family and our neighbours, señor, we were all there on 19 July, at the rally in the square. Our life, of course, is not a bed of roses. We have more than our share of troubles. You see for yourself what our housing conditions are like. And transport here is a disaster. But if it weren't for the "contras" and the blasted Yankees, we could live more peacefully. And prices are rising nevertheless, and we are grumbling, señor – that's only natural. But it's not the most important thing. The most important thing is that although we are grumblers, we are still Sandinistas in body and in soul. We are for the Revolution. And we will not desert it, no matter how hard it gets for us. Yes, señor,' he repeated firmly, 'we are Sandinistas. . . .'

One of the main signs of the times in present-day Managua is people carrying guns. Armed soldiers protect government buildings and industrial enterprises. The soldiers of the people's militia, sitting at the entrances to newspaper offices, shops and cinemas, never part with their arms. Literally at every step you take, you see on the walls of buildings and offices the patriotic slogan: 'Victorious Nicaragua will not sell itself and will not give in.' Some of the people one speaks to put on a show of defiance: 'Just let the Yankees try to poke their noses. . . .' Bravado is all very well, but just how seriously the Nicaraguans take the threat of a possible armed intervention from outside is demonstrated by the tanks and armoured cars concealed at strategic points in the capital and on the approaches to it.

It is enough to leaf through the local papers for a day or two to understand that the Nicaraguans are fully justified in their alarm. Here are a few reports which give an idea of the difficult times being endured by Sandino's motherland.

'There were 110 skirmishes with "Contras" in the first three weeks of July. The "Contras" were trying to enter our country from Honduras, in order to disrupt celebrations for the sixth anniversary of the victory of the Revolution. The mercenaries everywhere met with a rebuff.'

'The steamer *Rio Escondido*, on a regular civilian trip along the river Escondido between Rama and Bluefields, ran into a "Contras" attack: four passengers were killed, seventeen injured.'

'Three cars belonging to the Construction Ministry were ambushed by the "Contras" to the north of Jinotega: four people were killed, the rest disappeared without trace. . . .'

One other aspect of the internal political situation is particularly striking: the more aggressive US policy towards Nicaragua becomes, the more patriotic and anti-imperialist becomes the mood of the Nicaraguans, and the wider the protest movement against Washington's policy of state terrorism grows. Today this movement makes use of many different and concrete forms of action – from peasant self-defence and boosting the ranks of the people's militia, to demonstrations in front of the US embassy and the collection of signatures on petitions which are sent to the United Nations and other international organisations. Sometimes the movement takes on unexpected forms, such as collective, pacifist hunger strikes.

. . . In the district of Monseñor Lescano, one of the oldest, most densely populated, poorest and most militant in the Nicaraguan capital, on a street of the same name, stands a small church of unassuming appearance. It is also called Monseñor Lescano. For a month it attracted public attention not only in Nicaragua, but in many other countries too: this was where Miguel D'Escoto, a priest and Minister of Foreign Affairs in the Sandinista government, staged a hunger strike in protest against the White House's aggressive policy towards Nicaragua.

The interior of the church looks more like an exhibition of anti-war posters than a traditional Catholic chapel. Hanging along the walls, these posters are either childishly naïve or, on the contrary, strike you with their skilful graphics, or tear at your heart with their tragic simplicity.

On one, the outlines of a tank are crossed out. Next to it is a drawing of a dove with a green twig in its beak and the caption: 'Stop the war unleashed by the USA!' But probably the poster which makes the strongest impression is one against US intervention in Central America: a white dove is sitting on her eggs, protecting them with her body from a bomb, which a predatory eagle is preparing to drop.

Miguel D'Escoto would not speak to journalists. But he made an exception for *Pravda*'s correspondent.

'I am fasting as a mark of protest against the policy of aggression and state terrorism which the USA is carrying out against my country,' said D'Escoto. 'At the same time, it is also my protest against the slanderous imperialist propaganda campaign, which claims that there is no religious freedom in Nicaragua, and that religion is being persecuted. As a Nicaraguan I am faithful to my duty, and therefore I am trying to persuade people that the Revolution is bringing good, for it is being accomplished primarily for the poor.'

Believers and atheists alike took part in a movement of solidarity with Miguel D'Escoto. There were about forty other hunger strikers with him in the church. Among those who came to give him a word of encouragement or support, or to write something in a special book, were students and teachers, workers and peasants, soldiers and mothers of young men who fell in the struggle against tyranny or in battles with the 'Contras'. Some came at the end of their working day, others sometimes came straight from the battle areas. I observed a group of soldiers who appeared in their stained uniforms. Having signed the book of solidarity they pinned a poster to the wall, on which was written: 'The special purpose battalions are on the alert holidays or weekdays! The enemy shall not pass!'

The great majority of Nicaraguans think the same way.
[12 August 1985]

Broken Lives
by Vladimir Belyakov

[Review of *The White Book*, published in Moscow in 1985]

The book before us is an accusatory document, whose pages are full of facts about countless human tragedies. One after another, the fates of people who curse the day and hour they found themselves in a foreign land pass before the reader. They were lured there, separated from their homes and Motherland, and had their human rights and dignity trampled on by imperialism and Zionism, by those selfsame services and gentlemen from America and other countries who cynically don the guise of 'humanism'.

It is difficult to know which lines to quote from the letters included in the *White Book* – each line is more bitter than the last. Perhaps these ones? 'I cannot resign myself to the ways of this country, and if I ever manage to return, I'll kiss the very ground of my Motherland.' Or these? 'All our people who arrive here from the USSR weep, live like beggars, and cannot return. Some are ashamed, others have run into debt, some have ended up in psychiatric hospitals, and some have had their children taken from them to be drafted into the army.'

This is Israel. But perhaps those who end up in other countries fare better? 'The homeless roaming the streets, the unemployment, the uncertainty about the future, the widespread crime which has become the norm in this society – this is what we saw in America,' says one letter whose author encountered blatant racism and anti-Semitism in that country.

In New York, for example, a third of the companies building new houses will not rent their flats to people of Jewish origin, and about 700 business clubs in 46 states will not allow them to become members. What can one do? The USA is a 'free country'. . . .

About 3,000 of our former citizens drag out a miserable existence in the small town of Ostia, not far from Rome. They live from hand to mouth, trading at the local flea-market. Stories from people who live in this new ghetto call to mind the characters from Gorky's play *The Lower Depths*. It is difficult to believe that they too once had a proper home, regular work, an income, and that they enjoyed the respect of their comrades. All that is in the past. And in the future lies emptiness.

Of course these people now have to pay a cruel price for the thoughtless step they took. But they are also the victims of a determined ideological campaign by the ruling circles of the USA and other imperialist powers, who are veritable 'hunters' of human souls. Ingratiating radio 'voices' and other centres of ideological sabotage in the West invent malicious lies about our life, and promise a land flowing with milk and honey in the 'free world'. Documents published in the *White Book* clearly show how these falsehoods are fabricated.

The facts demonstrate that US officials – from the President down to embassy staff – do not shrink from taking part in the psychological war against the USSR. The Rabbinate and the Council of the Moscow Synagogue were even forced to send an indignant letter to the US ambassador, Arthur Hartman, condemning the behaviour of a number of American diplomats. It seems that these gentlemen repeatedly went to the synagogue specifically to lure believers into their nets, and to incite them to leave the USSR.

The fates of these people worry the 'champions of human rights' in Washington about as much as last year's snow. The main task for these ideological saboteurs is to spread anti-Soviet ideas and put about slander to the effect that people 'prefer Western freedom to Soviet dictatorship'. And those who swallow the bait are left to make out as best they can in a foreign land. They've played their part. . . .

The *White Book* was prepared by the Anti-Zionist Committee of the Soviet Public and the Association of Soviet Lawyers. Its strength lies in its strictly documentary approach. It exposes the organisers and inspirers of subversive acts against the USSR, who openly violate human rights and destroy people's lives.
[10 August 1985]

New Year Notes 1985

Prisoners of Reaction
by V. Korionov

Today these people are not among their families and friends, and are not joining in the New Year celebrations. They have before them not a New Year's tree shining with festive lights, but the bars of a prison cell. They are the victims of class vengeance, for their selfless participation in the struggle for the interests of the working people, for the triumph of the ideals of peace and democracy, national independence and socialism.

It would be hard to find a computer capable of calculating the number of these people. But from time to time some statistics filter out to the world press from one or other of the countries turned into concentration camps by the efforts of the American suppressors of freedom and their accomplices. And then we learn, for example, that in El Salvador at present there are approximately 5,400 political prisoners. But who can say with any accuracy how many freedom-fighters are languishing in the torture-chamber of the butcher Pinochet, whose crimes are generously paid for in dollars?

Today we cannot forget the names of those whom the powers that be would prefer to die in obscurity. Names like Leonard Peltier, the valiant fighter for the rights of the Red Indians doomed to extinction. He has been wasting away in the torture cells of American 'democracy' for more than eight years. Or Joe Harris, jailed for many years for defending the rights of black Americans. And Nelson Mandela, the unflinching fighter against Apartheid, who has been 22 years in the torture-chambers of the South African racists.

It is more difficult to list the names of all the Palestinian patriots thrown into punishment cells by Israeli soldiers, or detained in camps like the one at Ansar. The numbers of these freedom-loving people are huge. And we believe that the day will come when they will return to their peaceful homes.

A new category of prisoner has appeared in recent years, as US ruling circles have begun to force a course leading to the unleashing of nuclear war. These people are thrown into prisons merely because they do not want American MX or Pershing or Cruise missiles to start sowing death on the fields of Europe and in other continents.

We are celebrating the New Year under a peaceful sky, thanks not only to the socialist community [i.e. the Soviet bloc] and other peaceloving countries and nations, but also to those who, fearing neither prison nor death itself, have joined the fight against the forces of war, evil and oppression.

A Symbol of Courage
by A. Maslennikov, London

The year 1984 will go down in British history as the year of an unprecedented upturn in the struggle of the working people to defend their social and democratic rights.

The continuing strike of the British miners – the most persistent and prolonged in the chronicles of the British workers' movement – has become a symbol of unflinching courage, steadfastness, and readiness to put up with any privations in the name of preserving the workingman's dignity and inalienable right to live by the fruits of his own labour.

Flaring up at the beginning of March in protest against the government's plans to cut coal output by approximately ten per cent and, under this pretext, to sack about 20,000 miners, the strike has had a profound effect on the entire social and economic situation in the country.

For the 150,000 striking miners and their families the past nine months have been a time of severe ordeals. Having to exist on the wretched 'poverty benefit' paid out to the wives and children of the strikers has brought undisguised need into their homes. About 9,000 striking miners have been in police torture chambers, or have been fined or sentenced to lengthy spells in prison. The miners' leaders are subjected to increasingly cruel persecution.

But nonetheless the British miners are not giving in. Their determination flows from their unshakable faith in the justice of their cause, and also from the increasing material and moral support from other groups of workers, and from the broad democratic public. It is hard to disagree with the weekly *New Statesman*, which wrote that 'whatever the outcome of this struggle, the miners and those fighting alongside them in the mining communities will write an unfading, heroic episode into the history of the British trade union movement'.

[31 December 1984]

Notes

1. Seventy-Five Years of Truth: The History of Pravda

1. R. C. Elwood, 'Lenin and Pravda', *Slavic Review*, Vol. 31, 1972, pp. 358–9.
2. V. I. Lenin, *Polnoe sobranie sochineniy* [*PSS*] (Moscow) 5th edition, Vol. 48, p. 62.
3. *Pravda*, 22 April (5 May) 1912.
4. Lenin, *PSS*, Vol. 48, p. 78; also N. Krupskaya, *Vospominaniya o Lenine* (Moscow, 1968), p. 208.
5. Lenin, *PSS*, Vol. 48, p. 74.
6. Cited in V. E. Shlyapentokh (ed.), *Problemy sotsiologii pechati, 2. vyp.* (Novosibirsk, 1970). p. 27. [N.B. Dr Shlapentokh (as he is known in the USA, where he now lives) is referred to in the notes as Shlyapentokh where the writings in question were published in Russian in the USSR.]
7. Krupskaya, *op. cit.*, p. 224.
8. *Pravda*, 5 May 1922.
9. Krupskaya, *op. cit.*, pp. 203–4.
10. *Ibid.*, p. 223; D. Shub, *Lenin. A Biography* (Harmondsworth, 1966), p. 146.
11. A. F. Berezhnoy, *Tsarskaya tsenzura i bor'ba bol'shevikov na svobodu pechati* (Leningrad, 1967), pp. 220–1.
12. See Paul Roth, *Sow-inform, Nachrichtenwesen und Informationspolitik der Sowjetunion* (Düsseldorf, 1980), pp. 18–19.
13. Berezhnoy, p. 230.
14. Lenin, *PSS*, Vol. 48, p. 272.
15. Artem Gertik, in *Pravda*, 5 May 1922, says that *Luch*'s circulation was 10,000–12,000. See also Elwood, p. 378.
16. Fuller details of the press regulations are in Whitman Bassow, 'The Pre-Revolutionary *Pravda* and Tsarist Censorship', *The American Slavic and East European Review*, Vol. 13, 1954, p. 49.
17. *Ibid.*, p. 60.
18. Gertik, in *Pravda*, 5 May 1922.
19. Bassow, *op. cit.*, p. 50.
20. B. Ivanov, 'K 15-letiyu "Pravdy"', *Pravda*, 6 May 1927.
21. *Pravda*, 5 May 1922.
22. Elwood, *op. cit.*, pp. 358–9.
23. 'Zhandarmy o "Pravde"', *Proletarskaya revolyutsiya*, II, 1923, p. 463.
24. *Pravda*, 24 April 1912.
25. Adam B. Ulam, *Lenin and the Bolsheviks*, (London, Fontana), p. 414.
26. For a discussion of the speed with which *Pravda* was revived after the February Revolution, see P. Frank and B. C. Kirkham, 'The Revival of *Pravda* in 1917', *Soviet Studies*, Vol. 20, 1969, pp. 366–9.
27. A. G. Shlyapnikov, *Semnadtsatyy god*, Vol. 2 (Moscow, 1925), p. 180.
28. *Pravda*, 21 March 1917.
29. *Proletarskaya revolyutsiya*, No. 1, 1923, p. 221.
30. *Pravda*, 8 April 1917.

31. More detail in Roger Pethybridge, *The Spread of the Russian Revolution* (London, 1972), pp. 121–3.

32. *Ibid*.

33. Lenin, *PSS*, Vol. 34, p. 210.

34. N. Suchanov, *1917 Tagebuch der russischen Revolution* (Munich, 1967), pp. 677f, in Paul Roth, *Die kommandierte öffentliche Meinung* (Stuttgart, 1982), pp. 40–41.

35. Text of Press Decree in *Pravda*, 10 November 1917.

36. Mark W. Hopkins, *Mass Media in the Soviet Union* (New York, 1970), pp. 78–79.

37. Berezhnoy, *op. cit.*, p. 67.

38. *Pravda*, 16 March 1918.

39. A. Sol'ts, 'Sekretar' "Pravdy"', *Pravda*, 5 May 1922.

40. Stephen Cohen, *Bukharin and the Bolshevik Revolution* (Oxford, 1980), p. 62.

41. See E. H. Carr, *The Russian Revolution from Lenin to Stalin 1917–1929* (London, 1979), pp. 50–60.

42. E. H. Carr, *The Interregnum, 1923–24* (London, 1954), p. 319 (note).

43. *Ibid*.

44. *Pravda*, 15 December 1923.

45. Cohen, *op. cit.*, p. 155.

46. *Pravda*, 28, 29, 30 December 1923; 1, 4 January 1924.

47. Carr, *The Interregnum*, p. 322.

48. Carr, *The Russian Revolution . . .*, pp. 82, 117.

49. E. H. Carr, *Foundations of a Planned Economy, 1926–1929*, Vol. 2 (London, 1071), p. 61.

50. *Pravda*, 4 August 1929.

51. Cohen, *op. cit.*, p. 450.

52. See his 'Notes of an Economist', *Pravda*, 30 September 1928; also *Pravda*, 28 November 1928, 20 January 1929.

53. *Pravda*, 24 August 1929.

54. *Pravda*, 5 May 1922 and elsewhere.

55. A. Gayev, 'Kak delaetsya "Pravda"', *Ost-Probleme*, No. 37, 1953, pp. 1567f.

56. *Ibid*.

57. *Pravda*, 3 January 1930.

58. *Pravda*, 16 February 1983.

59. *Pravda*, 11 May 1937.

60. *Pravda*, 3 January 1937.

61. *Pravda*, 1 January 1937.

62. *Pravda*, 17 May 1937.

63. *Pravda*, 29 July, 1931.

64. *Pravda*, 7 November 1937.

65. A. Gayev, 'Sovetskaya pechat' na voyne', *Mitteilungen des Instituts zur Forschung der Sowjetunion*, No. 1, 1954, p. 53.

66. Hopkins, *op. cit.*, p. 101.

67. Gayev, 'Kak delaetsya "Pravda"'.

68. *Pravda*, 1 March 1948.

69. *Pravda*, 14 February 1948.

70. R. Medvedev, *Khrushchev* (Oxford, 1982), pp. 53–54.

71. Edward Crankshaw, *Khrushchev* (London, 1966), p. 199.

72. Circulation figures from the *Yearbooks [Yezhegodnik]* of the *Bol'shaya Sovetskaya Entsiklopediya*.

73. R. Medvedev, *op. cit.*, pp. 207–8.

74. *Pravda*, 23 November 1962, 23 December 1962.

75. *Pravda*, 12 May 1963.

76. *Pravda*, 17 November 1970, 13 September 1971.

77. See Michel Tatu, *Power in the Kremlin* (London, 1969), pp. 446–56; John Dornberg, *Brezhnev. The Masks of Power* (London, 1974), p. 203.

78. *Izvestiya*, 21 May 1965.

79. Zhores Medvedev, *Andropov* (Oxford, 1983), p. 45.

80. *Pravda*, 21 February 1965.

81. See Dina R. Spechler, *Permitted Dissent in the USSR* (New York, 1982), pp. 213ff.

82. *Pravda*, 8 October 1965.

83. *Politicheskiy dnevnik*, No. 31, April 1967 (reprinted by Alexander Herzen Foundation, Amsterdam, 1972, 1975).
84. *Pravda*, 30 January 1966; see Tatu, *op. cit.*, p. 484.
85. Stephen Cohen (ed.), *An End to Silence* (New York, London, 1982), p. 299.
86. *Komsomol'skaya pravda*, 30 June 1967.
87. Author's interview with V. Shlapentokh; Cohen, *An End . . .* , *ibid*.
88. G. T. Zhuravlev (ed.), *Marksistsko-leninskaya metodologiya i voprosy metodiki konkretnykh sotsial'nykh issledovaniy* (Moscow, 1977), pp. 75, 83.
89. Notably, the Central Committee resolution 'On the further improvement of ideological, political and educational work' of 26 April 1979.
90. Even *Pravda*'s editor, Afanasyev, noted the slackening of the discipline campaign under Chernenko; see *Zhurnalist*, No. 3, 1984.
91. See *Pravda* leader, 27 March 1985.
92. *Pravda*, 27 February 1986.
93. *Pravda*, 13 February 1986.

2. Pravda and the Soviet Mass Media

1. V. V. Uchenova, *Osnovy marksistsko-leninskogo ucheniya o zhurnalistike* (Moscow, 1981), p. 97.
2. *Pravda*, 5 May 1985.
3. *Ibid.*
4. See, e.g., Uchenova, *op. cit.*, *passim*.
5. V. S. Korobeynikov (ed.), *Sotsiologicheskie problemy obshchestvennogo mneniya i deyatel'nosti sredstv massovoy informatsii* (Moscow, 1979), pp. 32–33.
6. *Leninskoy 'Pravde' – 70 let* (Moscow, 1982), pp. 462–3.
7. *Reuters*, 5 August 1986.
8. Leonid Vladimirov, *The Russians* (London, 1968), pp. 88ff.
9. *Pravda*, 19 June 1985.
10. *Pravda*, 30 June 1985.
11. *Pravda*, 22 July 1985.
12. *Guardian*, 24 July 1985.
13. *Yezhegodnik bol'shoy sovetskoy entsiklopedii*, 1985.
14. See *Guardian*, 3 May 1984.
15. E. P. Prokhorov (ed.), *Sotsiologiya zhurnalistiki* (Moscow, 1981), p. 94.
16. *Govorit i pokazyvaet Moskva*, 10 April 1985.
17. L. N. Tsarev (comp.), *Sila slova* (Leningrad, 1981), p. 21.
18. *Summary of World Broadcasts* (BBC, Caversham Park), 8 May 1985.
19. *Yezhegodnik . . .* , 1984.
20. *Sovetskiy entsiklopedicheskiy slovar'* (Moscow, 1979); Hedrick Smith, *The Russians* (London, Sphere, 1976), pp. 433–4.
21. *Ibid.*
22. V. Stepakov, former editor of *Izvestiya* and chief of Central Committee Propaganda Department, and L. Vladimirov, former Soviet journalist now in the West; both cited in Paul Roth, *Sowinform*, pp. 211, 239.

3. How Pravda is Made

1. *Sovetskiy entsiklopedicheskiy slovar'*.
2. Herman F. Achminov, 'Probleme der Sowjetjournalistik',

Osteuropa, December 1967, p. 896.

3. BBC radio, 18 September 1983.
4. *Daily Telegraph*, 11 February 1985.
5. *Los Angeles Times*, 9 December 1983.
6. D. Georgiev, *Rezhissura gazety* (Moscow, 1979), pp. 190–2.
7. Author's interview at *Pravda* offices, 5 December 1983.
8. Anatoliy Karpychev, '"Pravde" – 70 let', *Zhurnalist*, May 1982, p. 6.
9. Interview at *Pravda*.
10. *Ibid.*
11. E.g., Georgiev, *op. cit.*, p. 63.
12. Full details of the various plans are in S. M. Gurevich (ed.), *Planirovanie raboty v redaktsii* (Moscow, 1979), *passim*.
13. Georgiev, *op. cit.*, pp. 66–73.
14. Karpychev, *op. cit.*, pp. 4–8; Gurevich, *op. cit.*, pp. 79f.
15. Vladimirov, *op. cit.*, p. 94.

16. *Literaturnaya gazeta*, 31 May 1960.
17. Karpychev, *op. cit.*, p. 7.
18. See John H. Miller, 'The Top Soviet Censorship Team? – A Note', *Soviet Studies*, Vol. XXIX, No. 4, October 1977, pp. 590–8. The details have changed slightly, but the principle remains the same.
19. *Zhurnalist*, July 1970; V. S. Korobeynikov, *Redaktsiya i auditoriya* (Moscow, 1983), p. 110.
20. *Le Monde*, 26 January 1985.
21. Korobeynikov, *ibid.*
22. *Summary of World Broadcasts* (BBC, Caversham Park), 12 July 1985.
23. Information board in *Pravda* offices.
24. See Zev Katz, *The Communications System in the USSR* (Cambridge, Massachusetts, 1977), p. 58.

4. All the Views Fit to Print: Content and Policy

1. *Pravda*, 12 March 1985.
2. *Pravda*, 26 February 1986.
3. According to the dissident Soviet historian Roy Medvedev, Gorbachov tried to persuade the Politburo, meeting two days after the accident, to give full and correct information, but was opposed by all except Vitaly Vorotnikov (Premier of the Russian Federation) and Viktor Chebrikov (head of the KGB). Only when the extent of the accident and of the worldwide reaction became clear did Gorbachov succeed in imposing his line. See Alberto Jacoviello's interview with Medvedev in *La Repubblica*, 31 May 1986.
4. *Sovetskaya Rossiya*, 5 January 1986.
5. *Pravda*, 13 June 1986.

6. *Pravda*, 30 May 1986.
7. *Literaturnaya gazeta*, 18 June 1986.
8. *Pravda*, 16 August 1986.
9. Hedrick Smith, *op. cit.*, pp. 455–6; Robert G. Kaiser, *Russia: The People and the Power* (Harmondsworth, 1977), pp. 215–6.
10. *Moskovskaya pravda*, 21 September 1986.
11. *Rude pravo*, 14 June 1986.
12. *Pravda*, 24 June 1985.
13. Gromyko's speech was published only in the brochure *Materialy vneocherednogo Plenuma Tsentral'nogo Komiteta KPSS, 11 marta 1985 g.* (Moscow, 1986).
14. *Pravda*, 16 April 1985.
15. *Pravda*, 2 June 1986.
16. *Pravda*, 18 December 1982.
17. *Pravda*, 21 March 1982.

18. *Pravda*, 14 May 1985.
19. See Daniel Tarschys, *The Soviet Political Agenda* (New York, 1979).
20. *Summary of World Broadcasts* (BBC, Caversham Park), 9 September 1985.
21. *Pravda*, 12 June 1985.
22. A. V. Chernyak, '*Partiynaya zhizn*'' – *glavnaya rubrika* '*Pravdy*' (Moscow, 1984), pp. 37–38.
23. *Plenum tsentral'nogo komiteta KPSS 14–15 iyunya 1983 goda; Stenograficheskiy otchet* (Moscow, 1983), p. 24.
24. Author's own survey. The periods covered were 1–14 July 1982, 17–30 June 1985 and 1–17 October 1986. All criticism, however mild, was counted, but not mere discussion of, say, economic problems. If an article was *mainly* critical, then the whole article was counted as 'criticism'; individual critical passages in other articles were also measured and added to the total, which was then calculated as a percentage of the overall space available for domestic news. In the 1982 period there were 29 'completely critical' articles (an average of 2 per day); in 1985 there were 45 (about 3 per day); and in 1986 46.
25. *Der Spiegel*, 25 February 1985.
26. *Pravda*, 8 February 1985.
27. *Summary of World Broadcasts* (BBC, Caversham Park), 7 January 1985.
28. See *The Times* and other Western newspapers, 4 January 1985.
29. *Pravda*, 13 June 1985.
30. *Pravda*, 27 September 1983.
31. *Pravda*, 5 October 1983.
32. *Pravda*, 23 September 1983.
33. *Pravda*, 22 June 1984.
34. *Pravda*, 2 October 1985.
35. *The Times* (London), 8 October 1984.
36. *The Times* (London), 4 February 1985.
37. *Pravda*, 7 January 1984.
38. *Pravda*, 27 November 1984.
39. *The Guardian*, 28 April 1986.
40. *Pravda*, 18 January 1982.
41. *Pravda*, 26 May 1986.
42. Dornberg, *op. cit.*, p. 241–2.
43. *Izvestiya*, 8 September 1983.

5. *Pravda and its Readers*

1. See, for 1968 – B. Yevladov, A. Pokrovskiy and V. Shlyapentokh, 'Chetyre tysyachi i odno interv'yu', *Zhurnalist*, October 1969, pp. 34–37; for 1977 – S. V. Tsukasov, 'Vremya zrelosti', *Zhurnalist*, December 1978, pp. 37–39.
2. Krupskaya, *op. cit.*, p. 224.
3. S. Tsukasov, 'Vremya zrelosti', *Zhurnalist*, December 1978, p. 37; V. S. Korobeynikov (ed.), *Sotsiologicheskie problemy obshchestvennogo mneniya i deyatel'nosti sredstv massovoy informatsii* (Moscow, 1978; for official use only), pp. 12–13.
4. *Sredstva massovoy informatsii i propagandy. Sovetskaya literatura 1982 g. (Referativnyy sbornik)* (Moscow, 1983), p. 143.
5. V. E. Chernakova, in Korobeynikov (ed.), *Sotsiologischeskie problemy* . . . (1979), p. 20.
6. Korobeynikov, *Sotsiologicheskie problemy* . . . (1978), p. 105.
7. K. R. M. Short (ed.), *Western Broadcasting over the Iron Curtain* (London, 1986), p. 6.
8. *Ibid.*, p. 21.
9. S. Tsukasov, in B. M. Morozov (ed.), *Sotsiologicheskie issledovaniya kak sredstvo povysheniya effektivnosti partiynogo rukovodstva pressoy* (Moscow, 1980), p. 12.

10. *Ibid.*, p. 30. E. P. Prokhorov, in 'Sotsiologicheskie issledovaniya funktsionirovaniya sovremennykh sredstv massovoy informatsii', *Vestnik MGU (Zhurnalistika)*, No. 5, 1979, pp. 19–21, also urges that more thorough surveys should be carried out to find out the reasons behind the reading preferences of *Pravda* readers, which, he says, 'give rise to concern'.

11. Author's interview at *Pravda*, 2 December 1983.

12. Author's interview with V. Shlapentokh, September 1983.

13. V. S. Korobeynikov, *Vozrastanie roli i znacheniya obshchestvennogo mneniya v zhizni sotsialisticheskogo obschchestva* (Moscow, 1979), p. 40.

14. Hedrick Smith, *op. cit.*, p. 453.

15. Mickiewicz, *op. cit.*, p. 69.

16. Stephen White, 'Political Communications in the USSR: Letters to Party, State and Press', *Political Studies* (March 1983), XXXI, p. 58.

17. *Ibid.*, p. 52.

18. Author's interview at *Pravda*, 5 December 1983.

19. V. S. Korobeynikov, *Redaktsiya i auditoriya* (Moscow, 1983), p. 177.

20. V. S. Korobeynikov, *Sotsiologicheskie problemy obshchestvennogo mneniya i deyatel'nosti sredstv massovoy informatsii* (Moscow, 1976), pp. 113–126.

21. Korobeynikov, *Redaktsiya . . .*, p. 177.

22. Author's interview at *Pravda*, 5 December 1983.

23. White, *op. cit.*, p. 52.

24. The paper referred to is *Taganrogskaya pravda*. See White, *op. cit.*, pp. 53–54.

25. Nicholas Lampert, *Whistleblowing in the Soviet Union* (London, 1985) reviewed in *The Economist*, 11 May 1985.

26. *The Economist*, 6 July 1985.

27. Georgiev, *op. cit.*, p. 223.

6. Getting the Message Across

1. *Pravda*, 19 February 1985.

2. *Pravda*, 18 January 1983.

3. *Pravda*, 19 September 1983.

4. Boris Groys, 'Schweigen ist Gold', *Süddeutsche Zeitung*, 15/16 January 1983, p. 112.

5. E. P. Prokhorov (ed.), *Sotsiologiya Zhurnalistki* (Moscow, 1981), p. 90.

6. Some of the ideas here were prompted by David Wedgwood Benn's interesting article 'Soviet propaganda: the theory and the practice', *in The World Today*, Vol. 41, No. 6, June 1985, pp. 112–115.

7. *Pravda*, 13 December 1982.

8. Stephen White, 'The USSR: Patterns of Autocracy and Industrialism', in Archie Brown and Jack Gray (eds.), *Political Culture and Political Change in Communist States* (London, 1979), p. 49.

9. Television versions of Gorbachov's speeches have tended to be longer and occasionally more 'revealing' (though still edited) than the press versions.

10. Lendvai, *op. cit.*, p. 45.

11. *Financial Times*, 3 September 1986.

12. See, e.g., *Pravda*, 15 March 1986.

Appendix 1

TABLE 1: *PRAVDA* 1912–1914 – TITLES AND PENALTIES

Name of paper and dates (Old Style)	Total issues	Issues punished	Issues confiscated	Fines incurred	Sum of fines (roubles)	Number of 'editors'
Pravda (*Truth*) (22.4.12 – 3.7.13)	355	73	52	21	10,300	21
Rabochaya pravda (*Workers' Truth*) (13.7. – 1.8.13)	17	14	12	2	1,000	1
Severnaya pravda (*Northern Truth*) (1.8. – 7.9.13)	31	24	21	3	1,250	3
Pravda truda (*Truth of Labour*) (11.9. – 9.10.13)	20	14	13	1	250	1
*Za pravdu** (*For Truth*) (1.10. – 5.12.13)	52	26	23	3	1,300	4
Proletarskaya pravda (*Proletarian Truth*) (7.12.13–21.1.14)	34	12	12	0	0	2
Put' pravdy (*The Way of Truth*) (22.1. – 21.5.14)	92	16	12	4	1,650	3
Rabochiy (*Worker*) (22.4.14; 5.5. – 9.6.14)	9	4	3	1	300	1
*Trudovaya pravda** (*Labour Truth*) (23.5.14; 30.5. – 8.7.14)	35	8	7	1	500	4
Totals	645	191	155	36	16,550	40

*Za pravdu was published in alternation with *Pravda truda*, and *Trudovaya pravda* with *Rabochiy*.

SOURCE: Whitman Bassow, 'The Pre-Revolutionary *Pravda* and Tsarist Censorship', *The American Slavic and East European Review*, Vol. 13, 1954, p. 63. Other sources give slightly different figures.

TABLE 2: *PRAVDA* IN 1917

Title	Dates	Number of issues
Pravda	5 March – 5 July	99
Listok 'Pravdy' (A Sheet of 'Pravda')	6 July	1
Rabochiy i soldat (Worker and Soldier)	23 July – 10 August	15 (plus a sixteenth of 6 copies only)
Proletariy (Proletarian)	13–24 August	10
Rabochiy (Worker)	25 Aug. – 2 Sept.	12 (circulation 50,000)
Rabochiy put' (Workers' Path) Pravda	3 Sept. – 26 Oct. From 27 October	46

SOURCE: *Epokha – gazetnoy stroke: 'Pravda' 1917–1967* (Moscow, 1967), p. 63.

TABLE 3: *PRAVDA*'S COVERAGE

Subject	1947/48	1956	1962	1965	1982	1985
			(Percentages)			
Domestic news (total)	60.2	52.5	62.9	70.3	66.0	68.2
Political	18.5	15.7	18.7	18.6	14.5	17.7
Economic	31.1	25.7	27.7	21.3	18.0	16.0
Public welfare	0.3	2.9	–	1.3	2.2	3.5
Arts	3.5	3.7	6.9	6.8	4.9	5.1
Science and education	1.7	0.8	3.7	11.0	6.5	3.1
Sport	0.6	0.7	1.5	2.4	3.5	2.1
Military	1.5	0.3	1.3	1.3	0.3	0.2
History	0.5	n.a.	1.2	5.1	0.7	2.9
Information (TV schedules, etc.)	n.a.	0.4	1.6	2.4	3.6	3.4
Photographs/illustrations	n.a.	n.a.	n.a.	n.a.	8.7	10.3
Miscellaneous	2.5	–	0.4	–	3.1	2.6
Foreign news (total)	39.8	47.5	37.1	29.7	34.0	31.8
Warsaw Pact	6.9	9.8	11.0	6.0	7.7	8.7
China and Albania	n.a.	6.0	0.7	0.1	0.2	0.3
Third World allies	n.a. }	0.8	5.6	3.1	{ 2.3	1.6
Other communist parties	n.a. }				{ 0.4	1.4
USA	3.4	3.2	6.7	5.5	5.2	3.3
Europe/NATO	13.3	10.8	5.1	7.4	6.0	4.1
Latin America	10.6	0.1	0.3	1.7	1.4	1.8
Africa	1.5 {	0.9	0.9	2.3	1.0	1.1
Middle East	{	10.4	1.8	0.9	1.0	1.0
Far East/Asia	2.9	2.8	2.2	1.8	1.7	2.2
United Nations/peace/disarmament	3.9*	2.8	2.8	0.7	7.1	6.3

* 'World affairs'.

SOURCES: Alex Inkeles, *Public Opinion in Soviet Russia* (Cambridge, Mass., 1967), p. 163 (for 1947–48); Gayle Durham Hollander, *Soviet Political Indoctrination* (New York, 1972), p. 43 (for 1956, 1962, 1965); author's own survey (for 1982, 1985).

TABLE 4: *PRAVDA*'S READERS ON A GIVEN DAY

Occupation	Percent
Workers	17.5
Agricultural workers (incl. management)	9.5
Engineers and technicians	17.5
Intelligentsia	22.0
Office workers	9.0
Service industry workers	2.0
Pensioners	15.0
Students	2.0

SOURCE: V. S. Korobeynikov (ed.), *Sotsiologicheskie problemy obshchestvennogo mneniya i deyatel'nosti sredstv massovoy informatsii* (Moscow, 1978; for official use only), p. 19.

TABLE 5: READING PREFERENCES OF *PRAVDA* READERS AND THE POPULATION AS A
WHOLE (1977)

	Percentage of Pravda readers	*Percentage of population as a whole*
International life	75	48
Morals and upbringing	69	47
Housing, pay and social security	48	32
Physical culture and sport	41	30
Legislation	41	26
Work of service industries & shops	40	27
Health care and the medical service	37	27
Industry, construction & transport	37	21
Agriculture	34	26
Environmental protection, natural resources	34	18
Party life, work of Party organisations	33	13
Culture, art, literature	32	23
Education	32	18
History of the Revolution & military-patriotic themes	31	17
Marxist-Leninist theory	30	9
Work of Trade Unions, Komsomol and other public organisations	29	17
Problems of science	29	16
Work of soviets, ministries, government depts & other state admin.	19	9
Other issues	13	9
'Don't knows'	1	12

SOURCE: N. E. Chernakova, in V. S. Korobeynikov (ed.), *Sotsiologicheskie problemy obshchestvennogo mneniya i deyatel'nosti sredstv massovoy informatsii* (Moscow, 1979), p. 19.

TABLE 6: WHO WRITES TO THE CENTRAL MEDIA?

	Percentage of letter-writers	Percentage of population
Workers	40	49
Engineers & technical staff	17	7
Office workers	4	7
Intelligentsia not employed in industry (i.e. doctors, teachers, etc.)	10	2
Workers in shops and services	2	7
Students	4	3
Pensioners	22	16
Housewives	1	9

SOURCE: V. S. Korobeynikov (ed.), *Sotsiologicheskiye problemy obshchestvennogo mneniya i deyatel'nosti, sredstv massovoy informatsii.* (Moscow, 1976), p. 120.

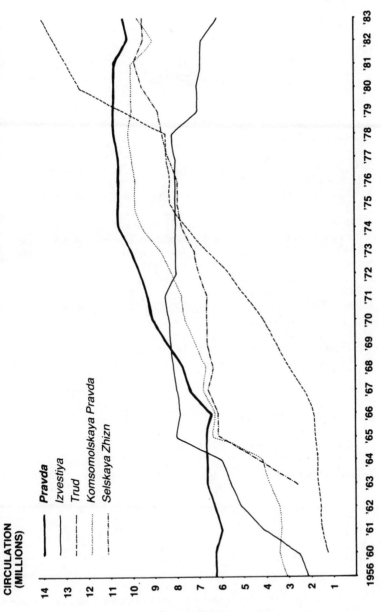

Circulation of Central Newspapers

Appendix 2

Editors of *Pravda**

I. V. Stalin, Ya. M. Sverdlov, M. Chernomazov, L. B. Kamenev, V. M. Molotov [1912–1914]

Molotov, A. M. Shlyapnikov, K. S. Yeremeyev, M. I. Kalinin [5–13 March 1917]

Stalin, M. K. Muranov, L. B. Kamenev [13 March–4 April 1917]

V. I. Lenin, G. E. Zinoviev, Stalin, Muranov, Kamenev [4 April–5 July 1917]

Sverdlov and others [6 July–9 December 1917]

N. I. Bukharin [10 December 1917–23 February 1918]

? [24 February–July 1918]

Bukharin [July 1918–October 1928 (nominally until April 1929)]

G. I. Krumin [1929–1930]

M. A. Savelyev [1930]

L. Z. Mekhlis [1930–1937]

A. N. Poskryobyshev [1937–1940]

P. N. Pospelov [1940–1949]

M. A. Suslov [1940–1951]

L. F. Ilyichov [1951–1953]

D. T. Shepilov [1953–1956]

P. A. Satyukov [1956–1964]

A. M. Rumyantsev [1964–1965]

M. V. Zimyanin [1965–1976]

V. G. Afanasyev [1976–]

*N.B. The editorship of *Pravda* during the early years was both collective and constantly changing; only the more important names are given here.

Index to Part One

Index to Subjects Covered in Part Two

Domestic

Foreign